HERE WE STAND
POLITICS, PERFORMERS AND PERFORMANCE

Colin Chambers

Colin Chambers, formerly a journalist and theatre critic, was Literary Manager of the Royal Shakespeare Company from 1981 to 1997. He was co-adaptor of *Tynan*, based on *The Diaries of Kenneth Tynan*, and his many books include *The Story of Unity Theatre*, the award-winning *Peggy: the Life of Margaret Ramsay, Play Agent* (published by Nick Hern Books), *The Continuum Companion to Twentieth Century Theatre* (editor) and *Inside the RSC*. He is Reader in Drama at Kingston University, London.

Colin Chambers

HERE WE STAND

*Politics, Performers
and Performance*

PAUL ROBESON
ISADORA DUNCAN
and
CHARLIE CHAPLIN

NICK HERN BOOKS
London
www.nickhernbooks.co.uk

A NICK HERN BOOK

Here We Stand
Politics, Performers and Performance
first published in Great Britain in 2006
by Nick Hern Books Limited
14 Larden Road, London W3 7ST

Front cover image of Robeson:
Leonard Mccombe / Time & Life Pictures / Getty Images

Every effort has been made to trace all copyright holders.
The publishers will be pleased to receive information
about any omissions and make the necessary arrangements
at the first opportunity.

Cover designed by Ned Hoste, 2H

Typeset by Country Setting, Kingsdown, Kent, CT14 8ES
Printed and bound in Great Britain by Biddles, King's Lynn

A CIP catalogue record for this book
is available from the British Library

ISBN-13   978 1 85459 920 9
ISBN-10   1 85459 920 8

CONTENTS

ACKNOWLEDGEMENTS

Thanks to: Günter Berghaus, Albrecht Dümling, Nick Hern, Bert Hogenkamp, Ben Jancovich, Michael Kustow, Andrew Lang, Rob Marx, Jim Miller, Michael Morley, Richard Nelson, Avi Oz, Michael Patterson, David Robinson, Moti Sandak.

INTRODUCTION: DREAMS AND NIGHTMARES

'I am a man of a thousand faces, all of them blacklisted.'
Zero Mostel, actor [1]

Different art forms have their own genealogies of dissent and conflict with authority, whether in poetry, sculpture, painting, photography, music, the novel, the cinema, dance or theatre. In the European tradition, since Plato spurned the undesirable poets at the gates of his city Republic, the strong link between control of the word and political power has rightly afforded a central place to the writer: the writer banned by censors, the writer in gaol, the writer in exile, even the writer executed.

Performers have featured less prominently in the lineage of rebels, yet, from shaman to troubadour, they boast a long history as outlaws and outsiders, the purveyors of society's dreams and nightmares. In Britain, the ancient poets would have been performers in the tradition of the bard or seer, and later came the minstrels and itinerant troupes; for centuries actors were classified by law as rogues and vagabonds, and for a period during the seventeenth century theatres themselves were closed down. In Catholic countries actors were denied not only the sacraments and Christian burial but also their rights as citizens. In China, actors and their descendants were prevented from entering public service, and in Japan actors were designated as non-persons.

While control of performance has been endemic to many territories and states, the relative scarcity of the performer in the annals of revolt may be rooted in the different role a performer plays in originating meaning to that of the writer, as well as in the nature, and historic suspicion, of performance itself.[2]

Performers are often regarded as mercenaries doing someone else's bidding, in essence no different from a prostitute;
this was, in fact, a literal association for many years, especially,
though by no means exclusively, for female performers.
Performance by extension is often presented as a venal trade
in illusion, pretence and insincerity, the very opposite of truth
telling. Legend has it that the first western actor, Thespis, was
asked by the Athenian lawmaker Solon if he was ashamed of
telling so many lies before so many people. The mud has stuck.
Common English usage reflects this bias, in the derogatory
tone of phrases like 'he's putting on an act' or 'she's only play
acting'; furthermore, when acting is used as an adjective (for
example, acting president), it means a temporary substitute,
not the real thing.

It is not surprising, therefore, that a performer who voices
political views is frequently belittled as a professional purveyor
of make-believe merely playing to the gallery in another role.
And if the performer happens to be very famous, then the
scepticism intensifies that any significant coincidence of political integrity and celebrity can exist.

EXTRAORDINARY PERFORMERS

The aim of this book is to explore that coincidence and its
contradictions, and, in the process, to investigate the special
and often dangerous comradeship that exists more generally
between performers and political commitment. I have chosen
to do this by first examining the lives of three performers, Paul
Robeson, Isadora Duncan and Charlie Chaplin, who, to vary-
ing degrees, risked their extraordinary skills and their celebrity to serve political ideas both in their work and in their
lives.[3] Behind my investigation lie several questions: how did
their political views inform their work, what compromises did
they make in their work, how much pressure and of what kind
did they come under because of their politics, what risks did
they take and how much did they suffer?

In the second part of the book, I explore the censorship of
performers and performance in different contexts, and, lastly,
I investigate wider questions of art and politics, the role of the
activist celebrity and the political potential of performance.

Of the three extraordinary performers whose lives I examine, Robeson's accomplishments cover the widest range – as athlete, orator, linguist, scholar and exceptional figure in theatre, film and music, both live and recorded. His political activism, as a citizen and, when he was able, as an artist, was the most consistent and committed. His life of solidarity, combining race, class and national struggle at home and abroad, is unmatched by any comparable figure, and few performing artists have conducted their careers with such a staunch struggle to express their political philosophy in their art.

Indeed, this book draws its spirit and its title, *Here We Stand*, from Robeson's autobiography, *Here I Stand*, published in 1958. Through another history of resistance and challenge, the title also echoes the (perhaps apocryphal) words spoken by Martin Luther in 1520 when he refused to recant and thereby heralded a religious and existential revolution that became known as the Reformation. While Robeson did not found or lead a movement, he became an emblem of a struggle of similar moment to which he was totally dedicated: universal emancipation of the oppressed.

This was a cause to which Duncan and Chaplin could also be said to have subscribed, although their commitment was less politically precise and potent than Robeson's. In this sense, Robeson can be seen as the paradigm of the politically committed performer, which, paradoxically, may be related to the fact that, unlike the other two, he was an interpreter rather than an originator.

Each, nevertheless, put his or her art at the service of society because of the political context in which they found themselves. Each linked the individual to wider identities and explored the interaction of individual personality and collective interests. In their art and in their lives they questioned national identity and its relationship to citizenship, ranging across gender, sexuality, race, religion, class, politics and culture at a moment when the place of such subjects on the historical stage was being fiercely contested. For instance, along with Duncan's promotion of the independent woman and Robeson's espousal of a black presence, all three performers presented workers as historical agents and work as worthy of artistic attention at a time when this was still contentious.

The cauldron of their creativity was America, a land of revolutionary democracy and breathtaking dynamism as well as equally robust conservatism. They were all inheritors of Walt Whitman's love of the 'common people', locating the strength of a nation, of all nations, in its people (however incomplete and racist Duncan's grasp of this was). All three appealed to an international identity beyond local features, and, in so doing, all three questioned what it is to be a human. They aimed at universality, Duncan through the exclusivity of her solo dancing, the single figure representing the whole, Chaplin through his silent, almost androgynous clown and Robeson through the symbolic breadth of repertoire and intensity of his unadorned voice.

The prevailing notion of art they all had to confront was the one closest to Duncan's own, namely the Enlightenment view that art was a special activity for the initiated few, akin to religion. This exclusive club was led by the white, Christian, European males subsequently fabled in literary criticism, complete with muscular doormen to keep out the riff-raff. Each had to come to terms with the consequences of that.

Robeson's challenge to the systems of control operating in his chosen cultural fields shaped the multifarious and interwoven strands of his life and work. He was involved briefly with the avant-garde but for the most part conducted his struggle within popular culture, where his skin colour was decisive and control was exercised over representation (the images he was allowed to portray) as well as over the physical conditions of performance and its reception (for instance, by pay, segregation, access to venues and boycotts).

His fame allowed him to use his performances to promote the causes in which he believed, but his fame also made it harder for him to find suitable artistic material for those performances, and the pursuit of those causes led him to forfeit both the fame that had been his lever and the ability to perform as he desired. When his celebrity was threatened, however, he did not accept obscurity but contested the attempt to render him anonymous by standing up for himself, his people and his politics. He symbolised both a society's discrimination as well as its success; he was both a confirmation and a challenge, and, at the deepest level, both hero and villain.

Duncan chose to belong to the 'high art' world, but whatever enlightenment she encountered rarely extended to her gender. When she became a celebrity and entered the popular domain as well, her womanhood defined reactions to her, and these were reinforced by negative responses to her political views. Only in the Soviet Union did Duncan briefly glimpse the mass audience that could give her work the resonance she desired, yet even here she was not able to realise her dreams.

Chaplin, although highly influential in the avant-garde, ignored 'high art' and immediately entered the world of popular entertainment, where he remained. He reshaped and dominated his own field, and helped break open the old, restrictive notion of art to allow cinema in. Having established himself as an artist with a social outlook, he found his sexual behaviour provided his opponents with a useful tool with which to attack his politics as well.

While Robeson, Duncan and Chaplin had different views on the function of art, each wanted to be taken seriously and to make an impact. Their appetite for ideas was linked to the force that drove them as performers, a connection that also drew them to politics and politicised expression in their art. In their different disciplines, they challenged the asocial notion of the neutrality of art and the autonomy of the performer's presence, aware that reception of their art was of crucial importance and that art cannot be understood on its own terms alone; interaction is implicit.

With different degrees of success, they attempted to direct or control that interaction, a process intensified by celebrity. At one moment or another they all sought to reach beyond their performance by buttressing the 'meaning' of their art with commentary, as if recognising the importance of direct contact with their audiences and wary of the possible limitations of their art – or of all art – if left to work 'on its own'.

Each had a particular and different way of relating to the politics with which they chose to associate and for which they took risks and were punished. In the process they all came to represent the dangerous 'other' to be avoided, demeaned and, if necessary, suppressed.

Duncan was always both herself and the transcendent 'other' to which she aspired and channelled her energy. Chaplin created a mythic, global figure, and, regardless of the guises in which he appeared, he remained the Tramp. Robeson appeared in conventional representational roles, but he was always present as himself. These different kinds of authenticity reflect the particular artistic platform from which each was able to operate politically. They relate both to the different art forms in which the three appeared and to the material they performed, as well as to their different relationships to its ownership, distribution and reception.

Whereas recorded media played a decisive role in creating the popularity of Chaplin and Robeson, a fact which allowed them to intervene in, though not control, the trajectory and reception of their celebrity, Duncan's renown was created largely through the mediations of others. As a consequence, her space for intervention was necessarily more restricted.

Duncan owned her body and displayed it as she chose. Chaplin owned his films and displayed himself in them as he chose. Robeson owned his voice (both actual and metaphorical) and, within the limits of his cultural outlets, he displayed that as best he could. For each, the area they controlled represented the space in which they could be authentic. For Duncan it was her art, for Chaplin his performance and for Robeson his conviction.

There was no political dance movement of which Duncan could have been a part – and, if there had been, she probably would not have 'joined' it – yet she inspired the creation of such a movement by allying her dance to grand political causes. Chaplin did not associate with the political film movements of the inter-war years, which were primarily documentary-based, and he did not inspire them directly, yet his example was a beacon to many. Robeson did become part of a left-wing theatrical and musical movement and its wider political expression, although always as an extraordinary figure even when trying to be a 'foot soldier'. To Robeson, however, the 'foot soldiers' were the true celebrities.

Celebrity is a means of reinforcing a dominant ideology, but it can also be a means to challenge it. That challenge may be commercially or politically useful to the dominant value system or it may transgress and pose alternative values. Celebrity may also do all these things at once. Although celebrity usually ignores or masks anomalies, or appears to resolve them without significant disturbance, when it becomes politically engaged, celebrity can reveal contradictions and comment on them with a special intensity; perhaps it can even suggest a resolution that might be unsettling.

CONTEXT

Paul Robeson, Isadora Duncan and Charlie Chaplin all used their celebrity in support of alternative ways of seeing and living. The story of each of these performers represents a unique and different historical experience in a pre-globalisation era that has disappeared. It was an era of unprecedented conflict that roughly spans the beginning of the modern epoch, symbolised by the First World War – and, out of that, the establishment of the Soviet Union – through the Cold War to the supposed end of history, with the collapse of the bi-polar world of 'Communism versus capitalism' and the arrival of globalisation.

Historical context is critical, but necessarily partial. We reassess, and, in so doing, recreate the past in terms of our present and where we think we would like to be going in the future. Although I am focusing on artists from an earlier period, I cannot avoid viewing them from the perspective of today and making of their stories something that suits my current purpose. Shaping my approach is the notion that society, culture, performance, ideas and history itself are processes of human activity that are realised in certain specific historical circumstances. These are not of any individual's choosing or making, and, while they do limit choice, they nonetheless do not prevent it; change is constant and we play an active part in it, however remote this exercise of agency appears to be.

Change for Robeson, Duncan and Chaplin meant different things, yet, whatever the differences, all three were broadly speaking to be found on what would have been described as the progressive or left-wing of politics, which, after 1917, was dominated by Marxism and, in particular, the Soviet Communist version of it. Robeson, Duncan and Chaplin were by no means alone in defining their politics – and on occasion being forced to define their politics – in relation to Communism, an inherently activist as well as utopian philosophy. None was a party member, unlike other major artistic celebrities such as Picasso, and each had a different relationship to the local and international variants of the ideology.

This terrain has largely been overshadowed by the massive failings and inhumanity of Communism rather than its positive achievements. Its idealism and its tyranny led to the paradox of the red banner being a mighty inspiration as well as an historic desecration of culture.[4] The extraordinary diversity and individuality of Communist-inspired culture has been lost, however, in the blooded shadows of the depredations perpetrated by ruling Communist parties, which undermined the commanding Enlightenment notions of progress, reason and the beneficence of art. The decisive damage to such notions was inflicted, however, by the systematic horrors of Nazi genocide, which were generated from within the heartland of the Enlightenment.

Beyond art, the terrible things done in the twentieth century in the name of ideology rendered the very notion of ideology highly problematic. It was, and remains, a slippery if vital concept, and one that is central to the second part of the book, which deals with broader issues of censorship and the politics of performance.

Here, I use ideology to mean a set of lived ideas and values that allows a substantial grouping of people to identify with each other and to co-exist as a group. Different ideologies vary in their internal consistency and ability to dominate, overlap or cohabit with others. At different moments one ideology may consolidate or supersede others, for example patriotism in time of war, while some may be of overarching importance, such as feminism, with its challenge to patriarchy and the self-elevation of maleness as the universal norm.

For many, ideology – especially when related to politics or religion – is regarded as a bad thing. It is seen as an external, exclusive and corrupting influence, something imposed from outside, rather than an ever-present part of the reality it seeks to construct, co-existing with other ideologies, itself subject to change as it is tested against lived experience. In extreme examples, ideology may be totalitarian in design but it is rarely lived in such a total way, even if it is highly pervasive and pro-

moted through overt force. Ideology works more hegemo-
nically by connecting the lived reality of individuals to wider
ways of understanding life in intersecting, interlocking processes embedded not only in obvious public manifestations
(e.g. political speeches or educational curricula) but also in
the everyday, in the personal and the private, in the apparently
normal or commonplace.

Such an understanding of ideology disputes traditional
notions of both art and politics, and gave rise to the identification by some on the left like Gramsci and Brecht of 'common sense' as a prime site for political struggle. It is a site in
which art – seen as cultural practice: a process not a product,
an agency as well as an effect – plays a significant role and,
therefore, itself becomes a critical arena of challenge.

Performance occupies a special place because it enacts and
embodies ideologies, whether supportive of the status quo or
not. The importance of performance lies in relation to how we
imagine ourselves (individually and socially) and how we
imagine our future, both of which are intimately bound up
with culture and the interactions of everyday life. If resistance
and challenge can be located in areas outside and in addition
to the conventional sphere known as politics, performance
can play a vital role in the complex process of how we perceive
human agency, social causation and the role of the individual.

This redefining of the political and aesthetic spheres and
the relationship between them forms the basis of the final
section of the book, which comes full circle with its exploration of issues concerning contemporary celebrity and engagement in political activity.

Many star performers of the twenty-first century make
sporadic appearances in the political arena, often on a single
issue. They rarely sustain their commitment or place their
intervention in the wider context of a coherent political philosophy, a trend exacerbated after the demise of the Soviet bloc
when totalising theories lost their pre-eminent status and
made way for post-modern and supposedly post-ideological
strategies.

Robeson, Duncan and Chaplin lived at a time when the
ideological battle lines were more distinctly drawn and there
was a great deal at stake for the individual who took a stand;

perhaps, as a result, fewer performers ventured to express political opinions as openly as they did. Each in his or her own way was a pioneer and had no role models to guide them in their chosen confrontations with authority and in the risks they took. None, however, was struggling alone. Despite their absence from these pages, the activists who were their contemporaries – whether famous or not – form an integral part of the story, as the title of this book implies.

NOTES

1. Quoted in Victor S. Navasky, *Naming Names*, New York, Viking Press, 1980, p. 178.
2. Bias against performance extends to artistic judgements, too. Performance poets, for example, are disregarded in relation to literary poets. Performing poets like Sergei Esenin, Hamish Henderson, Adrian Mitchell, Yevgeni Yevtushenko or Benjamin Zephaniah, unlike W.H. Auden (who said poetry never made anything happen), believed poetry could extend beyond the written word to change nations; to them, poetry can become the people and be a pleasure as well as a call to action.
3. There is no record of Robeson having met or seen Duncan, and it is unlikely their paths ever crossed. Duncan did meet Chaplin, when he was visiting the Côte d'Azur in the mid-1920s, and one of his celebrated party pieces at the time was an imitation of her involving streams of toilet paper. Chaplin and Robeson knew each other, and they even both appeared in 1926 in *Camille*, an amateur silent film made by the cartoonist and illustrator Ralph Barton. Robeson acts the part of Alexandre Dumas Fils and Chaplin a character called Mike, who plays the piano, pretends to be Salome and performs the 'Dance of the Rolls' from *The Gold Rush*. The distinguished cast of more than fifty includes the actor Sacha Guitry, the actresses Ethel Barrymore and Yvonne Printemps, the critic George Jean Nathan, the directors Jacques Copeau and Max Reinhardt, the lawyer Clarence Darrow, the publisher Alfred Knopf and the writers Sherwood Anderson, Paul Claudel, Theodore Dreiser, Sinclair Lewis, Anita Loos, H.L. Mencken, Ferenc Molnár and W. Somerset Maugham. The film can be seen as an extra feature on the DVD of Chaplin's *A Woman of Paris*, Warner Brothers, Z1 37976, 2003.
4. This paradox is part of a much bigger debate about the particular historical reasons why Marxist and Communist ideas attracted so many bright and passionate people, who engaged in sharp debate on an

astonishing range of issues: art, science, politics, modernism, realism, the nature of consciousness and illusion, as well as economics. The predominance of ideology in the 1930s did not preclude subtle and sophisticated debate; indeed, they were the prerequisites for the ideological ferment. The leftism of the time was many things at the same time and meant different things to different people.

PART ONE

PAUL ROBESON: THE ARTIST TAKES SIDES

'I do the singing and I do the acting
because it helps me make a statement,
gives me a platform to say what I believe.'
Paul Robeson [1]

In the three decades between the 1920s and the 1950s, Paul Robeson was arguably the most prominent African American in the world, but when he wielded that eminence in the cause of social and political justice, the price he paid personally and as a performer was devastating. How did he pass from rising star to voice of the nation and then demonised outcast, an extraordinary journey that has been hailed as both iconic and heroic?

It began by happenstance. He became a performer because of being black, and his blackness remained central to everything he did, whether as impediment or inspiration. However dubious or absurd the basis for racial categorisation is, the colour of one's skin was critical in a society that for the most part raised 'whiteness' above race as the God-given stamp of natural superiority.[2] Robeson challenged that throughout his life, and, having experienced the obstacles of racism in his education and professional life, he came to connect his people's struggle to class and national struggles at home and abroad. It was in such a context that his life as an artist and his life as a politically active citizen became as one.

CORE BELIEFS

He was born in 1898 and raised in Princeton, New Jersey, which one writer has described as being like the South but with better housing and education.[3] As Robeson grew up, he experienced not only habitual racism but an accompanying duality that tutored him for the future: he was both invisible to the white population as a supposed inferior and yet extremely visible, not only because of his skin colour but, in addition, because he was tall, upright, strong and striking.[4] The youngest of five children, he quickly learned the value of the local church-centred black community when his mother died not long before his sixth birthday, an appreciation that was reinforced when he stayed with black families while studying at Rutgers University. At Rutgers, to which he won a scholarship and which he chose in preference to an all-black college, he had no option but to be representative of his people. He was only the third black student to attend Rutgers, and only one other black student was enrolled while he was there.

The bad treatment he received in class turned violent on the football field, crossing the boundaries of the rules, but in that highly masculine world, and standing six foot two inches tall, he was able to win respect, though not acceptance, by fighting back. In so doing, Robeson became the first black student to play for the university football team. He had assimilated from his father the general survival strategy of showing restraint, but he also learned early from this display of strength the value in certain circumstances of replacing passive resistance with active retaliation.

Many of his qualities, in particular his epic and obstinate steadfastness, can be traced to the influence of his father, an escaped slave who joined the Union army as a labourer and who, after the civil war, gained a divinity degree and became a reverend. From this formidable disciplinarian, Robeson learned the absolute worth of honour, of pride in one's people and loyalty to one's convictions as well as a lifelong love of scholarship, a duty to challenge injustice and the adamantine core belief that he was as good as any white person.

He demonstrated this at college as an outstanding student who won many academic and sporting honours. He thought he would be able to continue this success after graduating from Columbia University Law School, but a less than triumphant future in his chosen profession became apparent when a white secretary at his law firm refused to take dictation from him because he was black.[5] Having discussed his prospects with the sympathetic yet realistic head of the firm – all-white with the exception of Robeson, including administrative staff – Robeson resigned, despite having no other employment in sight. The offer that eventually came from the Provincetown Players a few months later to appear in New York in the première of Eugene O'Neill's *All God's Chillun Got Wings* proved a decisive turning point.

The entertainment industry that Robeson was entering reflected the weft and weave of the society. Actors playing in 'blackface' were still commonplace, while opportunities for black performers (a broad and unscientific category) were strictly controlled by segregation and stereotyping, although the creativity of the artists often managed to transcend such strictures. Most employment came in bands, in novelty or speciality acts for vaudeville and revue, and in exotic dancing.

Robeson had been working at a variety of jobs to make ends meet while at law school, including some as a performer, although he did turn down a proposal to train as a professional boxer. He had been performing since an early age, in the collective singing in church, in school theatricals and in college oratory, for which he won prizes. While at Columbia, he had appeared in an amateur production of *Simon the Cyrenian*, a folk play by white writer Ridgely Torrence, which tells the story of the black man who carried Jesus' cross. Robeson said of this experience – idealistically but, compared to his experiences elsewhere, honestly – 'On the stage there was only the sky to hold me back.'[6]

Two years later, in 1922, on the strength of this performance, he had been pressed into reluctant service for his professional acting debut as an itinerant minstrel in *Taboo*, a plantation melodrama by white socialite Mary Hoyt Wiborg, which toured in Britain as *Voodoo*. A chance meeting had led him to join the successful all-black Broadway musical *Shuffle Along* by Noble Sissle and Eubie Blake, and, as well as singing at the Cotton Club in Harlem, a celebrated whites-only venue that featured black entertainers, he had appeared in the chorus of the Broadway show *Plantation Revue*. He had also led an all-black cast in a two-week revival of *Roseanne* by another white writer, Nan Bagby Stevens, which had played to black audiences in Harlem and Philadelphia.

The invitation to appear in the 1924 O'Neill première brought with it both opportunity and the chilling blasts of racism. Its theme of 'miscegenation' and the prospect of Robeson kissing the hand of a white actress provoked parts of the press and the Ku Klux Klan to issue grave warnings and calls to prevent the production opening in order to avoid a race riot. Piles of hate mail arrived for the actors at the little Greenwich Village theatre; there was even a bomb threat. In the midst of this furore, the theatre management found they had a gap in the programme to fill and decided to mount a brief revival of O'Neill's *The Emperor Jones* with Robeson in the eponymous role of the Pullman porter who becomes a dictator. This would play in May, in the week before *All God's Chillun Got Wings* opened. It was an enormous gamble and, for the novice Robeson, an extraordinary challenge. Many of the critics, both local and out-of-town, praised Robeson's performance in the highest terms, and this heightened expectations for the première of *Chillun*.

Only hours before *Chillun* was due to begin, the mayor departed from usual practice and refused a licence for the employment of child actors, who are required in the opening scene in which black and white children play together. Whatever the intention of this move, it did not stop the production. With police surrounding the theatre and steelworkers protecting the dressing rooms, the first scene was read from the stage. The rest followed as planned without a hitch or disturbance. The play fared less well at the hands of the critics than Robeson, who received more eulogies. His performing career had truly begun.

In contrast to the white press, however, there was sharp argument in the black papers and among black leaders over both the O'Neill plays and Robeson's performances in them.[7] Some judged the black actor Charles Gilpin, who had starred in the original production of *The Emperor Jones*, to have resisted the inherent stereotyping more robustly than Robeson. Robeson defended O'Neill's portrayal of race and his willingness to tackle related issues, as did other prominent African Americans, like the historian and activist W.E.B. DuBois. Whatever arguments they provoked, the two O'Neill plays gave lead roles to African American actors and helped end the practice of blackface.

Later in 1924, Robeson appeared in his first film, *Body and Soul*, in which he plays the double role of twins, an evil pastor and his equally decent brother. It was directed by Oscar Micheaux, a former shoeshine 'boy', farm worker and railway porter who became the leading black film director of the silent era. Micheaux had set up his own film company and worked tirelessly making and distributing his own films among black communities. *Body and Soul*, his thirteenth film, was heavily re-edited at the request of the industry's censor, set up by leading film companies in 1922 to regulate film production and distribution, paying especial attention to moral concerns.[8]

The film was disregarded at the time and Robeson was criticised for his portrayal of the corrupt and womanising preacher, the more interesting of his two parts and one in which he apparently showed a visceral, raw energy that is not seen in most of his film work.[9] As one subsequent commentator has argued, *Body and Soul*, with the complexity of its black characters and its depiction of a strong black woman and a rape, is a critique of the more simplistic O'Neill plays and, by extension, of Robeson's role in them.[10] Robeson, perhaps not surprisingly, does not seem to have been pleased with the film and never again worked with a black filmmaker.

AFRICAN AMERICAN FOLK MUSIC

In 1925, Robeson appeared in *The Emperor Jones* on Broadway. Three months later at the Provincetown Players' theatre, he gave what have come to be seen as historic concerts of African American folk music. He had already performed from this repertoire in Boston, his first formal concert, but this time in New York he was accompanied by the African American pianist and arranger Lawrence Brown, whom he had met when they both happened to be in London at the same time. It was the start of a long and productive relationship and heralded the beginning of their concert touring (in the course of which they routinely encountered racism in halls, hotels and restaurants). It also heralded the release of Robeson's first recordings in both the US and Britain, which included two best-selling songs, 'Joshua Fit de Battle' and 'Bye and Bye'.

The music of Robeson's people was already known in the concert-hall context, performed by black artists such as the Fisk Jubilee Singers, Roland Hayes and Marian Anderson as well as by white singers such as Oscar Seagle, Mary Jordan and John McCormack. The songs were regarded as offering a dignified antidote to the vaudeville exploitation of popular blackface artists like Al Jolson. For Robeson, singing spirituals and work songs such as 'Balm in Gilead' or 'Steal Away' was a liberalising project linking black and white. Such co-operation became a hallmark of the Harlem Renaissance of the 1920s, which followed the mass movement of African Americans to northern towns after World War I and celebrated African American heritage in the arts.

Robeson discovered that his physique – large head, broad, barrel chest and wide throat and nose cavities (the latter due to a football injury when his nose was broken) – allowed him to produce a full, deep and pure bass sound. The singing style he adopted to express this sound was, for its time, startlingly unelaborated. Reports even suggest that at first the simplicity he strove for embarrassed his middle-class and intellectual black audiences. This simplicity of style, however, created an effect that was far from simple. He gave his songs a good overall shape without losing detail. His singing was intense but not over dramatic. Its intimacy seemed to speak directly to each member of the audience while its epic gesture placed the audience in a collective context. His performance was imbued with the self-confidence the songs displayed in his own culture.

Although the songs abound with biblical reference – the only book the masters would allow the slaves to know – the songs are not passive or subservient, and this Robeson chose to emphasise with a stubborn lyricism that defied the conditions in which the songs were born. He saw that Christianity had been used to enslave his people but that it was also a means for them to affirm life and the struggle to be free. Many of the songs, like 'Deep River' or 'Go Down, Moses', carry references to this struggle against slavery that many white people might not have recognised. In that sense, Robeson was able to express something very different to his black audiences. He also wanted to demonstrate how rhythmically and tonally sophisticated the songs were. He distinguished them from the strictly measured tempo of Christian hymns, which he described as chorally primitive, as well as from other immigrant folk music that lacked the polyrhythmic intricacy peculiar to music with African roots.

Unlike Hayes and Anderson, Robeson in this period did not sing the European repertoire of opera and lieder. This was a technical choice as well as an aesthetic one. He felt he could not understand the psychology or philosophy of European classical music and that he lacked the necessary training, technique and, most importantly, range. Nor did he include the blues and jazz, which, like the work songs and spirituals he was performing, came from African American culture. He felt kinship with an anonymous and collective oral tradition rather than one stemming from the individuality of jazz and blues. He did record the 'St Louis Blues' but knew he could not sing this kind of music convincingly; when he recorded with Count Basie, the great jazz band leader and pianist agreed. Robeson enjoyed certain blues performers, like Bessie Smith, and later adjusted his view of jazz, admiring a range of artists from Duke Ellington to Charlie Parker and the Modern Jazz Quartet. However, Robeson never abandoned his aesthetic preferences based on the direct relationship of folk to its audience and to its message.

His singular focus was also a declaration of faith in, and a direct connection to, black creativity, a positive assertion of his role as an interpretive artist that he was to find increasingly constrained in theatre and film. In relation to his predominantly white audiences, he justified his repertoire choice by saying: 'Now, if I can teach my audiences, who know almost nothing about the Negro, to know him [sic] through my songs . . . then I will feel that I am an artist, and that I am using my art for myself, for my race, and for the world.'[11]

The nude statue of him completed by the Italian American artist Antonio Salemmé in 1926 and called 'Negro Spiritual' exemplifies the power and intended universal appeal of Robeson, and the merging of the man and the artist. It links his image as representative of the Harlem Renaissance to the traditions of the European Renaissance, echoing the classical adoration of the body beautiful. Yet the reception accorded the Salemmé sculpture by the establishment art world shows that the body beautiful if black was still disturbing. Having asked the sculptor to submit 'Negro Spiritual' for exhibition, the Philadelphia Art Alliance returned the offending object without displaying it.

Robeson's politics were as yet rudimentary but he knew that a black performer had to look beyond individual interests and had a responsibility, willingly embraced or not, to his or her people. He realised that the roles he played were going to be identified with him as a person in a way that rarely happened to white actors and that he would therefore face battles with both white and black audiences. At the same time, the fact that he generally received better notices than the plays or films in which he appeared only exacerbated the dilemma of how to find suitable roles and best use his talent. There were few plays available by black writers and plays by white authors usually dealt in stereotypes when it came to African American roles. He even talked of setting up his own theatre, but his skills did not lie in that direction. Survival and a career were more pressing, and his own ambition to make a greater impact led him away from coterie projects of either black or white artists towards more popular platforms.

CELEBRITY

He encountered sharp contradictions in this quest, however, because popular meant white-dominated, yet in the process he consolidated his status as an international celebrity. *Black Boy*, a play by Jim Tully and Frank Dazey drawn from the life of the black boxer Jack Johnson, was poorly received but Robeson received high praise from white critics for his 1926 portrayal of the pugilist while the black press despaired that Broadway continued to present ill-informed pictures of black life. Robeson later commented that white audiences would not have accepted the play at all if it had expressed how and what Johnson had truly lived and felt. Robeson did reject David Belasco's play *Lulu Belle* as too formulaic and Paul Green's *In Abraham's Bosom* as too negative but accepted the role of Crown in a 1928 revival of Dorothy and DuBose Heyward's musical play *Porgy*, a part he had been asked to create but which he had been forced to decline because of a European tour. He did not enjoy the experience of the revival, having to push his voice too hard to be heard over the chorus.

The invitation to play the river man Joe in *Show Boat* in its 1928 London transfer at Drury Lane offered an escape, and it was this that persuaded him to lay aside the doubts he had about the role, which he thought boring. He liked the relative liberalness of London, despite the occasional – and for that, the more shocking – racism he encountered.[12] The engagement also allowed him to plan further European concert tours. The part of Joe had been written with him in mind but he had already been contracted elsewhere at the time of the original production. In addition to having little to do in the musical, Joe is presented as idle and fatalistic, and, although the libretto does tackle racial mores, his song 'Ol' Man River' contained lyrics and references to 'niggers' to which Robeson objected. Nevertheless, 'Ol' Man River' is the show's framing motif, and such was Robeson's outstanding success with it that he not only became a star in Europe as well as in America but the song became the one with which he is most popularly associated. He changed the words during the course of his performing career, swapping 'niggers' for 'darkies' and then dropping those references altogether and altering the lyrics in line with his growing political consciousness.[13]

In *Show Boat*, which played for 350 performances, Robeson was engaging with popular theatre in what was the key musical of its period, yet, as expected, he was criticised by black commentators, even though his performance appears to have transcended the cliché of the role he played. Central to the argument was the extent to which his skills were seen to reinforce or counteract the stereotype. Robeson's successes, still rare for a black performer, had made him a prominent figure in the Harlem Renaissance, which, though vibrant and historically very significant, has been criticised as a black cultural movement under white patronage because of the preponderance of rich white supporters. The debate, familiar to marginalised groups, over whether or not to work within the mainstream (in this case, white-dominated art forms) arose against the background of enormous emigration from the countryside, which had led among urban African Americans to a strong interest in black folk culture. That folk culture, however, was often an imagined one and created by white southerners, like the authors of *Simon the Cyrenian* and *Porgy*. For the black artists involved there was an inherent political danger of being satisfied with the mere assertion of African American identity (or even its superiority) and not engaging with the need for change.

Robeson and other leading black cultural figures believed in the multivalent American myth that placed a premium on opportunity and the ability to take advantage of it: individual achievement was critical and individuals could affirm their identity in the market place of culture, which was idealised as a panacea for racial strife. The singer Florence Mills, the only black performer other than Robeson to appear on the cover of *Vanity Fair* in the 1920s, believed that every white person who was pleased by her performances was a friend won for her race. Robeson was aware of the limits but believed the self-respect gained during the Harlem Renaissance, however restricted and exclusive, was an important achievement upon which to build.

Initially, Robeson was driven to succeed in white culture because he had been so successful at school and college in so many fields that being thwarted in his chosen career of law made him even more determined. Although he did not regard wealth as a measure of success he knew he was admired by many black people for achieving it, and this, he felt, obliged him to give something back to them from within the system that had afforded him this wealth. He believed that as he had overcome obstacles to achieve at the highest levels, others could too.

His own accomplishments had been built on projecting an image of himself as a performer in which his physique and his voice were deployed with a dignity that appealed to a common humanity. His presence or charisma was defined by the creation of 'authenticity', a perceived 'truth' and 'naturalness' with which he could speak intimately and directly to his audiences. Both Robeson and his colleagues (who mistrusted overt and actorly skills) regarded him as an instinctive performer, in terms that describe an ability, and perhaps a deep inner impulse, to express a fundamental truth, as if truth were a nugget to be dug out from under layers of social conditioning rather than being socially created too. It was in such essentialist terms of expressing an inner truth – one's innermost nature – that the power of his performance was said to transcend the limitations of the plays and films in which he appeared and to find its harmony in his concert singing. That Robeson was described as crossing the border between acting and life was a tribute to the success of his strategy and his strength as a performer as well as an expression of the artistic under-representation of black people at the time.

The essentialist view supported the idea that African Americans were vital and natural whereas whites were enervated and alienated. Robeson sometimes echoed this dualistic approach and used it as a defence against possible criticism of his technical shortcomings by stressing his 'naturalness'. At other times, he recognised the importance of technique. As an actor and a singer, he was aware of and concerned about his technical limitations, especially as they contrasted with his strong physical image and apparent vocal power. He worked and trained hard to develop this 'naturalness' in movement, gesture and particularly voice.

The voice places a performer just as it places a person, not only geographically but also in relation to social power. Robeson developed a delivery and articulation that was distinct from both classical opera and vernacular idiom, what might be described as 'English English' rather than 'American English' or black American.[14] He wanted to be listened to by white audiences, while avoiding association with white elitism and exotica; from black audiences he wanted to command respect and represent achievement to them, which at that time could not be conceived in terms of a 'street' voice. Despite the image of authenticity he projected, he was not singing the songs as originally sung, which involved collective call and response, different intonation and more intricate syncopation. He was presenting a different kind of authenticity in following the concert-hall tradition that 'evens out' the music. He was thereby distancing himself from the rougher sounds of popular black music that he was unable to capture. He compensated by his phrasing and passion, and produced a remarkable sound, which was acknowledged as being distinct from but as beautiful, moving and effective as that of a classically trained opera singer. It was a voice that came to carry its own moral weight.

GROWING POLITICAL AWARENESS

By the end of the 1920s, Robeson had become an international star. In Europe, he mixed in high society and met the likes of James Joyce, Gertrude Stein and Ernest Hemingway as well as leading politicians. This celebrity status, however, did not bring him artistic satisfaction. In the following decade, his discontent deepened as his political understanding and consequent political activism burgeoned; he was shaping a worldview of social change that allowed him to find a meaningful context for his art and to fit the particular struggle of his people into a relationship with other struggles.

His milieu began to alter during this period of politicisation in the 1930s, and he increasingly offered his name and his presence to a multitude of causes, from those involving international solidarity to those concerned with the rights of trade unions, the unemployed and his own people.

He spent much of the 1930s in Europe, especially in Britain, where, through contact with African students, anti-colonial leaders such as Nnamdi Azikiwe, Jomo Kenyatta and Kwame Nkrumah, and indigenous working-class activists, he learned about and became interested in Africa and class politics. Robeson traced his father's roots to the Ibo tribe and his mother's to the Bantu people and associated his pride in his culture and its ancestry with the national pride he found among organised English, Scots, Welsh and Irish workers. In particular, and not surprisingly, he developed a warm affinity for the Welsh mining communities, whom he first encountered in 1929 in the shape of a male voice choir singing in London in protest against poverty and unemployment. He visited south Wales and discovered parallels with his own people in a performance tradition derived from community, work and church, created by and through struggle.

In the face of the rise of the Nazis and the military rebellion in Spain against the democratically elected Republican government, Robeson became a committed anti-fascist. He developed an abiding sense of solidarity with the Jews, whose period of slavery in Africa gave rise to a biblical lexicon of oppression and liberation that his own people drew on in songs (which he sang) such as 'Go Down, Moses'. He performed benefits for Jewish refugees, having seen the destitution of Jewish communities in Europe and hatred in the eyes of storm troopers in Berlin when he stopped there on his way to Moscow in 1934. He had fond memories of the culturally alive Berlin he had visited in 1930. The contrast he felt on the later visit, combined with the warm reception he found in Soviet Russia, remained crucial for him, both because it coincided with his own political awakening and because he had experienced it himself first hand. On arriving in Russia after leaving Nazi Germany behind, he said: 'I feel like a human being for the first time since I grew up. Here I am not a Negro but a human being.'[15]

In Moscow he met artists like the Soviet filmmaker Sergei Eisenstein and the black American-born actor Wayland Rudd as well as black American Communists such as William Patterson. Robeson was conscious of the achievements of a land that had suffered serfdom more recently than his people had suffered slavery and yet seemed more intent on social justice than America. Later Robeson visited Soviet Asia and was impressed by the situation of minority populations. The 1936 Soviet constitution, which outlawed racial discrimination in stark comparison to the anti-Semitic laws passed in Germany, and the subsequent Soviet role in supporting anti-fascist and national liberation struggles won Robeson to the pro-Soviet camp. He was never publicly to condemn the appalling treatment of Soviet citizens, the minorities or the dissenters, yet his private criticisms of aspects of Soviet life, including its anti-Semitism, and the tension between his public statements and private knowledge must have contributed to his illnesses in the 1950s and '60s.

FILMS

The different strands of his artistic life took different turns during the years of growing political awareness. The improved working conditions and closer relationship to audiences that he found in small-scale theatre and political song balanced the frustrations of the star system in film. He appeared in 1930 with his wife Eslanda in a silent, avant-garde film *Borderline*, which deals with racism in a Swiss border village. It was made using montage techniques by the Pool Group of white artists associated with a cinema journal *Close Up* and the Harlem Renaissance.[16] It was largely ignored on its release but has subsequently become a minor classic of experimental cinema. Apparently, Robeson, who was not in sympathy with what he regarded as the mystique of modernism, did not think very highly of *Borderline*, and he showed no inclination to pursue this type of film.

The advent of the 'talkie' offered Robeson a direct route to a mass audience and in 1933 he turned towards mainstream, albeit still independent, cinema to make his first commercial – and sound – film, *The Emperor Jones*. The African American actress Fredi Washington was forced to 'darken up' when amorous scenes between her and Robeson had to be reshot at the demand of the industry censor's office, who thought the light-skinned Washington looked white in the original versions. While Robeson's role was a welcome departure from the usual comic or musical parts offered black screen actors, aspects of his performance fed the very idea of atavistic primitivism he was trying to challenge in his politics.

When the film was released, the criticisms Robeson had received following the stage version were repeated even more sharply, and he became wary of, yet still attracted to, the potential of film. Despite his misgivings about the role of Joe in *Show Boat*, he agreed to appear in the second film of the musical (1936) because of the extra power he thought his resulting income and celebrity would bring. The remake, which was an improvement on the original 1929 version and restored the critique of Southern racism that had been lost, proved very popular, but the studio rejected Robeson's request to be granted approval of the final cut, and Hollywood did not follow through by offering him the leading roles he was looking for.

Robeson turned to Britain instead and pursued two of his favourite themes – Africa and the working man – but with only mixed success. He rejected an offer to appear in *Aida* in order to make the film *Sanders of the River* (1935), in which he plays an African chief and which he strongly believed would further understanding of African culture. He claimed it became an apology for British imperialism only in the editing stage, and he refused to perform at the première. Many black commentators, including friends of Robeson, did not accept the editing excuse, and he subsequently recognised the inherent bias of the project, coming to hate the result, which, even more exasperatingly, proved popular. He tried unsuccessfully to buy all the prints and stop its distribution, and refused to appear in three subsequent films from the same stable, Alexander Korda's London Film Productions.

The following year he recorded the theme song and prologue, rewritten by himself, for what turned out to be a rather mild documentary film on South Africa, *Africa Looks Up* (known in the US as *My Song Goes Forth*). For *Song of Freedom*, that same year, 1936, Robeson insisted on final approval. He plays the bespoke part of a dockworker who becomes a concert singer but who is unknowingly the heir to an African kingdom. Despite its limitations, especially the absurdity of the plot, the film does offer positive depictions of a multi-racial East End of London, of a black relationship (between Robeson's character and his wife, played by Elisabeth Welch) and of the possibility of an autonomous black future in Africa. Even his black critics praised *Song of Freedom*; it was later shown during the struggle for independence on the Gold Coast and by the Nkrumah government of what had now become Ghana at its second anniversary celebrations in 1959. The honesty of the film's portrayal of black people made it one of only two of his films Robeson liked – the other being *The Proud Valley* (1940). Neither received wide distribution in the US.

In spite of his attempts to get script changes to *King Solomon's Mines* (1937), another hidden identity film in which he plays a servant who is discovered to be a tribal leader, the result was insultingly stereotypical. He gained greater control over *Jericho* (1937, also known as *Dark Sands*), in which, as a medical student drafted into the army in Egypt, he becomes a hero and, escaping injustice, ends up as a Tuareg tribal chief. In *Big Fella* (1937), directed by J. Elder Willis, who had directed *Song of Freedom*, Robeson plays a singing dockworker again, this time in Marseilles, and he won script changes that emphasised the goodness of his character. The film, which includes several strong black characters, received little distribution, however.

Song of Freedom and *Big Fella* also express Robeson's growing interest in class and celebrate the dignified virtues of the male proletarian, as does the film *The Proud Valley*, an optimistic, idealised portrait of the archetypal worker, the miner. It tells the story of an unemployed African American David Goliath (the film's original title), who ends up working in a south Wales mine and becomes part of the community fighting to save the colliery from closure. He dies in a pit tragedy, saving the son of the (white) man who gave him a home. A deeply emotional and sentimental film, its attempt at a realistic portrayal of working-class life, in which skin colour was less important than human solidarity, made it remarkable for its time. In Britain, its reception was hampered by a ban on any mention of Robeson in newspapers owned by press baron Lord Beaverbrook in reprisal for pro-Soviet comments Robeson had made.

The series of feature films Robeson made in the 1930s represents an enormous if frustrating and frustrated effort to reach a mass audience with positive images that countered white visions of the uncultured, lazy or sly black person that were rooted in slavery. His intentions are submerged under cliché because the mostly simplistic parts he plays commonly express values which white cinema found acceptable and therefore permitted. His role as singer/entertainer, for example, was entirely suitable – and he liked singing on film because he did not have to project as he did in a live performance. The topics of Africa and the working man were perceived as distinctively different and also acceptable for a black performer. Yet, although sometimes attacked by the left and even by black critics for his cinematic performances, Robeson does display on screen what the writer James Baldwin calls 'hints of reality, smuggled like contraband' as he tries to wrestle with the stereotype to turn it to his advantage.[17]

Robeson's attempts to reach outside the stereotype suggest not so much the specificity of black struggle but an appeal beyond skin colour or culture to the universal. This appeal comes through his masculinity (which is seen as the all-encompassing value rising above gender in the way that 'white' supposedly transcends race), but also through his expression of 'female' values. His physicality – handsome, tall, athletic – is exhibited as admirable and fits an idealised picture, which he tempers with openness, decorum and integrity. In this, he was attempting to reconnect the emotion and the intellect, which he believed the Renaissance in western Europe had separated, a division he linked to subsequent white domination over colonial subjects justified by the Enlightenment. He also believed he was countering a contemporary obsession with the black body, which was being denigrated by commercial exploitation. Yet it is precisely his black body that many of the filmmakers were interested in, and the end result often achieves little more than a forceful projection of dignity. This, however, was an achievement in itself in that era.

At the same time, Robeson's presence is destabilising, especially for a white audience used to images of the body being strictly policed in both its sexual and its labouring roles. Despite Robeson's own strong sexual allure, he instead shows restraint – gentleness or spirituality even – yet this is not always a protection against erotic disquiet. His size and stature, his demeanour and carriage, suggest another potential threat to white typecasting. Here is a possible alternative, a possible leader, someone searching for a different future. Robeson's images had to be controlled, to be seen as impressive rather than alarming. Nevertheless, penetrating the self-restraint he developed off screen, he expresses on screen an immense potential for anger and action. The films have to contain these tensions, but in so doing they also reveal them, and this provides the power of his performances.

Robeson felt he had done what he could in the cinema.[18] Film scripts he saw were usually poor but he knew that if he were to wait for the ideal one, he would have to wait for ever – always the dilemma for a performer of other people's work. For instance, a plan by Eisenstein to make a film with him as the Haitian hero Toussaint l'Ouverture failed to materialise and Robeson felt obliged to accept other, less appealing work while trying to maintain a degree of influence. 'To expect the

Negro artist to reject every role with which he is not ideo-logically in agreement,' he told a journalist, 'is to expect the Negro artist under our present scheme of things to give up his work entirely.'[19]

Yet, having worked without satisfaction in minority film, both black and experimental, as well as in mainstream feature film, that is precisely what he did: he decided to leave the film world altogether.

He was not the first or only black actor to retreat wounded from the film industry: for example, Bert Williams and Charles Gilpin in the days of silent movies and Daniel L. Haynes in sound pictures. Robeson was the first, however, to attempt to create a body of significant black characters who measured up to the white characters in his films. For Robeson this was not enough. He saw that all the characters in the films were stereo-types, regardless of colour, but that meant they were still re-flecting the power structure of society. Whatever his individual successes, he had not been able in general to affect the films as a whole. He came to recognise that even as a black celeb-rity, and regardless of his own commitment and fortitude, he could not defeat the dominant film system and that to mount a serious challenge would require an equally serious challenge to the social system that underpinned it.

THEATRE WORK

In the theatre during the 1930s Robeson found greater con-tentment. He gave two highly praised performances of *The Emperor Jones* in Berlin in 1930 but after that, as in his film work, he gravitated to Britain where the decade began with West End success as Othello. Understandably, he had always aspired to act this part (and had performed extracts at school), but he was nervous of his ability to do justice to the role as well as to history – records suggested few black actors had been allowed to play the Moor since the American Ira Aldridge in the nineteenth century. Robeson, nevertheless, triumphed in the part, which remained a symbol of his own life, a connec-tion underscored by the fact that he played it in three different productions and that in his regular concert repertoire he included Othello's last speech before he stabs himself:

Soft you; a word or two before you go.
I have done the state some service and they know't.
No more of that. I pray you, in your letters,
When you shall these unlucky deeds relate,
Speak of me as I am. Nothing extenuate,
Nor set down aught in malice.

By way of preparation for his first essay – in London in 1930, with a twenty-two-year-old Peggy Ashcroft as Desdemona – Robeson studied phonetics, English pronunciation and the history of the role on stage. He took voice and diction classes with Amanda Ira Aldridge, one of Ira's daughters, whom he had met in London in the 1920s and who had given Robeson the earrings her father had worn for the part. Unfortunately, the short rehearsal period was fraught, the production was weak and poorly cast in several roles, and Robeson thought the end result clumsy and his own performance not that good. The director was the inexperienced Ellen van Volkenburg, wife of the producer Maurice Browne, who had persuaded Robeson to play Othello and had cast himself disastrously as Iago. A measure of the problems was Robeson having to resist Browne's insistence that as Othello he arrive in Cyprus singing.

Some (white) critics complained that Robeson was too civilised, as if the presence at last of a black actor in the role required him to fulfil their preconceptions of racial behaviour. Others either praised him as outstanding or damned him as pedestrian. Robeson did feel awkward, however, because there had been much press speculation about him having to kiss a white actress and this had affected his composure. A proposed US transfer never materialised; the dates were wrong for Robeson and, more importantly, Browne was against it. Furthermore, Robeson told the BBC how difficult it would be for him to perform the play in the US because of his kissing a white woman and handling her roughly.

His next appearance in the West End the following year lasted only five performances; the revival of O'Neill's *The Hairy Ape* had to be cancelled because of Robeson's nervous exhaustion. After returning to the US a year later to star in a revival of *Show Boat* on Broadway, he turned his back on mainstream theatre for the rest of the decade. Instead he found nourishment and self-expression in London's non-commercial 'little theatres', innovative venues usually bankrolled by a wealthy patron, run on small budgets and offering cheap seats as well as new drama in reaction to the ossification of the West End. Thematically, he trod similar ground to that of his film work yet it was in such theatres that Robeson found politically sympathetic figures and was able to work in collective circumstances that reflected his new political interests.

He appeared in a 1933 revival of *All God's Chillun*, which began at the small Embassy Theatre but transferred to the West End. He gave a benefit performance of the production for Jewish refugees, a gesture which he later said marked the beginning of his political engagement. He played an African chief in Peter Garland's *Basalik* (1935), which reprised the cod African milieu of some of his films, a heroic worker in *Stevedore* (1935) by Paul Peters and George Sklar, the Haitian leader in the C.L.R. James play *Toussaint* (1936, also known as *Black Majesty*) and a trades unionist in Ben Bengal's *Plant in the Sun* (1938), in which black and white workers unite to defend themselves and their union.

Robeson rejected a lucrative West End offer as the star in *The Sun Never Sets* at Drury Lane in order to appear in *Plant in the Sun*, which was staged by the Communist-oriented Unity Theatre. He admired the connection the play made between class and race and even accepted a part written to be played by a white actor, as if to underline the overriding importance of class-consciousness and the equality of the races. Robeson also enjoyed the absence of star billing at Unity, a non-professional group, of which he had been an original general council member since the company had opened a new theatre the year before. Unity did not publish the names of the actors in its programmes, an echo of his association with the anonymity of folk culture, although the theatre understandably used his presence to attract publicity.

TAKING SIDES

His musical development during the 1930s also directly reflected his politicisation and, consequently, saw a broadening of his repertoire. Without losing their place, the work songs and spirituals ceased to be his dynamo. Indeed, his signature tune, 'Ol' Man River', is not drawn from that stock and, in the version he sang from the late 1930s on, it bears the marks of his own intervention arising from his solidarity with Republican Spain. This crystallised his new political opinions about the weakness of international capitalism, which had failed to protect the Spanish government against the fascist uprising, and the need for solidarity across nations, colour and even class.

Following the ancient folk habit of adapting songs – which he had practised before and was to continue to do – Robeson had already substituted lyrics by the time of the 1935 film of *Show Boat*: he no longer sang about 'niggers' or 'darkies' working on the Mississippi, and the river had become 'the ol' man I don't like to be'. Now he went further in expropriating his signature tune. He transformed it from a white version of a work song, which conveyed defeatist acceptance, into a protest song of resistance. He turned 'Ol' Man River' on its head through a change of lyrics and the way in which he sang it. The passive 'I'm tired of livin' and scared of dyin' ' became 'I must keep fightin' until I'm dyin' ' – a call to arms emphasised in tone of voice and body gesture that marked a decisive break with the Robeson of the past. When he sang this version in London's Albert Hall at a concert for Spanish refugee children in 1937, he declared to a rapturous audience, 'The artist must take sides. He [sic] must elect to fight for freedom or slavery. I have made my choice. I had no alternative.'[20]

In 1938, he went to Madrid to sing for the troops of the International Brigade, the volunteers who were fighting on the side of the Spanish government against the fascists. In the Lincoln Brigade, which grouped the volunteers from America, he saw black and white fighting together unlike in the segregated US army, and fighting furthermore not as conscripts but as willing participants, in another continent for a common cause. After this visit, he concluded that there was no standing above the conflict: 'The battlefront is everywhere.'[21]

The readjustment of his singing repertoire did not downgrade the work songs and spirituals but gave them a new and, to him, stronger context. When he had toured Europe in the twenties, he had found similarities between black folk music and the folk music of that continent, particularly in central Europe stretching from Poland and Hungary through Romania to Bulgaria and Albania. He repeated these discoveries as he learnt about Celtic folk music, ancient Hebraic chants, flamenco in Spain, and, through Larry Brown, the presence of folk idioms in the classical music of Bartók, Dvořák (who pointed American art music toward its own folk heritage), Janáček, Kodály and Mussorgsky. All this confirmed for Robeson the existence of a global body of music based on a five-tone (pentatonic) scale, which validated the universality of the songs of his people and reinforced his belief in the common threads linking the human race that lay behind much of his politics and art.

Learning in Britain about his African roots nurtured his interest in etymology; this study alongside his musical investigations confirmed his ideas of a universal humanity. His singing became a bridge between peoples within that humanity, an expression of his support for the ideas of the Popular Front and for internationalist politics. Black folk music would be interspersed with speeches from plays and songs of other cultures – Slav, Mexican, Russian, Chinese, African, Jewish, Welsh and Gaelic – as well as with songs from the contemporary left-wing scene. For instance, he would sing 'The Song of the Peat-bog Soldiers', which had been taken up internationally from Nazi concentration camps by the left, or 'Joe Hill', which, in its metaphor of the militant who lives on after death, captures Robeson's own aspiration for political longevity and effectiveness beyond the moment of performance.

He also now drew on classical music, which he sang like folk music without decoration; there were, for example, arias from Mozart's *The Magic Flute*, Beethoven's 'Ode to Joy' and Smetana's 'Freedom'. Chosen because they were consistent with his worldview, all these additions were often accompanied by spoken commentary and sung in English as well as in the original language. He also added commentary to his African American repertoire, with reference to leading figures in the struggle to abolish slavery, as if acknowledging that the singing voice he had developed was not, of itself, always able to bring out the politics of the songs. The achieved simplicity of his style for all his songs regardless of origin was a reminder that his politics at root were a matter of conviction rather than ideological nuance and that context was critical for him in his ambition to make his art useful.

Appropriately, he broadened his audiences and the choice of venues he sang in as well, often appearing at rallies or political gatherings in the open air, and in provincial music halls and cinemas with very low admission prices. He concentrated particularly on events for the labour, progressive and national liberation movements, from Aid Spain concerts to benefits for the defence of China against Japanese aggression and campaigns to register black voters in the South. In such circumstances, he found a different and more rewarding relationship to his audiences than at his more formal concerts, and, for Robeson, this became an important aspect of trying to make his art politically effective.

WAR

In 1939, he returned to stay in the US because of the war, which, at first, he believed America should spurn. He supported the Nazi-Soviet pact and Soviet entry into Poland and Finland as justifiable responses to the West's attempts to isolate the Soviet Union. Yet he still espoused Popular Front ideas and presented himself as an optimistic patriot in the spirit of Roosevelt's New Deal, which had seen progress from the Harlem Renaissance in the autonomy of black artists and their wider presence in a range of artistic ventures. Robeson saw criticism of his country as the highest form of loyalty and invoked the traditions of the constitution and American revolutionary democracy. He believed the true interests of America lay in the unity of black and white people and placed great emphasis on their two mass organisations, the church and the trade unions respectively.

The protean nature of his celebrity can be seen by the extraordinary popularity he achieved with 'Ballad for Americans', despite recently making remarks about America keeping out of the war, which had provoked sharp criticism even from friends. The ballad, written by Communist Party member Earl Robinson with lyrics by the poet John LaTouche, celebrates the dynamic social pluralism of the US. It embraces the 'melting pot' idea of multi-ethnic America, and carries sentiments ranging from 'Our Country's strong, our Country's young, / And her greatest songs are still unsung' to an echo of Marx, 'Man in white skin can never be free / While his black brother is in slavery'.[22]

When rehearsing for its radio broadcast, Robeson persuaded Robinson to lower the song's pitch – Robeson could best achieve his personal voice in the lower keys because, if he was using a microphone, he did not need to push for greater volume (something that occasionally troubled him in the unamplified concert auditorium). The broadcast in November 1939 on CBS radio was an immediate success; the studio audience gave him a twenty-minute ovation. His appearance at the Hollywood Bowl singing the ballad resulted in a record attendance there. The disc sold 30,000 copies within a year and both the Republican and Communist Party Conventions of 1940 chose the song for their theme. It was a rare moment when the mood of the left was in tune with the general mood, and Robeson had achieved one of his dreams, to epitomise the whole nation.

His colossal celebrity did not guarantee artistic success, however, as was shown in 1940 by the failure of the musical play *John Henry*, his first foray on Broadway since the revival of *Show Boat* eight years earlier. His wife Eslanda Robeson and Larry Brown had warned him the script by the white Southern writer Roark Bradford was poor, but Robeson wanted to reconnect to black American folk culture and ignored their advice. It was badly received in pre-Broadway try-outs and, despite good reviews for Robeson, the show closed in New York after seven performances.

He stayed true to his decision to abandon the film industry, spurning several offers, until two quite different American projects enticed him back. Both appeared to suit his political aspirations but only one came close to succeeding. This was the full-length documentary film *Native Land*, made by the independent, left-wing production company Frontier Films to expose infringements of trade-union and civil rights. He had already given a modest sum to help the makers of the film, which began production in 1937 but which, because of financial problems, was not completed and released until 1942.

Robeson became involved at the end of the process, to sing and provide narration, which he rehearsed for six weeks as if it were a play. But, because of Pearl Harbor in December 1941, America was at war by the time the film was seen, and its reception was badly affected by a new mood of national unity.

The other film was the multi-episode *Tales of Manhattan* (1942), which came to Robeson replete with stars such as Henry Fonda, Edward G. Robinson and Ginger Rogers. Robeson believed the film would deal in a sympathetic way with rural poverty among African Americans and suggest a communal solution.[23] He agreed to appear in the final 'sharecroppers' section and subsequently wished he had stuck by his decision to retire. It was a repeat of his *Sanders of the River* experience; he condemned the false image of happiness and equality projected in the film and joined those protesting against its distribution. He believed state intervention was required to break the studio system, which was too dependent on the lucrative market of the racist South. Now his retirement from film was final.

His disappointment with the film industry was mitigated by the opportunity at last to play Othello on stage in his homeland. Keenly conscious of his social duty as an artist, it was important to him that a black performer conquered the artistic heights of the established artistic scene at a time of national solidarity. Robeson also felt that, in contrast to his first attempt a decade previously, he was now ready to play the Moor. When the idea of this second attempt was mooted the experienced classical director Margaret Webster, who had seen the London production and, like Robeson, had thought it poor, could find no New York management willing to take the risk. Instead, she began the production, with Uta Hagen as Desdemona and Hagen's husband José Ferrer as Iago, as a limited summer try-out in Cambridge, Massachusetts. It was well received, with *Variety* stating: 'no white man should ever dare to presume' to play the role again.[24]

It took another fourteen months to open the production in New York. The delay was not due to a lack of backers, who, in response to the reviews, were eager to support the production, but to Robeson's existing obligations. In the meanwhile, he used his celebrity to get six weeks' rehearsal instead of the fortnight for the Cambridge try-out and to have Hagen and Ferrer reinstated after the producers had sacked them. His interpretation went further than before in treating Othello as a great 'Negro warrior' isolated and then undermined in an alien world rather than a man undone simply by sexual jealousy. His status as an outsider was the key to his vulnerability, Iago's hatred and Desdemona's daring in marrying him. Robeson worked very hard to overcome his self-consciousness on stage, to achieve tonal range, and, as he put it, 'not to sing my lines, but to speak them musically.'[25] He also tried but with less success to overcome the self-possession he had learned as a survival strategy in life so that he could act the anger of the role on stage.

The opening performances out of town divided the critics but, nevertheless, there was the tangible feeling of a special occasion for the Broadway première. The reception was rousing, the daily critics were complimentary and, despite mixed reviews in the weekly press, the production went on to set a Broadway record for a Shakespeare play of 296 performances. This was followed by a tour of 45 cities for 36 weeks, avoiding the South except for black colleges and unsegregated theatres. Regardless of the quibbles about his acting skills, Robeson had won over those who had criticised him for misusing his talents in sub-standard Hollywood and Broadway vehicles. While he did not agree that it was the ringing endorsement of American democracy a few black commentators proposed, the production was clearly a theatrical and racial landmark.

HERO'S FALL

As it turned out, *Othello* was also both the summit and the conclusion of his American stage career. He made only one further theatrical appearance and that was more than ten years later and in Britain. He had begun the 1940s as a national symbol, evidence that a black person could succeed in America. He ended the decade as the country's most persecuted and reviled African American, openly condemning the system that had glorified his individual achievement because it had failed the overwhelming majority of his people. Unsurprisingly, during these years his political activities increased. They ranged from chairing the Council on African Affairs and backing striking car workers to protesting against the imprisonment of Communists and campaigning for the desegregation of major league baseball. His unswerving political beliefs led to an inevitable and escalating conflict with the state and its acolytes.

As Robeson's popularity grew and honours were bestowed on him, he was being increasingly investigated by the FBI as a suspected enemy of the state. The Bureau found the film *Native Land* to be 'obviously a Communist project', and his contribution to it led the House Committee on Un-American Activities Chairman, Martin Dies, to accuse Robeson himself of being a Communist.[26] This was in the same year that the Secretary of the Treasury cited him for distinguished and patriotic service to the US. In 1943, Robeson received the Abraham Lincoln Medal for notable and distinguished service in human relations as FBI chief J. Edgar Hoover added his name to the security index of those to be arrested in the event of national emergency. In 1944, at the height of Robeson's popularity, an article in *The American Magazine* called him America's 'Number One Negro' and a year later he won the Springarn Medal, the highest decoration for a black person, while the FBI were bugging the telephones of the leadership of the Council on African Affairs, which they already believed to be run on behalf of the Communist Party.

During the war, Robeson had vigorously supported the campaign to open a Second Front and encouraged American-Soviet friendship but the underlying differences between the two systems made the wartime alliance a very brief affair, and those who continued their support for the Soviets, as Robeson did, became targets of aggression and contumely. With Roosevelt's death in April 1945 a great deal changed both in America at large and for Robeson personally. Democrat contender Harry Truman's victory paved the way for a period of vicious anti-left activity under the anti-red banner. Abroad, the American reluctance to pursue de-Nazification alarmed Robeson, who saw the end of the anti-fascist war bringing not a flowering of freedom but the start of the Cold War and the systematic thwarting of national liberation and anti-colonial struggles.

The class and international solidarity Robeson had promoted since the 1930s when American workers had found a new level of class-consciousness did not survive into the Cold War except in small pockets of the left. Robeson rejected the premise of Churchill's 'iron curtain' speech and explicitly related the liberation of his people at home with the liberation struggle abroad and the wider fight for Socialism. Robeson stepped up his battles against racism in the US, in particular against lynching and segregation, not only among his own audiences but also in the armed forces and in society in general. In 1946, he was called before a Californian Un-American Activities 'fact-finding' committee and asked if he was a member of the Communist Party; he replied he was not but defended his right to join any legal party and characterised himself as 'an anti-fascist and independent'.[27] The following year came the first of several attempts on his life.

THROWN TO THE LIONS

Also in 1947, three-quarters of the way through a national tour, Robeson declared he would stop giving concerts for two years and would sing only for causes in which he believed. 'I must raise my voice,' he said, 'but not by singing pretty songs.' The FBI took this announcement as a challenge and stepped up its efforts to prove him a member or affiliate of the Communist Party. Journalists attacked him with great clamour. Hedda Hopper, the right-wing columnist who also pursued Charlie Chaplin, attacked Robeson for having sung the Russian 'People's Battle Song'. This was 'abusing the precious heritage of freedom'. A right-wing columnist, George E. Sokolsky, who was nationally syndicated, wrote venomously but realistically: 'If Robeson chooses to be both singer and propagandist, that is his risk. Those who favour causes must risk the consequences of opposition.' He added, chillingly, 'Better men than Paul Robeson have been thrown to the lions.'[28]

The cause Robeson favoured was black emancipation and the liberation of all the oppressed, but he was punished for his

support of what his enemies saw as the atheistic foreign ideology of Communism – a stark contrast to the spiritual quality
of his own performances and his close association with black
churches, neither of which his enemies could comprehend.

As Robeson had retired from filmmaking, his persecution –
the desire to rub out a star – must have had deep roots. Certainly, the process of harassment intensified. Meetings and
concerts were cancelled with greater frequency, several trade
unions turned their back on him, municipal auditoria became
closed to him and his records were withdrawn from shops.
Robeson, nevertheless, still retained enormous if dwindling
popularity and used his beleaguered celebrity to attack laws
that required oaths of loyalty, that outlawed the closed shop,
that were used to imprison Communists and that promoted
white supremacy.[29] The personal cost, however, was increasingly high. He was starved of earnings (one estimate said his
income dropped from the late 1940s to early 1950s by a
staggering 96 per cent) but more importantly to him he was
being denied his audience.[30]

In the autumn 1948 presidential election, Robeson was
backing Henry Wallace of the Progressive Party, an apostle of
post-war cooperation, against the incumbent Truman when
he decided to return to giving professional concerts.[31] A US
tour comprising 85 appearances was booked but collapsed
when the country became even more anti-Communist in the
wake of Truman's victory. Robeson turned to Europe instead.
During his tour there he spoke at a Paris peace conference in
1949 and, prefiguring Muhammad Ali's rejection of the
Vietnam War ('No Vietcong ever called me nigger'), was mis-
quoted as saying that African Americans would not fight for
the US against the Soviet Union.[32]

What he actually said is disputed; apart from a film of the
conference, which has not been found, there is no accurate
record. The press version of his speech reported him as saying
it 'is unthinkable . . . that American Negroes would go to war
on behalf of those who have oppressed us for generations . . .
against a country [the Soviet Union] which, in one generation, has raised our people to full human dignity of mankind.' Another version offers a quotation from a different part
of the speech: 'Our will to fight for peace is strong. We shall

not make war on anyone. We shall not make war on the Soviet Union.'[33]

When asked about the speech, Robeson said that he was referring to all those who had created the wealth of America, but the exact message was less important than the fact that he had criticised America abroad and in relation to an enemy power. The reaction he aroused was furious, and not only in the white media and political circles. A series of black figures – political, sporting and cultural – disavowed him in the press and before the House Committee on Un-American Activities (HUAC). This rejection by black leaders was made both in genuine disagreement but also opportunistically because, by distancing themselves from Robeson, they could appear respectable and hope to gain white support in their fight for civil rights, or, in the case of sportsmen and entertainers, protect their careers.[34] It did not dent Robeson's enthusiasm for continuing on his path; he did still have considerable support within the black political community, but it served to increase his isolation.

His use of his talent had generally been acceptable for nearly three decades – until he was deemed to have gone too far and had to be punished. He was dangerous because he represented two enemies in one, the red and the black; he appealed not only to the left but also to a popular audience and, even rarer, to a popular audience that comprised both black and white, indeed that crossed ethnic and cultural identities. To suppress him, the state had to suppress both his art and his politics. He had broken the tacit rule that said artists should avoid confrontational politics, a contravention more dreadful for an African American and even more terrible for an illustrious one.

Robeson's persecution was not just personal but part of the wider anti-Communist campaign of punishment and deterrence, which included a strategy to quell the radical black left. His wife Essie Robeson, as well as many friends and acquaintances, were called before HUAC or the McCarthy hearings, and others like W.E.B. DuBois also had passport problems. Black leaders such as the trades unionists Ferdinand C. Smith and Revels Cayton were harassed, the Communist Party was heavily attacked and several of the organisations with which

Robeson was associated were driven out of business as 'red front' groups.[35] Critical to this assault was the biased trial of Communist Party leaders, overseen by a judge who had taught Robeson at law school, which convinced Robeson that an exclusively constitutional route in the political struggle was pointless.

This view was underlined by the general failure of the law to prevent lynching and by the legal defeats suffered following the Peekskill atrocities of 1949. The Civil Rights Congress (successor to the National Negro Congress) had organised a fund-raising concert just outside Peekskill, a quiet town some twenty miles north of New York, at which Robeson was to sing. He had done this before, but this time the local paper published calls for action against the event and rioting gangs associated with veterans' organisations aided by the police stopped it happening; a week later Robeson was only able to sing at a second concert there because trades unionists and other supporters formed a guard. Crosses were burned on surrounding hills and two effigies of him were hung from nearby trees. The audience was attacked at the end, in certain cases with the help of the state troopers present and in other cases without the troopers intervening; nearly 150 people needed treatment. In the wake of a national outcry, a grand jury investigation found the cause of the riots was Communism. Robeson and twenty-seven others sued county officials and veterans' bodies for damages, but the New York Supreme Court eventually dismissed the suits.

PASSPORT CONFISCATED

In 1950 Robeson suffered more effective though less violent censorship than had occurred at Peekskill. He became what was reported to be the first American to be banned from US television when NBC stopped his appearance on 'Today with Mrs Roosevelt'. Censorship went further still when, after denouncing US participation in the Korean War, he refused to sign a document saying he would not speak in public abroad and the State Department revoked his passport.

The removal of Robeson's passport, enforced for nearly a decade, was an attempt to make him a non-person, once he had ceased to be useful to the prevailing system as an emblem of a successful black man and, worse still, was challenging the very foundations of the system that had made him a success. Although only a small number of Americans held passports, the withdrawal of Robeson's presented both a real and a symbolic attack on his freedom: mobility had been the means of escape from slavery and it was also the means for black and other oppressed American artists to find work, usually in Europe. This route was now denied him. Among other engagements, it cost Robeson the opportunity to make a film of *Othello*, another about Ira Aldridge and to appear in *Pericles* at Stratford-upon-Avon.

In 1952, although an American citizen did not need a passport to visit Canada, he was prevented by the immigration service from crossing the border to attend a mineworkers' convention in Vancouver. He decided instead to address them via long-distance telephone relayed through a public address system. Following the miners' suggestion, Robeson gave a 'Peace Arch' concert across the US-Canadian border later that year with people gathered on both sides of the divide to hear him sing. An estimated 25–30,000 people turned up on the Vancouver side at White Rock, although less than five thousand attended on the US side at Blaine. Robeson repeated the event annually for the next three years, and it became important in his campaign to stay in the public eye.[36]

He was also stopped from travelling to Moscow in 1952 to receive the Stalin Peace Prize, a snub that led a protesting Charlie Chaplin to comment: 'To deny a great artist like Robeson his right to give his art to the world is to destroy the very foundation upon which our culture and civilisation is built.'[37]

Deprived of access to cultural and political engagements abroad, Robeson found that offers of work at home had also dried up. The media and his opponents – black and white and certain sections of the labour movement he had supported – attempted to delete him from public life. In 1953, he and DuBois were omitted from the first ever children's book of famous American Negroes (written by erstwhile friend and admirer, the black playwright and poet Langston Hughes), in 1956 Robeson was excluded from the list of All-American

football teams for 1918 and as late as 1970 the National Football Foundation failed to include him in its Hall of Fame.

Robeson countered this cultural boycott by establishing his
own apparatus, singing in black churches as well as for the left
and those still sympathetic in the labour movement, setting up
his own record label and writing a regular column in the
Freedom magazine, which he and DuBois founded.[38] He even
broke his boycott of the cinema by singing the title song to
Song of the Rivers, a documentary film made for the World
Federation of Trade Unions, which, apparently, was not
shown in US.[39] Friends in Britain launched a 'Let Robeson
Sing' campaign and, in response, he sang to thousands in
Wales, Manchester and London via a telephone link. Solidarity spread; India held a Paul Robeson day and the government's demand for the return of his passport endangered
India-US relations. A hero abroad, a world cultural figure on
the level of Pablo Neruda, Bertolt Brecht and Charlie Chaplin,
he became ever more cut off at home. White liberals deserted
him, and he himself advised acquaintances like Sidney Poitier,
Harry Belafonte and Dizzy Gillespie to be careful of – and
even to avoid – his company in order to protect their careers.

Prevented from performing as and when he chose, Robeson's life and his struggle with the state had become the main
performance, and it was taking its physical toll. In addition to
a urinary tract infection, he suffered in 1956 an emotional
collapse. Against his doctor's advice, he agreed to appear
before HUAC that year but was not allowed to read a prepared statement. He did use the opportunity, among other
things, to place his Paris comments in context. Making reference to the Bandung conference of African and Asian nations
held the previous year, which he was unable to attend because
of his travel embargo, he linked the situation facing 15 million
black people in America to the plight of coloured peoples
around the world, who, he believed, would not go to war to
defend western imperialism. When asked why he had not
stayed in Russia, Robeson replied, 'Because my father was a
slave, and my people died to build this country, and I am
going to stay here and have a part of it just like you. And no
fascist-minded people will drive me from it.' He accused the
committee of being the 'non-patriots . . . the un-Americans',

and they in retort voted to cite him for contempt.[40] The House of Representatives, nevertheless, disagreed. He refused to sign an affidavit declaring he was not a Communist, an act which would have returned his passport, and the Supreme Court refused his appeal against its confiscation.

As HUAC and McCarthyism revealed, Robeson had not been alone – either among black or white people – in embracing a utopian, pro-Communist worldview in the 1930s following the failure of capitalism in the Depression. For anyone wanting to become politically active, the Communists had represented a major force because their philosophy was to change the world. Robeson's defence of Communists and the Soviet Union was motivated by a belief that they were the most reliable opponents of racism, fascism and imperialism, which he considered more heinous than the defects of the first Socialist state.

This accounts for the different yardsticks he used in making his political judgements and the apparent disparity between the validity of his domestic and foreign agendas. He thought the Soviet Union was under siege by the West and, just as in wartime, innocent individuals might suffer in the process of the majority struggling to achieve a noble aim. That was the price of history seen from the point of view of an activist who emphasised collective rather than individual struggle, who himself continued to suffer injustice in his homeland and whose people continued to be discriminated against and lynched.

His opponents preferred deficient American democracy to whatever the Communists were offering. In 1956 Soviet leader Nikita Khrushchev's revelations about Stalin gave more ammunition to Robeson's detractors. Robeson, however, had personal experience of good people in the ranks of various Communist parties, and when anti-Communist persecution forced him, like many others, to make a stand, to him there was only one choice. He was not going to assist the enemies of his people and fail those who, unlike him, had chosen to be Communists, many of whom he had worked with and sung for. His stand was not a matter of duty but of conviction, of honour.

He was trapped in a symbiotic relationship with his adversaries; the more they intensified their attacks and won over leading black figures to isolate Robeson, the more he felt the need to defend the principles by which he stood. The more he did this, the harder it became for him to make public any criticisms he may have had of the Communists, even should he have wished. He had predicated his image of authenticity on truthfulness, and if this were to be undermined, he would have been unable to occupy a political position that would not have destroyed his whole persona; he chose to retain his dignity instead.

There were other strategies. Many white progressives like the musician Larry Adler, who left for Britain, and even some American Communists, did not agree with mixing art and politics in the way Robeson favoured, although singers such as Pete Seeger did; he offered robust support to Robeson and in turn was himself blacklisted. The African American singer Marian Anderson, whose repertoire combined spirituals with European opera, was deeply religious and, rather than attack racists, chose to shame them by her restraint and the excellence of her art. She was not opposed to Robeson, who was a friend, and said that people like him were 'very, very necessary'.[41]

Despite the severe setbacks he suffered in the 1950s, he steadfastly remained politically active. For example, he presented a petition to the UN on behalf of the Civil Rights Congress charging the US with genocide against black people, he denounced US intervention in Guatemala and its efforts to discredit the Kenyan independence movement, he attacked apartheid South Africa and US support for the regime (which was designed to protect its uranium supply), and, long before it became a national issue, he opposed US interference in Vietnam.

HERE I STAND

His autobiography *Here I Stand*, written with Lloyd L. Brown, formed part of this campaigning and offered a powerful riposte to those trying to silence him. It serves as a personal manifesto and explains his politics and belief in Socialism as well as his attitude to Communism. On this latter point, he asserts the primacy of black people in the struggle for their own liberation rather than the primacy of a vanguard party, a view that was not well received by the US Communist Party, although it did not represent a departure for Robeson. The book describes the break with his father's politics of gradualism and accommodation. Robeson affirms his place in the black community and praises collective black action, which, he points out, is often led by women. He dismisses the notion that 'the time is not right' to make immediate demands, and quotes Frederick Douglass, the outstanding black leader of the abolitionist movement: 'if there is no struggle, there is no progress. Power concedes nothing without a demand. It never did and it never will.'[42]

Here I Stand appeared in August 1958, issued in the US by Othello Associates, a small, black, New York publishing house established for the purpose, and through them in four foreign countries – Britain, Romania, the German Democratic Republic and the Soviet Union. No reviews appeared in the American mass media, but the black press did comment on it and welcomed the message that Robeson was above all a 'negro'. Despite the campaign to bury him, sales reached 25,000 within a year.

Publication turned out unexpectedly to be a celebration, marking the beginning of his rehabilitation. In May he had performed to a capacity audience at Carnegie Hall, his first appearance in a New York concert hall for nearly a decade. In view of the huge white presence, he had followed this with a second sell-out concert aimed at attracting a larger black audience. A fortnight later he had sung at the packed Mother AME Zion Church, where his Republican-supporting brother Ben was the pastor.[43] It proved to be his last concert in the US because, the following month, he had won his passport back, thanks to a ruling in a different case. The Supreme Court had at last decreed that the State Department could not deny a passport to a US citizen on the grounds of political belief.

Robeson immediately went abroad to thank those who had done so much to support him, and, despite MI5 attempts to persuade the Home Office to bar him, enjoyed a triumphant tour of Britain.[44] His repertoire choices now took on a fresh relevance linked to his experience of internal exile and the battle to travel. 'Ol' Man River', for instance, came to symbolise a personal as well as a collective struggle and 'Jacob's

Ladder', which he sang with renewed relish, summed up his personal victory. His visit included an historic appearance during Evensong in St Paul's Cathedral. Unusually, a collection was allowed for a non-religious cause – a South African defence fund – and, in what was reported to be the cathedral's first secular recital, he became the first black person to feature as a singer there.

The following year, he made his last appearance on stage, fittingly as Othello in the centenary season at Stratford-upon-Avon, which was both an honour and a vindication of his stand. Appropriately, Sam Wanamaker, a fellow victim of US anti-Communist persecution, played Iago. Directed by Tony Richardson with Mary Ure as Desdemona, this third interpretation of the role by Robeson reprised his romantic reading of the noble Moor as an outsider destroyed by a hostile host culture. Richardson's production, however, had a contemporary tone at odds with this reading. The critics on the whole sided with Robeson and the public unequivocally did; the entire seven-month run was immediately sold out and on the opening night he received fifteen curtain calls.

This production was followed in 1960 by a trip to New Zealand and Australia. Both had suffered local McCarthyism, and he pledged support for the Maori and Aboriginal causes. It turned out to be his final singing tour. His health had been faltering since the mid-1950s when he had prostate surgery and suffered with kidney problems and shingles. He was to spend the next three years in and out of various medical and psychiatric establishments in the Soviet Union, Britain and the German Democratic Republic.[45] During a bout of depression, he slashed his wrists and, for a time, he received electroconvulsive therapy and a diet of drugs that he believed did him permanent harm. His fragile psychological state was in stark contrast to the general image of him suggested by his powerful physique and was an indicator of the extreme pressure he had come under, which had sapped his uncommon fortitude.

The US state had not finished with Robeson, however. He was in a London clinic when he needed to renew his passport. Unexpectedly, he was required to sign an affidavit denying he was a member of the Communist Party of the USA or had been a member in the preceding twelve months. He stood by his constitutional rights and, as before, refused. It took much persuasion from Communist friends at Essie Robeson's behest to get him to change his mind so that he could remain in London to continue his treatment and avoid another debilitating legal wrangle.

In 1963 Robeson decided to return to the US after a five-year absence and he announced his retirement. Yet a year later the FBI renewed its investigations into him and only closed its file in 1974, two years before his death.[46] He lent his support to Martin Luther King Jr and the new generation of black activists that had emerged independently of Robeson, many of whom had either dismissed him because of his association with the Communist movement or were unaware of his political stance. It was only later recognised that Robeson had anticipated the black power movement but without promoting black separatism.

His public appearances became rarer and were soon mostly confined to the funerals of friends and selected celebratory events. His supporters say that the image of Robeson as a bitter, disillusioned recluse during his years of retirement is a myth manufactured by the mass media, which had played its significant part in creating his isolation. According to his son, after illness had robbed Robeson of his artistic gifts, he felt no obligation, even to his admirers, to appear in public or to see anyone outside of his circle. For a performer who could no longer perform, and whose aesthetic had become remote to many African Americans through the advance of jazz and black popular music, his identity had become frozen, and that identity was not the one he had once inhabited. Being unable to perform, he was not able to regain the identity he sought.

He died of cerebral vascular disorder in 1976, aged seventy-seven. An estimated 5,000 attended his Harlem funeral, where the presiding bishop, a childhood friend, described him in Christ-like terms as a man who had tried to live with dignity but 'bore on his body marks of vengeance'.[47]

Robeson's gradual and fitful rehabilitation had gathered speed in the last years of his life but, despite major advances, has still not returned him to the degree of popularity he once enjoyed in his own day or to a level commensurate with his achievements. While he was still alive, his supporters organised several celebrations, including one in 1965 sponsored by among others John Coltrane and James Baldwin, who said, 'In the days when it seemed that there was no possibility in raising the individual voice and no possibility of applying the rigours of conscience, Paul Robeson spoke in a great voice which creates a man.'[48]

Who's Who in American History included Robeson in 1967 and in 1968 there were celebrations for his 70th birthday in 27 countries. In 1971 Columbia Records released *Paul Robeson in Live Performance*. The magazine *Ebony* listed him in 1972 as one of the ten most important black men in American history. In 1978, two years after his death, the Hollywood Chamber of Commerce rejected his name for a star in the Walk of Fame but, following lobbying, conceded the following year, when he was also the subject of an Oscar-winning short documentary, *Paul Robeson: Tribute to an Artist*, narrated by Sidney Poitier.

The 1998 celebrations of his birth centenary renewed interest in his legacy, which has been commemorated at different times by colleges, museums, festivals and books as well as by the naming of a mountain in Soviet Kirghizia after him. The British link continued with the Welsh band the Manic Street Preachers recording 'Let Robeson Sing' in 2001 and the following year the unveiling of a blue plaque at his Hampstead home in north London. In 2004, the Columbia recording of Robeson's Othello was added to the Library of Congress registry of historic recordings; nothing by him had been included before.

REASSESSMENT

The closeness of his persona and his art, bonded in later years by an unshakeable political commitment, guaranteed that the meaning of his life was fought over both while he was still alive and after his death. The white media, central to any celebrity, at first applauded his 'natural' talent and the inner nobility he projected regardless of the stereotypes he portrayed. It even praised him in the 1930s and early '40s as an outstanding performer who was also a man of principle, but, with the post-war rise of anti-Communist hysteria, his challenge to the US system confined him to the wilderness before a re-evaluation began of him as a tragic figure after his career had been ruined.

This process of reassessment has largely denied the specific details and context of Robeson's politics and has cast him still as the 'noble savage' who was too trusting of the 'reds'. This is the kind of co-option, or neutralising by acceptance, that comes with recognition and society's desire to forget as it assuages its guilt. Robeson was a reminder of principle, of how one should behave, and that is uncomfortable. He was fully conscious of what he did and never reneged on his commitment, despite its cost. Among those who acknowledge this, there is an understandable tendency to turn him into an inspiring role model (something he wished to avoid) and the allied danger of smoothing out his complexity as well as the complexity of his situation. Such an approach is not surprising, as the image he wished to project was as simple as the message he wished to convey: 'My views, my work, my life are all of one piece.'[49]

In fact, it was not quite that simple. In the world he occupied, before the intrusive celebrity mania of a later period, 'my life' did not in general mean 'my private life', which did not impinge too directly in public unless it could be used against him. From time to time, real or alleged affairs with white women made the headlines, but he benefited from the indulgence afforded men and, overall, the coverage did little public damage. More seriously, his infidelity nearly led to divorce in 1930, but an accommodation was reached with his wife Eslanda that saw Robeson continue to conduct a string of affairs, some at the same time, while relying on her as the rock upon which he based his life of honour and dedication. To have left Essie, especially for a white woman, would have destroyed his standing among African Americans.

On the ideological front, his inconsistencies were often those of the international Communist movement, and the attitudes that lay behind them may now sometimes seem more unpopular than they were at the time. For example, he did not extend the right of free speech to Trotskyists, but this aroused little adverse comment in the media. Similarly, his view of the war in 1939 was shared by many, albeit from different standpoints, and there was a large body of opinion in the US that was pro-Stalin and supported the Nazi-Soviet pact. *Time* magazine made the dictator its man of the year in 1939 and praised his statesmanship in signing a treaty with Hitler, and it made him man of the year again in 1942.

As with any person, Robeson's ideological journey took shape and developed with the ebb and flow of the politics of his time, but, although history suggests he was wrong on certain matters, he did not take political positions to curry favour. At one moment he may have stressed internationalism, at another his black roots, yet such a shift of emphasis did not mean a rejection of any of his core beliefs. The one for which he suffered most was his insistent backing of the Communists and the Soviet Union. Arguments continue over Robeson's relationship to Communism, usually ignoring the historic significance of the Soviet experiment and the importance of the Communist Party of the USA in black political representation, particularly in Harlem, where the CP was for a period very strong and enjoyed widespread support.

The price Robeson paid in public for his loyalty is evident, but it is not clear to what extent he privately suffered for his steadfast support of the Soviet Union. There has been much animated speculation, and equally vigorous rebuttal, concerning the impact on his health of his knowledge of the shortcomings of Soviet society and of the Sino-Soviet split. There is evidence that the unravelling of the Soviet myth did seriously contribute to his dilemma and distressed him profoundly.

He reportedly clashed in private with Khrushchev over the treatment of Jews and came closest to open criticism in coded performance. In 1949 in Moscow – at a time of heightened Stalinist anti-Semitism, which had claimed the life of one of Robeson's friends, the actor Solomon Mikhoels – Robeson sang the Warsaw ghetto resistance song in Yiddish and mentioned Mikhoels by name. Again, in 1960, at a Moscow ball bearings factory, he sang in Yiddish and affirmed his love of Jewish culture. In the US, however, he always said he had not seen any anti-Semitism in the Soviet Union.

Robeson had other differences with the Soviet Communists – and knew personally as early as the 1930s of people in the Soviet Union who had wrongly suffered – but he suppressed his disagreements in public because he believed that was for the greater good. He also disagreed with aspects of American Communist policy, but when his passport was returned and the media reported he had lost his faith, he felt he had to stand by those who had stood by him.

CULTURE AND ACTIVISM

His consistent dedication and solidarity was his strength, but it also became a weakness because it did not allow for creative development, only offering more of the same. Given the nature and timing of his struggle, that may have been sufficient; as a celebrity, even a fallen one, there was always going to be an emphasis on him as an individual, but he balanced that by favouring the collective and found sustenance in that choice. Yet he never believed he had done sufficient service for his people. Even at school, he was aware of being representative but he also grew tired of this burden. At the same time, he was worried about being separated from the black community, especially since the white working class, to whom he looked to be partners in a progressive popular alliance, could not be relied upon.

He was also sensitive to African American criticism of associating too closely with white culture and not appearing in more work by black creators. Yet he was the first black performer to sustain an active resistance to and engagement with the way American culture represented 'non-white' people and to do so from within the system that he was at first dependent upon. He felt he had to be twice as good as whites to succeed, and succeed he did, becoming the first to be both a saleable symbol of black America to white America and an inspirational symbol to black America of its ambition and desire. His appeal was fashioned in transcendent, humanist terms of common decency, the very notion to which white society aspired but, for the most part, failed to achieve. Robeson lived the contradiction of the American dream and symbolised the problem of 'difference'. Many of the shortcomings of the productions and films in which he appeared as well as the power of his stage and screen performances derive from this tension of being emblematic of both discrimination and liberation.

Robeson pushed the limits of culture and of activism, appreciating the need for and the limitations of both. For all his political activity, he never abandoned performance and was not suited to be a full-time political activist, which became an option particularly when his travel was blocked. For him, politics and performance went hand in hand. As a black performer the restrictions on what he could achieve were especially severe, and when he was able to choose, he did not always make the best choice; but his fight to gain cultural power was nonetheless vital.

He joins an honoured list of black performers, including Bert Williams, Josephine Baker and Eartha Kitt, whose celebrity and appeal to both black and white audiences was accompanied by punishment for their politics, in a manner more familiar to harassed writers like James Baldwin, Chester Hines and Richard Wright. Many black artists, from Ruby Dee, Ossie Davis and Lena Horne to Harry Belafonte, Oscar Brown and Sidney Poitier, have acknowledged Robeson's influence and pioneering role, fighting battles that made it easier for future generations. Yet it would take another couple of decades after Robeson's decline for black stars to be able to appeal to white as well as black audiences on anything like their own terms.

The opera singer Willard White, who tours a Robeson show, believed he was more popular and significant in his day than Martin Luther King or Nelson Mandela. James Baldwin paid this tribute: 'Robeson lives, overwhelmingly, in the hearts and minds of the people . . . who gained from him the power to perceive and the courage to exist.'[50]

He stands in a proud American tradition of popular political fighters; indeed, one of his most celebrated recordings was of the song 'The House I Live In', which challenges by evoking an ideal and diverse nation of free and equal peoples.[51] The first line asks 'What is America to me?' – a question that Robeson's life continually posed.

As biographer Martin Bauml Duberman observes, Robeson's life is a peculiarly American tragedy. The fact that such interest has continued in him after his death is a tribute both to his legacy and to the continuing need to make connections between culture and activist politics, between art and meaning.

In a world where there is a profound social yearning to bridge the gap between rhetoric and lived experience, Robeson's life in all its complexity still stands vividly present in all our futures.

NOTES

1. Robeson to Uta Hagen, quoted in Martin Bauml Duberman, *Paul Robeson*, New York, Ballantine Books, 1990, p. 273.

2. Categories such as black and white are not used uncritically, and nor are other terms, the usage of which has changed over time, such as negro and African American. Robeson and his contemporaries, for example, commonly used the term negro. I also use the word actress, but only as a means of emphasis.

3. Ron Ramdin, *Paul Robeson: The Man and his Mission*, London, Peter Owen, 1987, p. 14.

4. This duality is described and explored by many black writers. It is related to what W.E.B. DuBois called 'double consciousness', which gives African Americans an intensified awareness of looking at themselves through the eyes of others (i.e. white society) and constantly living the contradiction of being both black and American.

5. According to Duberman (p. 55), the stenographer is reputed to have said, 'I never take dictation from a nigger.'

6. *ibid.*, p. 585, n. 18.

7. Marcus Garvey, leader of the Universal Negro Improvement Association and said to be one of the models for O'Neill's portrait of Brutus Jones, was (perhaps unsurprisingly) among the black leaders to criticise Robeson. Garvey and his followers continued to be critical. Robeson, who was never an assimilationist, had no sympathy with Garvey's brand of black Nationalism.

8. Officially known as the Motion Picture Producers and Distributors of America, the film regulation body (1922–45) was created by the major film companies to improve the industry's image and provide internal regulation, including a strict moral code. The office was headed by Will H. Hays (1879–1954). A Production Code, listing all the subjects forbidden to films, was begun in 1930 and lasted until 1966, when it was replaced by a ratings system.

9. Thomas Cripps, in *Black Films as Genre*, Bloomington and London, Indiana University Press, 1978, points out (p. 66) that, as *Body and Soul* is only available in post-censorship form, the original can only be analysed through secondary sources.

10. See Charles Musser, 'Troubled Relations: Robeson, Eugene O'Neill, and Oscar Micheaux', in Jeffrey C Stewart (ed.), *Paul Robeson:*

Artist and Citizen, New Brunswick, New Jersey and London, Rutgers University Press, 1998, pp. 92–102.

11. Quoted in Eslanda Goode Robeson, *Paul Robeson, Negro*, New York, Harpers & Brothers, 1930, p. 97.

12. A notable incident of the occasional racism Robeson encountered in London was at the Savoy Grill in 1929 when he and Eslanda were refused entry because of their colour. A friend of the Robesons gave the story to the papers, and subsequently a protest meeting was called by Africans and West Indians living in London, which was attended by a Labour MP, who raised the matter with the Prime Minister.

13. Duberman (p. 604, n. 14) says Robeson sang 'niggers' in 1928, whereas Paul Robeson Jr, on the radio programme *Soul Music*, BBC Radio 4, 14 March 2006, says his father sang 'darkies' on stage but acknowledges the use of 'niggers' in Robeson's 1930 recording of the song (mistakenly referred to as 1927 by Paul Robeson Jr).

14. See discussion in Doris Evans McGinty and Wayne Shirley, 'Paul Robeson, Musician' in Stewart; Joseph Dorinson and William Pencak (eds.), *Paul Robeson: Essays on His Life and Legacy*, North Carolina, Jefferson and London, McFarland, 2002; and Richard Dyer, *Heavenly Bodies: Film Stars and Society*, Basingstoke, Macmillan, 1986.

15. Quoted in Marie Seton, *Paul Robeson*, London, Dennis Dobson, 1958, pp. 94–95.

16. The Pool Group comprised Bryher (Winifred Ellerman), her bisexual husband Kenneth Macpherson and her lover (and Macpherson's), the poet H.D. (Hilda) Doolittle, according to Duberman, p. 130. Previously they had made three short films. *Borderline* was the only feature they completed before disbanding.

17. James Baldwin, *The Devil Finds Work*, London, Corgi, 1978, p. 104. He cites the cinema's treatment of Robeson and Ethel Waters (p. 103) as the most powerful examples of 'cowardice and waste' in not offering black American actors a serious challenge to deliver their best. Of Robeson, he says (p. 105), 'There is the truth to be found in everything I saw him do.'

18. Thomas Cripps, in *Slow Fade to Black – The Negro in American Film 1900–1942*, New York, Oxford University Press, 1977, p. 220, says Robeson tried to raise funds in 1929 for an independent black film company, the Tono-Film Corporation, which he was to run with lyricist/composer Noble Sissle and arranger/composer Will Vodery, but the venture came to nothing.

19. Quoted in Philip S. Foner (ed.), *Paul Robeson Speaks: Writings, Speeches, Interviews 1918–74*, London, Quartet Books, 1978, p. 513, n. 6.

20. *ibid.*, p. 119. The change of lyrics and the way he sang them can be judged by comparing different recordings and descriptions of his performances.

21. Paul Robeson, *Here I Stand*, Boston, Beacon Press, 1988, p. 52.

22. 'Ballad for Americans' began life as 'Ballad of Uncle Sam', written for a Federal Theatre Project revue *Sing for Your Supper*. Earl Robinson also co-wrote 'Joe Hill' and 'The House I Live In', two other songs with which Robeson was closely associated. See n. 51.

23. Robeson may have been influenced by a wider mood of optimism. Leaders of the National Association for the Advancement of Colored People (NAACP) met Hollywood executives in 1942 to secure better treatment of and for black people in the film industry and to confront the racism of the guilds. Such collective attempts to influence the film industry were rare; in 1915 the NACCP did campaign against the D.W. Griffith film, *The Birth of a Nation*, and its sympathetic portrayal of the Ku Klux Klan. A mass pageant, *Fifty Years of Freedom*, was presented as a counter to the film, 1915 being the fiftieth anniversary of emancipation.

24. Quoted in Duberman, p. 265.

25. *ibid.*, p. 275.

26. *ibid.*, p. 261. For the making of the film and details of Frontier Films, see Russell Campbell, *Cinema Strikes Back: Radical Filmmaking in the United States 1930–1942*, Ann Arbor, Michigan, UMI Research Press, 1982, and William Alexander, *Film on the Left: American Documentary Film from 1931–1942*, Princeton, New Jersey, Princeton University Press, 1981. The House Committee on Un-American Activities or HUAC (rarely its actual acronym, HCUA) was an investigating committee of the United States House of Representatives (1945–1975). It is often referred to as the House Un-American Activities Committee, hence the usual abbreviation HUAC. In 1969, the House changed the committee's name to the Committee on Internal Security. The House abolished the committee in 1975 and its functions were transferred to the House Judiciary Committee. See later, in 'Would-be Gaolers of the Imagination: Contexts of Coercion and Control' for more on HUAC.

27. Quoted in Foner, p. 180.

28. Robeson and Hopper quoted in Duberman, p. 317, and Sokolsky *ibid.*, p. 320.

29. There were a raft of measures Robeson and others on the left protested against, such as the Alien Registration Act (a.k.a. the Smith Act) 1940, which made it illegal to teach, advocate or encourage the overthrow of the US government. (It was used against Trotskyists and pro-Nazis, both with Communist Party backing, before it was turned on the CP.) President Truman's executive order on loyalty (1947) was aimed at organisations deemed 'totalitarian, fascist, communist or subversive . . . or as seeking to alter the form of government of the United States by unconstitutional means.' Disloyalty did not necessarily require membership of such bodies but merely 'sympathetic association'. The

Communist Control Act (1954) made CP membership illegal. Other acts against which Robeson protested were the 1947 Taft-Hartley Act, passed over Truman's veto, which outlawed the closed shop and required a statement of non CP membership, and the 1948 Mundt-Nixon Bill, which required the registration of Communists and was incorporated into the 1952 McCarran-Walter Act, which restricted immigration and, according to Robeson, was aimed at 'non-nordic' peoples.

30. Ramdin (p. 171) says income dwindled from over $100,000 in 1947 to about $6,000 in 1952, echoing figures from Sterling Stuckey's introduction to the 1988 edition of *Here I Stand* (p. xxx), which says Robeson's income plummeted in this period from over $100,000 a year to less than $6,000 a year and remained there for nearly a decade.

31. Democratic candidate Harry S. Truman was expected to lose in 1948, but he beat the Republican favourite Thomas E. Dewey. The third party candidate, Henry A. Wallace, opposed the Cold War, the Marshall Plan, which secured US hegemony abroad through loans, and the unfettered power of big business. He wanted to introduce a minimum wage and end the House Committee on Un-American Activities 'witch hunt'. He also opposed racial discrimination. He was Roosevelt's Secretary of Agriculture (1933–40) and vice-president (1940–44) but was dropped by the Democrats in the 1944 election in favour of Truman. Wallace served as Secretary of Commerce (1945–6) until Truman, who became President on Roosevelt's death, fired him for being too critical of foreign policy.

32. Muhammad Ali was quoted as saying this in 1966 in response to being asked by a reporter why he was refusing to go to Vietnam. His attempt to apply for conscientious objector status on religious grounds resulted in an extensive legal and political fight. He was eventually convicted of draft evasion and stripped of his boxing title as world heavyweight champion. In 1971, the United States Supreme Court overturned his draft conviction.

33. The press version of Robeson's speech to the Congress of the World Partisans of Peace (a.k.a. Paris Peace Congress, with 2,000 delegates from 50 nations) is in Foner, p. 537. Duberman (p. 342) quotes: 'Our will to fight is strong. We shall not make war on anyone. We shall not make war on the Soviet Union' from a translation of the French transcript held in the Robeson Archives, Howard University.

34. African American leaders such as Walter White and Roy Wilkins of the NAACP attacked Robeson as a Kremlin stooge. Jackie Robinson, the first African American to play major league baseball thanks to a desegregation campaign in which Robeson was a leading figure, also criticised him before HUAC. Later (in his autobiography *I Never Had It Made*, as told to Alfred Duckett, New York, The Echo Press, 1995) he

said he had come to respect Robeson and recognised that he had sacrificed his career, wealth and comfort in trying to help his people. Noble Sissle helped the FBI monitor Robeson. African Americans appearing before HUAC were primarily there to denounce Robeson rather than to reveal suspected Communists or their associates. The actor Canada Lee, who was banned from some forty television shows despite averring his anti-Communism – a move it seems he may have made because of his poverty – denounced Robeson, though he never appeared before HUAC. According to Victor S. Navasky, in *Naming Names*, New York, Viking Press, 1980, p. 189, Lee was rewarded with a part in *Cry, the Beloved Country* (1952). Lee died penniless the year the film came out. Folksinger Josh White, who made 'St James Infirmary' popular, criticised Robeson for supporting the Soviet Union and was apparently rewarded with work. The singer Harry Belafonte was offered the lead opposite Dorothy Dandridge in *Carmen Jones* (1955) but had to clear himself first with HUAC. He went to Robeson, who said he should do what he had to because employment opportunities were scarce. Belafonte was not required to 'name names' but he was visited by a HUAC representative. See later, in 'Would-be Gaolers of the Imagination: Contexts of Coercion and Control'.

35. Organisations that disappeared included the National Negro Congress, the Civil Rights Congress and the Council on African Affairs.

36. *Peace Arch Concerts* (CD), Folk Era FE 1442, 1998.

37. Quoted in *Let Paul Robeson Sing!*, education and resource pack, Theatre Museum, London, 2001, p. 23.

38. The monthly newspaper *Freedom* was launched in 1950, disbanded 1955. Othello Recording Company released the albums *Robeson Sings* (1952), *Let Freedom Sing* (1954) and *Solid Rock: Favourite Hymns of My People* (1955).

39. Robeson sang the title song for *Song of the Rivers* (a.k.a. *Unity* and *Seven Rivers*) with lyrics by Bertolt Brecht. It was recorded at the Harlem house of Robeson's brother. The film, compiled by leading documentary maker Joris Ivens, tells of the workers' movement along six major rivers. It features music by Shostakovich, and Picasso designed the poster.

40. Foner reproduces the statement HUAC refused to let Robeson read, pp. 433–6. The Robeson quotations are to be found p. 427 and p. 433.

41. Quoted in Dorinson and Pencak, p. 160.

42. Robeson (1988), p. 89.

43. Selections from the concert at the Mother AME Zion Church can be heard on *Paul Robeson in Live Performance* (LP), CBS 61247 (along with selections from the Royal Albert Hall concert, 10 August 1958).

44. MI5 was interested in Robeson because it had set up a special department to study 'negro political movements' in the empire near the

end of the war and was alarmed at growing links between the US civil rights movement and black anti-colonial politicians. MI6 was also interested in Robeson as chair of the American Council for African Affairs and a key figure in the pro-independence movement.

45. There is a growing body of literature exploring the notion of 'racial madness' and the extreme and particular psychological pressure that leads to the unrepresentatively high numbers of black people in white countries in mental institutions.

46. Robeson's FBI files (2,680 pages) are available on the web: http://foia.fbi.gov/foiaindex/robeson.htm

47. Quoted in Duberman, p. 550.

48. Quoted in Foner, p. 44.

49. Robeson (1988), p. 3.

50. Quoted in Paul Robeson Jr, *The Undiscovered Paul Robeson: An Artist's Journey 1898–1939*, New York, John Wiley and Sons Inc., 2001, p. xiv.

51. Earl Robinson, composer of 'Ballad for Americans' (see n. 22), co-wrote 'The House I Live In' during World War II with lyricist Lewis Allen. In 1945, the song was made a hit by Frank Sinatra, who sang it in an Oscar-winning movie short (written by Albert Maltz, later one of the Hollywood Ten). Lewis Allen was a pseudonym used by Abel Meeropol, a Communist high school teacher who also wrote 'Strange Fruit', the anti-lynching song made famous by Billie Holiday (see later, in 'Would-be Gaolers of the Imagination: Contexts of Coercion and Control'). In the 1950s Meeropol and his wife adopted the sons of Julius and Ethel Rosenberg after their parents were executed for spying.

ISADORA DUNCAN: THE NECESSARY ICONOCLAST

'A desire for the unattainable is perhaps the happiest of states'
Isadora Duncan in her twenties[1]

Isadora Duncan was a liberator in the arts and in society at a traumatic moment in the early twentieth century when an old order was forced to surrender to a new reality. Perhaps, if she had been a man, the story of her as an idealist iconoclast, as an utopian resister, as a messenger of that birth of the modern, would easily have outrun the more familiar version of her as a mystical drama queen destroyed by the staples of modern celebrity, an excess of vanity, champagne and sex. Duncan was banished from history after her death and then gradually rehabilitated from the 1960s on, in the era when the personal became recognised as political. She offered up a life and a legacy which have been both absurdly adulated and disproportionately derided.

Dispute runs deep over her influence on custom, clothes and culture, not to mention on the narrower world of dance, on what she stood for, literally, on stage, and, emblematically, through her art and biography as a bequest to subsequent generations. Although the precise nature of her commitment to herself, to her creativity and to her causes may be hard to characterize and is marbled with contradiction, there can be little doubt that it was a monumental commitment and that performance lay at its heart. This commitment, however, is not usually associated with politics, especially when narrowly defined, but that would be to overlook a crucial dimension. What were her politics, however intermittent, and when did she embrace them in her life and art?

THE BEGINNINGS

The threads are woven into a complex journey through the different periods of Duncan's life, during which she remade her image of herself several times. Beginning in 1877 with her birth in San Francisco to parents who had travelled west in the gold rush, her journey passed from apprenticeship to international renown as a society and art dancer, and subsequent identification with grand ideals: liberty in World War I, and, in its wake, the defining social and political experiment of the period, the new world promised by Soviet Russia. She describes the arc of this journey in her autobiography, *My Life*: 'As a child I danced the spontaneous joy of growing things. As an adolescent, I danced with joy turning to apprehension of the first realisation of tragic under-currents; apprehension of the pitiless brutality and crushing progress of life.'[2]

At the start of the journey, the descriptions of which she was careful to control, lie a number of inter-connecting factors: class (a 'genteel' poverty after her parents divorced), gender (confinement by patriarchy to an inferior sphere), skin colour (privilege), location (a burgeoning West Coast interest in the environment and healthy living), aspiration to culture (the 'improving' high arts, the Romantics' view of nature as an authoritative source of creativity and action) and nationality (after the trauma of civil war, the US forged its identity in a rapidly industrialising and increasingly powerful democratic republic).

For Duncan, to dance was to be, and any separation of Duncan the person from Duncan the performer had to be obliterated. The later disparity between her non-dancing and dancing life made it all the more imperative for her to avow this simultaneity of person and performer and to choreograph her biography, many details of which remain uncertain.

'From the first I have only danced my life,' she wrote in her autobiography, confirming the image she had sought to promulgate of a complete identification between her art and her life.[3] Sustaining and asserting this indivisibility, which becomes her politics, led her to offer a fanciful account of her expressive origins. She began to dance in her mother's womb, she writes, hypothesising that it was probably a result of her pregnant mother's diet of iced oysters and champagne. With this image she foretells her future and projects herself as a force of nature, transcendent in exactly the way that she believed art, and especially her art, to be.

Duncan danced Duncan. Self-sufficient, self-assertive, she danced in the spirit of the liberating poet Walt Whitman: 'I celebrate myself, and sing myself.'[4] She said she danced naked and alone by the ocean and 'it seemed as if the sea and all the trees were dancing with me.'[5] As with Robeson's 'naturalness', her 'natural' dancing was the result of great and enduring effort, and it became more 'natural' as she became more expert over time.

Her poetic description of herself as the progeny of 'wind and wave and the winged flight of bird and bee' buried the facts of her impecunious and nomadic upbringing. Father was a poet as well as a publisher of poets but also a drunk, a 'womaniser', a failed banker and a fraudster who had left the household by the time Isadora was three. As a result, Isadora's mother, thirty years younger and a struggling piano teacher, was often forced to move home with her four children – Isadora (the youngest), her two brothers and her sister. It was a peripatetic existence that Isadora was to extend into her adult life, as was her facility for persuading others to part with their money on her behalf. She claimed to have left school at ten and honed her social performance skills in cadging credit from the butcher and the baker.

As a child she began the habit of reading widely. This took her beyond dance and art into philosophy and science, and from a tender age she was ready to announce herself as someone with strong opinions, candidly expressed, displaying rebellion and class-consciousness. Inspired by her freethinking atheist mother, she declared in front of her class that Santa Claus did not exist but was an invention for rich mothers who could afford to perform the role.

The household was filled with Beethoven, Mendelssohn, Schubert and Mozart, Shakespeare, Burns, Shelley and Whitman; Botticelli's 'Primavera', a painting that associates nature with dancing, hung on the wall. She knew early on that art could flourish amid poverty and aspired to the higher, sublime realms of life. Art was a temple where the soul could find freedom from the constraints imposed by society. In an existential, almost biological, way she followed Whitman and connected Art (with a capital A) to life and democracy. For her, personal truth was the key to truth in art because life nurtured art. 'I burned with apostolic fire for my art,' she said. 'I wanted to make over life, down to its least details of costume, of morals, of way of living.'[6] With this evangelism, art offered an enlightenment that in theory was available to all, even if at that juncture its appeal still bore the marks of elitism. She saw both art and nature in 'white' terms, their benevolence and civilising qualities defined in contrast to the perilous primitivism of the 'non-white' world, even though it was black people who were often described as being 'natural'.

The development of her distinctive dance was not, as her account proposes, a fully formed natural phenomenon. She says she danced as a small child and studied from the age of four, but not in the usual, formal sense; she left her ballet class after the third lesson. There is evidence, however, that she continued to study ballet through her teenage years, although she pretended otherwise. She claimed that at the age of six she taught a group of toddlers to wave their arms and from eleven to sixteen taught the fashionable ballroom or 'fancy' dancing, as the Duncans called it. During these years, the Duncan siblings founded a school of the arts and Isadora began to teach what she described as 'a new system of body culture and dancing'.[7]

Her experiments with 'free' dance were heavily influenced by images from ancient Greece, an inspiration then in vogue which connected nature to physical and spiritual well-being and which Duncan embraced as validation of her yearning for betterment and self-expression. Her sense of movement, gesture, structure and display was also shaped by the contemporary fad for rhythmic callisthenics and physical culture, especially exercises based on the ideas of the French teacher François Delsarte, who emphasised minimalism and efficiency and sought to join emotion and motion. She also drew on her experience of civic and children's pageants and tableaux vivants, which were commonplace in America at the time and which she called 'mimodramas'.

It seems likely she first appeared in public in 1889 at the age of twelve in a civic parade and a year later gave her first public dance performance alongside her siblings at a local church. Three years later she began her apprenticeship in professional theatre, an initiation which was much more vulgar than her later sylvan image implies. The Duncan children toured the principal theatres of California with a variety act comprising burlesque, melodrama, comedy, dancing, singing and some high-minded offerings (the recitation of poems and selections from Shakespeare).

In 1895, aged eighteen, she left San Francisco with her family because her birthplace would not accept her art – one producer said it was not suitable for theatre and belonged in church. 'Clan Duncan' went to Chicago in the belief that this progressive town would rise to Isadora's revelation but the responses were the same. Female dancers had to be erotic. Indigence drove her to the music hall where she performed briefly as the Californian Faun. Propelled to New York as her only remaining refuge, she found work with Broadway's leading producer Augustin Daly and remained with his company for almost two years despite not being able to perform as she wanted. The nearest she came was in the role of First Fairy in *A Midsummer Night's Dream* when she was given a solo spot. Costumed (against her wishes) in glittering tinsel wings, she proved popular with the audience but not with Daly, who dimmed the lights on her performance for the duration of the tour.

When she could take no more of such indignities she returned to solo performance in private salons but fared poorly. She lived in often dire circumstances with the family, without whom she would not have survived the early years of experiment. A turning point came when she performed for the popular composer Ethelbert Nevin, who had burst into her rented studio to forbid her to use his music in her performances. He agreed to see her dance and was enchanted. Accompanied by Nevin and others in a concert at New York's Carnegie Hall in 1898, she at last reaped the reward for her persistence. She danced three of his *Water Scenes*, 'Narcissus,' 'Ophelia' and 'The Water Nymphs', and, in what could be seen as her growing sensitivity to the limitations of immanent transcendence, she ended the performance with a lecture.

This was to become a feature of Duncan's appearances, implicitly acknowledging that meaning is not isolated and self-evident but constructed through performance and the process of communication. She had also come to realise that, although she could choose the music that formed the essential collaboration of her performance, she could not compose it. In that respect, she was an interpretive as well as a creative artist. Within the collaboration, she controlled her domain, as she alone was responsible for the movement and look of her body in the given space. However, since the music was an aspect of making meaning she could not fully control, she used her speeches in an attempt to ensure that the music as well as the dance meant what she wanted it to mean.

TO EUROPE

The burden of her Carnegie Hall lecture challenged the separation of the mind and the body, a central concept of the Enlightenment. Furthermore, she proclaimed that dance was not dancing but movement expressive of thought, and asked, 'how shall it be brought to life as an art?'[8] Duncan believed that, because America thought artistic dance still meant ballet, she could best answer her own question by turning to what she saw as the deepest source of her inspiration – Europe. In the US she had not been able to find the necessary audience either among those who saw her in Daly's company or in the salons of the rich. She despised both the role of the popular – and, therefore, sexual – dancer and that of tame entertainer of the well-to-do who, she believed, exploited her art to gain social prestige rather than personal illumination. America, the most dynamic country in the new world, gave birth to the innovator Duncan but could not appreciate her. She had to go to the old world for recognition and yet there she was seen as a product of American modernity; she 'danced America' in the way that Whitman had 'sung America'.

In London, her first stopping place (which she had visited with Daly's company), she faced the same dilemma as in the US: how to be seen as a serious artist and to find the right audience? She solved the former problem but not the latter. An artistic elite with pre-Raphaelite and moneyed connections who also associated nature and mysticism took her up, and through them she began her climb to celebrity across Europe. Paris, the hub of artistic innovation in the West in the early years of the twentieth century, became her main base for the rest of her life.

Duncan longed for the modern but often cast her craving as a backward-looking fantasy, appealing to an illusory bygone age of untrammelled virtue and innocence, an individualist oasis in the face of the degradation of the mass who, it was believed, had no time, unlike the rich, to contemplate the relationship between body and soul. Only later does she attempt a political resolution of the tension between the individual and the mass, and then only with the mass as worthy of salvation in a grand plea for them to come to her way of understanding. For the time being, transcendence was sufficient; art was both a flight from the social world and a return to it on a different, ethereal plane. Political engagement with that world could wait.

Despite this attachment to otherworldliness, she could not evade the issue of gender, a central thread in her lifelong creation of 'self'. Taking her cue from her mother, she challenged in her dance and in her non-dancing life, in a way that only a woman could, the social definitions of male and female and the separation of the private from the public. She launched her vision in opposition to the male-dominated perception of the female dancer, both in contrast to the arcane world of ballet, which she detested as ugly, unnatural and imprisoning, and the readily available world of popular dance, which she dismissed as a 'leg business', a low entertainment inhabited by covert prostitutes. She used her body to mark out the space she wished to inhabit as a woman, to assert her control over that space and to affirm the role of woman as an active, social agent.

Like the actor Henry Irving in Britain, another fan of Whitman, Duncan wanted to be respected as an artist and to raise her discipline to the equal of those other arts that were considered noble. Like Irving she was not the first to desire this but the first to register her desire on a significant social scale. Unlike Irving, hers was a solo path that did not aim to change the social apparatus of dance directly; it is impossible to imagine her (if she had been English) becoming the first dancer to be created a dame, in the way Irving became the first actor knight. Recognition had to come on her terms, otherwise not at all.

Her fame allowed her to perform as much on her own terms as possible and to audiences who might value her on those terms. She was hailed wherever she went but also attacked, and she was rarely satisfied. There was a constant need to raise funds, which placed her at the mercy of sympathetic rich individuals, but still she refused to compromise. She declined a Berlin manager's huge fees to appear in music hall, even when the fee was doubled: 'my art is not for a music hall among acrobats and trained animals'.[9] Attendant personal and professional difficulties, which were often transformed into widely reported scandals, disrupted the flow of money. Allied to her carefree attitude to finance, this seemed to increase rather than decrease her determination to succeed in laying the foundations for 'a different dance' and establishing a school that would perpetuate her ideals.[10]

Indeed, from within this maelstrom, in the years before the outbreak of World War I, Duncan did establish the fundamentals of 'a different dance'. She was not alone in doing this. The 'art dancer' became not only a phenomenon but also a commercial prospect. Duncan influenced certain contemporary performers such as Ruth St Denis, who developed her own 'exotic' style derived from the Orient, while some like Maud Allan earned a living imitating Duncan. Others, such as Loïe Fuller, with whom Duncan worked and from whom she learned, were as different and as distinctive as Duncan herself. Fuller, who had become popular in European music halls in the 1890s, also 'danced nature' but used innovative lighting and costume to create her flame or flower. A protégé of Fuller's, the Japanese actress/dancer Sado Yacco, impressed Duncan at the 1900 Paris Universal Exposition with her fluid movements and fusion of emotion and control. Another female experimenter, Valentine de Saint-Point, developed a Futurist 'Métachorie' or metadance, which was described as a 'kinaesthetic incantation', a form of almost robotic gestures accompanied by a narrator reciting her poems while mathematical equations, geometric shapes and revolving coloured light were projected on to her silhouette. Nevertheless, of such pioneers it was Duncan with her flair for celebrity who made the deepest impression.

Drawing on her reading of Darwin and Nietzsche, she gave a stirringly utopian speech in Berlin in 1903, later issued as 'The Dance of the Future', which has been taken as a seminal manifesto of modern dance. It denounces ballet, the high art dancing favoured by her audience, as the enemy of art. Duncan opposes ballet because it separates the mind and the body and is mechanical. She calls it 'living death' because each action is an end in itself that dies as soon as it is done.[11] In contrast, she developed dance as a fluid succession of seamless movements, yet set within a conceptual frame that is the opposite of fluid, inspired by the apparent permanence of sculpture.

She still couched her views in explicit and portentously sacred terms; art which is not religious is not art but mere merchandise. Hers was not an alternative way of dancing to ballet, but something altogether different. Dance not only had to suit the human body, unlike ballet, but also had to suit the particular individual, in terms of age, shape and personality. Dance had to be serious in intent, reaching beyond even the higher calling of art to the liberation of the individual. Duncan looked forward to a time when a dancer would not require external motivation from either word or music because the inner self would become its own musical dynamo, the creative source. The dancer of the future, seen as female, would be 'the highest intelligence in the freest body'.[12]

In distinction to ballet's focus on the centre of the back at the base of the spine, Duncan's bodily gesture was rooted in her notion that 'the central spring of all movement' is the solar plexus, 'the crater of motor power, the unity from which all diversities of movements are born' through which she learned to concentrate all her force.[13] She created with her body from the solar plexus but her physicality was not obsessed with muscular dexterity or technical spectacle, as are both ballet, the template against which she was rebelling, and modern dance, which she helped shape. She rejected the athletic in dance and criticised those like Emile Jaques-Dalcroze, the influential Austrian teacher of eurhythmics, who, she believed, were peddling gymnastics. Her approach to releasing the body chimes with aspects of early Stanislavskian teaching in emphasising the importance of preparation and emotional recall. Her physicality presented itself as naturalness, but was the result of training (however inconsistent) and refinement of technique that at first struck commentators as artificial and only later achieved the stamp of spontaneity.

She moved towards a dance that dispensed with traditional narrative in favour of metaphoric moral expression in which rhythmic flexibility replaced musical accuracy. She dropped sentimental and popular pieces such as 'The Blue Danube' and substituted more agonised or 'elevated' pieces such as 'Orpheus'. Although Fuller danced to Chopin, it was Duncan who became associated with the use of music by the great composers. To Duncan, the association was natural, but given the eminent standing of the likes of Brahms and Beethoven, it was a risky strategy and, indeed, the very elite, without whom she could not survive and whose definitions of art she had embraced, chided her for this temerity and lack of discrimination. In Russia, which she first visited in 1904, musicians thought dancing to such music a profanation. Her identification as a dancer with her music, nevertheless, became integral to her purpose. One of her patrons, Prince Peter Lieven, said, 'She was the first to dance the music not dance *to* the music.'[14] As Duncan attempted to dissolve her presence as an individual into the music itself, the very corporeality of her dance seemed to deny its physical presence.

In the same way that performance comprises a tension between the performer simultaneously being the performer and not the performer (a character, for example), the dialogue between the two registers of Duncan's dance – her body and the abstraction to which her bodily expression aspires – forms the tension at the core of her performance. Although it was a dialogue that developed through her life as both the display of her body and the abstraction to which she aspired changed, the tension remained central. As with any performer, an emphasis on the physical requires adjustment to the inherent predicament presented by the body through the different stages of the ageing process. Duncan's awareness of this, coupled with her growing awareness of the body's sexual and biological reality, reinforced a desire to find in dance a social meaning beyond the transient.

As she became accepted, she felt less need to defend her dancing and more concerned with the 'meaning' she aspired to through performance. She did not see herself as a dancer in the traditional sense, or, as one writer put it, she was the subject of expression not an expressive subject.[15] Her body came into performance only in order to become something else: the physical became the platform for the immaterial. This becoming was both self-expressive and impersonal, connecting by way of symbol or metaphor to the other, evanescent truth. Her self-effacement was more powerful because of her presence, a dynamic drive for impersonality fuelled by an apparently contradictory belief that she was creating more than mere or random sensation. She was not being neutral but believed she was creating important signs or symbols, hence her desire to overcome the ephemeral nature of dance through transcendence.

CONTACT WITH POLITICS

Her frustration with the limitations of transcendent expression – embodying idealised beauty, for example – led her to seek to achieve a reconnection to the social world, in other words to achieve a potentially political effect. Duncan's changing aspirations, which had been altering her dance, had also brought her into contact with politics. Dance to her was life, therefore, in one sense, it was of necessity political, but she had no conventional political belief, either in a party, in a movement (e.g. as a suffragist) or in the state, although she did believe the state should support all children. Since arriving in Europe, she had been making political gestures and on occasion supported certain causes spontaneously but without any sense of longer-term obligation to those causes.

In Budapest in 1902, dressed in a red tunic and no doubt influenced by her new-found love for a local actor, Oszkár Beregi, she danced a revolutionary 'Hymn to the Heroes of Hungary' to Liszt's 'Rakoczy March', named after an Hungarian aristocrat who symbolised the country's struggle for national sovereignty. In her autobiography, she says she performed the march in the open air when she was on a tour through the country and came to a town where she learned that seven revolutionary generals had been hanged.[16]

She visited Russia at the end of 1904 not long before the eruption of the January 1905 uprising, which was sparked by a massacre of unarmed protesting workers. She returned ten days after this 'Bloody Sunday' and witnessed a funeral procession (which in her autobiography she mistakenly reports as that of the slaughtered protesters): 'The tears ran down my face and were frozen on my cheeks as this sad, endless procession passed me . . . If I had never seen it, all my life would have been different.' What use was her art? she asked herself. She wanted to identify her simple tunic and unadorned art with those attending the funeral, and she compared them unfavourably with her audiences of bejewelled dilettantes. A few days later, she visited a sweet factory and was outraged at the conditions in which she saw the workers. Looking back on the funeral she wrote, 'I vowed myself and my forces to the service of the people and the downtrodden.'[17] While this was hyperbole, it remained an important benchmark for her, and later in the Soviet Union she danced to Russian revolutionary songs and dedicated her performance to the memory of the 'Bloody Sunday' victims.[18]

Just prior to her first Russian visit, she had achieved another of her aims by opening a boarding school in Berlin, situated in the southern suburb of Grünewald. The nineteenth century had seen the rise of the conservatoire and a growing fascination with artistic systems, which spread in the first decades of the following century. In the theatre, the new role of director brought with it attempts by major proponents like Copeau, Stanislavsky and Meyerhold to categorise, systemise and teach their methodologies, and in movement, the early codification undertaken by Delsarte was superseded by the notation of Rudolf Laban, who admired Duncan and drew on her dancing in his own work. In contrast, Duncan saw her school as providing an education for life through self-knowledge rather than the teaching of technique or a fixed system. For her, systems were subservient to a wider ethic and were to be judged by their ability to release the individual pupil, 'a beautiful human being, a dancing child'.[19] In addition to daily physical exercise, students were taught history, mathematics, natural science, literature and languages as well as singing, music, drawing and dance. The programme represented a child-centred approach in the forefront of progressive educational ideas.

Isadora and her sister Elizabeth, who appears to have been the better teacher, had taught local San Franciscan children dancing and had opened a school with their brothers in their youth. The Berlin school, under the operational direction of Elizabeth, survived more than three years before the money ran out. Isadora faced continuous battles to fund the school as it moved from site to site in Germany, France, the US and Switzerland as well as in the Soviet Union. She came to believe the existence of her school was an entitlement, as if the world owed it her, and, because of this attitude, the refusals of support sharpened her anger. The school also embroiled her in several serious and exhausting family disputes, mainly with Elizabeth, who continued to run the one in Strasbourg after Isadora's death.

This project of her school, where she was able to be mother and artist as well as teacher, absorbed the kind of energy she might otherwise have expended on social and political activity, where she would have been required to act in concert with others rather than alone as the single source of authority. To her, the school was a political project, always flawed yet essential, the transcendent made material and, she hoped, a living legacy. Its bequest to history, however, was insubstantial compared to Isadora's own influence or to that of the contemporary Denishawn Dance School in the US, run by Ruth St Denis and Ted Shawn, which trained key figures in modern dance such as Charles Weidman, Doris Humphrey and Martha Graham.

Duncan's other expression of a political mission related to her art came in her attempt to change the environment in which she performed and to attract a new kind of audience. As with the school, economics frustrated her experiments, combined with social constrictions and the lack of available venues. On stage, she was able to control the space she inhabited, how it was dressed and how it was lit; typically, she appeared barefoot in a white tunic on a bare stage curtained with blue material. In this, Duncan predated the minimalist

'empty space' and 'poor theatre' notions of the 1960s, implicitly handing more power to the audience as the authority to
make meaning. She rarely appeared in 'poor' auditoria, however, and her on-stage minimalism only survived thanks to
those who had plenty, a contradiction that became increasingly
hard for her to bear.

On her first return visit to the US, in 1908, Charles Froh-
man, the most powerful theatre manager since Daly died, mistakenly put her on Broadway in an August heat wave and
without adequate advance publicity. It was the wrong theatre,
the season had to be curtailed and she briefly concluded from
this failure that her art could only appeal to a certain restricted
public. This realisation of the importance of venue and promotion eventually turned into a desire for a permanent theatre
company. She was due to form one in Paris at Le Théâtre du
Beau in 1914, funded by money from the wealthy Paris Singer.
She hoped it would be 'a meeting place and haven for all the
great artists of the world', but the outbreak of war and her
rupture with Singer prevented it from happening.[20]

The following year in the US, she threatened to leave her
homeland unless someone built her a theatre. Otto Kahn, an
international banker and major arts patron, offered her the
Century Theatre by Central Park, known locally as 'million-
aires' theatre' because of its rich backers. Hankering for what
she believed to be the democratic character of Greek theatre,
Duncan attempted to counter the theatre's affluent image and
the hierarchical design of its proscenium auditorium. In order
to get closer to the audience and to involve them more in the
performance, she took out the first fifteen rows of the stalls to
make room for a vast apron stage and draped parts of the
auditorium with the same material she used to surround the
stage. She sat the musicians on the right of the stage and put
the chorus in a box. She closed the other boxes – symbols of
privilege – and introduced a cheap-seat policy for the upper
balcony, charging only a dime. 'Do you think it is right to put
human beings on the ceiling, like flies,' she said, 'and then ask
them to appreciate Art and Music?'[21] Having hired a 65-piece
orchestra and a 180-strong choir, her unusual repertoire of solo
dances, religious pieces and Greek tragedies proved to be a
critical and financial disaster.

She did not, however, abandon the aim of enlightening the masses by the exercise of her patrician humanism. Duncan assumed her values and tastes could, and should, belong to everyone. This implied the ending of class distinctions by wishing it, and she certainly did that. During her 1915 New York visit, she claimed Beethoven and Schubert as 'children of the people', poor men who were inspired by and belonged to humanity, and she gave a free concert in Jacob Adler's Grand Theatre on the Lower East Side. 'A theatre without a box office – so refreshing,' she remarked.[22]

Her relationship to class, however, was uneasy. Historically, notions of class were still uncertain, and class ideology was only just beginning to come to prominence. Duncan was not working class herself, although she came from a poor background, and in her own field she despised as demeaning and oppressive the dancing provided by members of that class for the enjoyment of other members, namely the chorus line and erotic performance. Reaching a popular audience was important for her, nevertheless, yet her main interest to a working-class audience was probably her notoriety. She never attracted a mass audience in the West, and in her art she still addressed herself to universal humanity rather than to a specific class. Her idea of humankind was abstract and unrelated to a class component until she went to the Soviet Union, but class necessarily influenced the establishment of her dancing as art.

IDEAS OF LIBERATION

Duncan's notion of political change was still rooted in the individual rather than in social forces, but she was committed to change nonetheless; and the commitment was unrelenting. She developed her idea of personal liberation as a critique of capitalist society and its culture, proposing in the abstract a more radical vision. Her idealistic appeal to liberty for all based on liberty for oneself has its corollary in her idealised performance aesthetic, which still bore an iconography associated with the ruling class.

The contradictions were highlighted during these tours to the US when she became the symbol of bohemian libertarian politics, centred in New York's Greenwich Village. In the shadow of Whitman, a distinct if ideologically diverse movement yoked self-expression to national freedom, and Duncan's dance, being abstract, was able to bridge the various political and artistic currents, embodying a militant, free spirit as well as female emancipation. Max Eastman, editor of the left-wing magazine *The Masses* and a leading figure of this movement, described her as 'America fighting the battle against Americanism'.[23] He likened her rebellion to Whitman's revolt against puritanism, and said she was 'an event not only in art, but in the history of life.'[24]

Her idea of liberation and national freedom was complicated and compromised by her racism (she used 'nègre' as a term of abuse) and by her related and contradictory opinions on sexuality. She was searching for dance worthy of modern democratic America – the America of Abe Lincoln, as she put it, without recognising the irony that he was known (however imprecisely) as the Great Emancipator because of his fight against slavery. Her notions of art and civilisation were those of the WASP elite and precluded the artistic expressions of non-white people, which she dismissed as 'primitive'. 'Primitive' carried connotations of sexual impropriety. To Duncan, popular dance forms deriving from African American culture, which started from the waist rather than the solar plexus, were not art. They made her dance look old-fashioned and offended her view of the body and sexuality as being 'fine' and 'pure', a response not consistent with her own sexual behaviour and experience. When she danced the tango, for instance, she found herself entranced and described the experience in erotic terms: 'From my first timid steps I felt my pulses respond to the enticing languorous rhythm of this voluptuous dance, sweet as a long caress, intoxicating as love under southern skies, cruel and dangerous as the allurement of a tropical forest.'[25]

She joined in the reactionary moral backlash against 'jazz' dancing and its sanitised white versions in so-called 'animal dances' like the foxtrot, which broke sexual taboos and the restraints of socially acceptable, public body gestures. She called for censorship of sexual representation in jazz and ragtime, and said the American dance she strove for would have nothing in common with the 'ape-like convulsions of the

Charleston' or the 'sexual convulsion of the Negro'.[26] Her attacks on ballet were far milder at a time when there was an unhealthy whiff of Anglo-Saxon body worship and eugenics in the American air. She was not a proponent of eugenics, but in her German school, Elizabeth and her lover were. It is not surprising that Nietzsche and Wagner were gods to Isadora and that her adoration of Art and Beauty had dangerous advocates among fascists.

Ironically, the body became the location of her attempts at liberation, which, in their turn, caused moral uproar. The reality of the body, she believed, should be unremarkable and consequently, as part of her 'natural' image, she performed with her feet, arms and legs uncovered. Her loose tunic came down to just below her knees, was gathered at the bosom and tied at the waist. It had baggy sleeves that allowed her arms to move freely. This attire represented liberty in the age of the corset, lace and button, an age in which the body was the site of containment and even imprisonment, a key element in the social apparatus that determined sexual and gendered behaviour. Duncan not only challenged the dominant male preconceptions of ballet and its sexually restrictive view of women, she also revealed in public what was supposed to be hidden, both literally by baring her limbs and symbolically in terms of how women could move and be seen.

In both her dance and her life, gender and sexuality became central. Her defiance in this sphere questioned notions of traditional politics, which separated the gender roles and defined political activity as belonging to the rational domain of men rather than to the emotional world of women. She became a threat to all kinds of authority; her behaviour caused outrage even within bohemian circles.

Flesh was still the symbol of the Fall, and her chaste displays without erotic intent proved to be highly disturbing, causing moral panic in both America and Europe. Faced with probably more bare skin than the average burlesque performer revealed but in the context of a concert hall, members of her audiences booed, hissed, threw things at her and walked out. Her lifestyle influenced such reactions, particularly when it was discovered that, while unmarried, she was pregnant and yet had continued to dance. In Germany, where her students had been banned from performing in costumes similar to hers, the female patrons of her school announced they could not continue to support an institution led by someone with such a loose idea of morals. She evidently had confused the twin images of woman as mother and whore to the point at which her bourgeois supporters were scandalised into serious retreat.

Her own sexual desires, however, challenged her presentation of the body as sexually innocent and tested her commitment to art (as opposed to lovers, husbands, children) in a way that applied uniquely to women, yet her sexualised sense of femaleness also renewed her art by opening up the world of social commitment to which she aspired in her dance. She lectured on women and motherhood and came to see giving birth as a superior form of creation to that of the artist. She defended a woman's 'right . . . to love and bear children as she pleased' (which meant being unmarried if one chose) but her outlook on sexual matters caused a breach with her mother, who had warned her daughter not to trust men or to marry, and it became the issue that caused her reputation to be cast in a hugely negative light.[27]

LOVERS

It is believed Duncan first had sexual intercourse in Hungary in 1902, the year she conceived her first baby and touched the 'tragic under-currents' of life when she miscarried and had a breakdown. This intermingling of pain and pleasure was to continue throughout her life and featured in the two significant but contrasting relationships that followed; one with Edward Gordon Craig, the actor turned designer and theatrical revolutionary, and the other, entering the world of affluence, with the millionaire sewing-machine heir Paris Singer (called Lohengrin in her autobiography).

Duncan met Craig in 1904 and instantly discovered a 'soul mate'. She was a celebrity, aged 26; he, the spoilt son of Britain's most famous actress Ellen Terry, was 32 and a habitual philanderer. Sex and art combine. They are both questioning their art, and he encourages her to rethink her repertoire while she inspires him in the writing of his influential work,

The Art of the Theatre. She bore two children, her first and second but his ninth and tenth. Motherhood forced her to face again but more intensely the contradiction between being a woman and being an artist. In America, she had decided to leave a Pole she loved in order to tour, and then discovered he was already married. In Hungary, she had been nearly suicidal at leaving her actor lover and vowed to serve art and not to sacrifice it for love.

With Craig, she discovered that while art and maternity were compatible, in so far as they were both creative, art and love were not, being exclusive and selfish in their demands. She looked after Craig for two years and helped him in his work, even when they had parted, introducing him, for example, to leading figures in European theatre like Firmin Gémier, Konstantin Stanislavsky and Eleanora Duse. Craig had placed Duncan on a pedestal above even his mother and Duse because he believed she was creative while they were only interpretive. Leaving him was an act of survival for Duncan but also an assertion of her own self, of her autonomy as a woman and as an artist.

Singer changed her world in a different way. He provided her with a prosperous and privileged way of life as well as a studio decorated by leading couturier Paul Poiret, who, with Mariano Fortuny – another fashion artist Duncan had inspired – designed her Greek tunics. She enjoyed the lavish lifestyle but was also embarrassed by it. She might talk Marx and Whitman to Singer but was self-conscious that the world she shared with him was endowed with such wealth. Contrasting this luxuriant prosperity with the struggles of her youth, she concluded that the rich could not be happy, a conclusion that led her to idealise manual labour and pronounce that money carried with it a curse. In relation to Singer's circle, particularly the British aristocracy, Duncan wrote, 'No wonder I felt inclined to become a communist.'[28] Repeated sexual scandal finally drove Singer away from her, but he continued to come to her financial rescue after their break-up.

The accidental drowning in the River Seine in 1913 of her two children (by Craig), aged three and six, along with their governess, devastated Duncan. It was possible that at the summit of her ability, aged 35, life might conquer art and she might never perform again. Her reaction was to become pregnant once more during a brief affair. The baby was born in Paris the following August just days after Germany had declared war on France. The baby died after a few hours, a catastrophe Duncan associated with the outbreak of the war, and this, following a suicide attempt, propelled her back into her art but with a fresh purpose. The loss of her children – she was not to have any more – and the savagery of war combined to shake her dance into a new arena: the personal became the political with renewed intensity. She retained, however – and never fully shook off – a mystical and religious element; in homage to her first children Deirdre and Patrick she continued to dance Schubert's 'Ave Maria' for the rest of her life.

The war offered Duncan the opportunity she had been seeking to commit wholeheartedly to a cause. It was sufficiently important and encompassing to match the grandeur of her aspiration. She resumed dancing in January 1915, six months after the death of her third child and, from this point, her dances become allegories of triumph through adversity over repression. She reasserts the value of human agency however buffeted by history and transforms herself from a dancer into a tragedienne. Turning her private anguish into public anger, she created four monumental pieces during the war that could be said to mark the beginning of dance as social protest.

The first of these dances was 'La Marseillaise', a national anthem rooted in revolution that stood as a global call to fight for freedom. Inspired by the sculpted Marseillaise on the Arc de Triomphe, Duncan performed it wearing red, the colour of blood and of revolution. In the dance, according to one report, she sees the enemy advance, she kisses the flag, she tastes blood, she is all but crushed under the attack but rises triumphant with the terrible cry 'Aux armes citoyens'. At the end, she 'stood, filled with patriotic fury', her left breast bared in evocation of Delacroix's painting 'Liberty Leading the People'.[29] She had caught an echo from Greek tragedy – the mourning mother imploring the citizens to wage battle – and turned it into a contemporary image of militant civilisation. Arnold Genthe, who took an iconic photograph of Duncan embodying 'La Marseillaise', said of the dance that it was 'something no painter could do with colours and no sculptor in bronze or marble.'[30]

She also linked the patriotic and the maternal in César Franck's 'Rédemption', a dance she had begun working on before the death of her children. One account of this, the second dance, says she lay still on the floor, then slowly rose to full height, arms outstretched, motionless and used just her neck, throat, shoulders, head and arms to show despair turn to hope.[31] There are similar descriptions of the third dance, to the 'Pathétique' from Tchaikovsky's Sixth Symphony, which she presented as 'the story of the present world struggle'.[32] In this dance, according to one description, Duncan moved from the spring song of peace to the approach of battle and on to the frenzy of physical heroism, ending with an epic lamentation for the slain.[33]

The end of Romanov rule in Russia reinforced her new approach. She dedicated the next concert she gave to the Revolution, and when America joined the war a few weeks later and Duncan was able to declare the conflict a battle for the democratic ideal, she created her dance of Tchaikovsky's 'Marche Slave', the fourth of her monumental pieces. She used the imperial pomp of the music to achieve an opposite effect. According to one report, she stood alone, dressed in a short red garment, head bowed, knees bent, hands apparently tied behind her back. She groped, stumbled in despair, and fell, 'a peasant shuddering under the blows of the knout'. The moment of release was not a sudden spreading wide of her arms. Instead, she brought her arms forward slowly and 'we observe with horror that they have practically forgotten how to move; they are crushed by long serfdom. The expression of frightened, almost uncomprehending, joy with which Isadora concludes the march is another stroke of her vivid imaginative genius.'[34] One critic described 'Marche Slave' as 'sculpture in transition', and when Ellen Terry saw the dance in London in 1921, she thought it an amazing conception: 'I never saw true tragedy before,' she observed.[35]

In these dances, Duncan aspired to epic gesture and, rather than identifying with the music, she worked against it. She tapped into a vein of resurgent nationalism in the countries where she performed and in these dances exploited the tension between the energy of national movements united in a global battle for good and the simplicity and stillness of her controlled performance. The free flowing, ethereal movements of her earlier dance gave way to a new, sculptured and more austere 'rootedness'. She was a tribune of the people, standing her ground. Despite dissenters who attacked Duncan for the political slant of her art, she mostly met an ecstatic response. She had found her pitch; audience, art and performer had become one in a common commitment.

The politicisation of Duncan's art was accompanied by gestures of social conscience. She gave her school, which was then situated in Paris, to Les Dames de France as a military hospital during the war. She sent money to children whose fathers were artists but had been called to fight. She helped refugees, especially the children of the Turkish-Balkan war. She donated box-office income to war relief and to the French and German Red Cross. She read to wounded soldiers, wrote their letters and ran errands for them.

There were episodes of a more sharply political character, too. In neutral Greece, when German officials called for a toast to the Kaiser in her hotel, she says she played 'La Marseillaise' on her portable gramophone, and she sang the anthem in the streets of Athens on anti-government demonstrations. Asked by students in Argentina to dance their national anthem on the night they celebrated the freedom of their country, she had the words translated (according to her version of the incident), wrapped the national flag round her and danced the suffering of the once enslaved colony and its liberation from tyranny. Reports of this escapade suggested she had been drunkenly dancing the tango with gigolos beforehand, and the ensuing scandal almost resulted in her concerts being cancelled.

When her visit to America in late 1914/early 1915 took on a confrontational character, Duncan interpreted it as a consequence of US isolationism, which was keeping her country out of the war. Trouble started when younger pupils from her school in France who had travelled to America were held on Ellis Island, the immigration centre for New York, because Duncan did not have the proper guardianship papers for them. Problems continued when, after performing 'La Marseillaise', she claimed she was prevented from performing it again because of US neutrality. In addition, she petitioned – to no avail – the mayor of New York to free a woman gaoled for killing her illegitimate children. Her unsuccessful season at the Century Theatre, which lost money, ended abruptly when her students were evicted from the theatre on the orders of the fire department because they had been sleeping in the building. Customs threatened to confiscate her trunks in view of the debts she had accrued, and she was able to leave her homeland only when they had been paid by a rich benefactor. She denounced the US and sailed from the quay waving the French flag and singing 'La Marseillaise'.

During her next visit to New York, however, she triumphed at the Metropolitan Opera House in March 1917, a month before the US entered the war, with a patriotic, anti-isolationist finale. As she finished dancing 'La Marseillaise' she removed an outer red robe to reveal the Stars and Stripes, and, on cue, the orchestra joined in with 'The Star-Spangled Banner'. One reviewer described the fervour with which she was greeted as the 'height of pandemonium'.[36] She had bridged the two revolutionary traditions of France and America, both born at the same historical moment, her stance evoking the Statue of Liberty, a famous gift from the one country to the other. For Duncan, this represented her own journey, an alliance of the old and new worlds. This was no longer a time for art and artists, she believed, but for trenches and soldiers. 'If I were only a dancer,' she said, 'I would not speak. But I am a teacher with a mission.'[37]

Paradoxically, just as she adopted a political position, it disenchanted her natural political confederates. Whereas in 1915, she had been celebrated on the cover of *The Masses*, now, almost two years later, the intellectual New York left, which was mainly anti-war, found her pro-war views, as well as the stridency with which she presented them, hard to swallow. Her bohemianism had become suspect and smacked of being erratic and egocentric.

After the war, she offered her dance to France as a 'consolation to the sorrowing and to the afflicted', but France was not to support either her school or her art. Even her treatment of 'La Marseillaise' was now criticised as disrespectful.[38] She sold her school building to the French government, which wanted it not as a hospital any longer but as a factory to make asphyxiating gases for the next war. Her plans to open a school in Athens in 1920 under a new, pro-Allied government were thwarted by the unexpected death of the recently installed king and the subsequent change of regime. Having failed to establish her school in western Europe or the United States, she looked to the Bolsheviks, who, she thought, needed her talents the most.

Before the Revolution, she had hoped her school might become part of the Moscow Art Theatre, but she could not find the money and had turned instead to the Imperial Ballet, where she met opposition from prominent figures such as Rimsky-Korsakov, who, in common with several other composers, questioned her use of their music as dance accompaniments. Now, the Russian Revolution seemed to offer not only a better prospect for the school than the capitalist countries but also a politically desirable one. She hoped the Revolution would deliver 'one great blow' to capitalism, which, she said, 'stands for monstrous greed and villainy.'[39]

INTERNATIONALISM

The nationalism of her politics in World War I gave way to internationalism. When the Bolsheviks came to power, she saw a continuum between her American ideals and those of the Soviets. She claimed Whitman as the first Bolshevik, not in a party political sense but in an emotional sense. Soon she would call herself a Bolshevik, but more by way of solidarity than in doctrinal alliance. Her own politics might be described as libertarian or even anarchistic (rather than in the more precise sense of her being a follower of anarchist philosophy), although later she would say she was neither anarchist nor Bolshevik. Cleaving to the radical tradition of modern America's roots, her preferred self-image was that of a revolutionary, both as an artist and as a person, although for her, the ultimate ideology or authority never was and never could be a party or a state but an ideal expressed through herself.

The head of the Soviet Trade Commission in London saw her dance 'Marche Slave' and went backstage, where they discussed the possibility of her opening a school in Moscow. She sent her proposal to the Commissar of Education, Anatoly Lunacharsky:

> 'I shall never hear of money in exchange for my work. I want a studio workshop, a house for myself and pupils, simple food, simple tunics, and the opportunity to give our best work . . . I want to dance for the masses, for the working people who need my art and have never had the money to come and see me.' Lunacharsky sent a telegram back: 'Come to Moscow. We will give you a school and a thousand children. You may carry out your big idea on a big scale.'[40]

Neither pleas by Russian émigrés nor scare stories of satanic reds butchering babies deterred her from going. She said she knew nothing of politics but believed Soviet Russia to be a new world where art could not be bought with bucks. She was aware of the risk to her reputation in the West that an alliance with the Bolsheviks posed (although contrary to her expectation it did not damage the box-office takings for her farewell performances), but she seems to have been unaware – despite what her exile friends disparagingly told her – of exactly what would greet her in strife-torn Russia. To her, it represented a fresh start, an opportunity to close the door on the excesses of her past and lead her back to a true path.

At the Russian border, she was so excited that she asked (fruitlessly) if she could join the Communist Party straight away. The train took her on to Petrograd, as St Petersburg was then called, which she had not visited since 1913. She found it in July 1921 looking miserable. When she arrived in Moscow, there was no official reception. She was met only by soldiers and suspicion. Lunacharsky later explained he had not really believed she would come, let alone arrive on time.

Life in Moscow for Duncan was very tough. Gone was the Singer lifestyle, a pampered existence of careless luxury. She agreed to live in a primitive summer cottage, but only lasted a few weeks before moving into the building that had been designated for the school, which was located in the abandoned mansion of a tea plantation owner and an émigrée ballerina. More delay followed as government offices already stationed there had to be moved out. Duncan set about masking the gaudy decorations and preparing for her first pupils. The country, however, was suffering the consequences of encirclement by the West and the depredations of civil war, in particular a severe famine. She was forced to scale down her project and return to fund-raising. This was a permissible activity thanks to the introduction of the New Economic Policy, which allowed a measure of private enterprise.

The Isadora Duncan State School opened in December 1921 with a staff of sixty, including plumbers, doctors, porters, cooks and secretaries as well as instructors, but the promise of 1,000 students was reduced to the reality of forty because the state could not afford to feed, clothe and heat the larger number. Despite the jolt to her idealism and sadness at the enforced retreat, she understood the thinking, and it did not shake her commitment. Notwithstanding the problems, the school extended its reach beyond the pupil intake and worked with hundreds of local children.

Duncan easily fell into adopting the style and rhetoric of the Bolsheviks, but the political reality was quite different. The first reception she attended appalled her because of the opulence on display; she accused those present of having removed the rich simply to replace them. Lunacharsky explained this behaviour away as the consequence of going through an understandable phase of early militant Communism, yet admitted that she had touched a raw nerve and was in certain respects correct. Duncan nonetheless retained her utopian idealism. She told Stanislavsky to commit suicide or begin life again as a Communist and in her turn received similar apocalyptic advice from Nikolai Podvoysky, who had been in charge of the storming of the Winter Palace and had become Commissar for Physical Education. After telling her that, when discussing her invitation, Lenin had said Russia needed her assistance in the work of the cultural revolution, Podvoysky pronounced to her face that all she had been through– the acclaimed appearances at grand theatres and the public celebrity – was false. She must now dance for the masses and not seek any gratitude. She could have happiness in her performances but she must not forget that Soviet happiness was hard, grim and built on a bonfire. He added that she had arrived a century too soon, to which she replied that her revolution had to happen right now.

Along with the economic strictures, she found antipathy towards her in certain official quarters, for example on the People's Commissariat for Food, which believed she was a luxury the state could not afford. The school faced ideological as well as bureaucratic antagonism – she was particularly criticised for her mystical tendencies and musical taste. Many musicians held to their pre-revolutionary aversion to her use of music not specifically composed to accompany dance, and innovative artists like Vsevolod Meyerhold shared the views of the western avant-garde, who now found her art outmoded. When she announced that she was going to dance 'Marche Slave', she was told she could not because it contained extracts from the Tsarist national anthem. She won the argument that the piece in itself was not important but her treatment was; her performance of it at the celebration of the fourth anniversary of the Revolution in front of Lenin proved triumphant. The programme ended with her leading a chorus of 100 children, who appeared one after another in red tunics dancing the 'Internationale'. As she requested, the audience, Lenin included, stood and sang. She repeated the programme for an audience of peasants and workers, who, it is reported, were moved to tears and at the close refused to leave until she had returned to the stage.

Even more emblematic of the new world in which Duncan believed was her performance in Petrograd in front of an audience of sailors that included the crew of the battleship *Aurora*, the guns of which had signalled the start of the October Revolution in 1917. The lights failed, the audience howled, Duncan asked for a lantern, which she held aloft like a revolutionary beacon, and to deafening applause she danced as the sailors sang revolutionary songs. She described this experience as more thrilling than first hearing Gluck's *Orfeo* or Beethoven's Seventh Symphony. The vitality of the new relationship between audience and performer that Duncan found in the Soviet Union, not just in Moscow but elsewhere (in the Ukraine, for instance), sustained her creativity and gave her the ability to endure the harsh conditions.

Duncan's performances expressed the continued mix in her ideologies. At the fifth congress of the women's section of the Communist Party, an event where babies are committed to Communism, she danced 'Ave Maria' alongside the 'Internationale'. Yet the new dances she created, at a time when her own body was old for a dancer, denote a new stage in her development, continuing the monumental gesture she initiated during World War I but more socially and politically grounded.

She created dances to two études by Scriabin, 'Mother' and 'Revolutionary', which were a direct response to the Volga famine. Having queued to see Lenin's body on his death in January 1924, and moved by the grieving of the mourners, she danced two revolutionary songs in his memory. Later that year she composed dances for her pupils based on revolutionary, folk and workers' songs: 'The Young Guard', 'With Courage Comrades, March In Step', 'One, Two, Three, Pioneers Are We', 'The Young Pioneers', 'Warshavianka', 'Dubinushka' and 'The Blacksmith' (also known as 'Forging the Keys of Freedom').

'One, Two, Three' is a happy round, danced to a folk tune and designed for young female pioneers. The others concern necessary sacrifice, struggle and ultimate triumph. 'Dubinushka', for example, has two lines of workers hauling a rope together rhythmically, a symbol of solidarity and collective endeavour. The movements of the front row are earth-bound while those of the back row reach upward, a juxtaposition that Duncan often used to represent servitude and liberation, and in this case reinforced by a beam of light angled across the dancers' arms. In 'The Blacksmith', the dancers are lying prone, one rises – the eponymous hero – and, in response, they all arise; they beat at the forge and release themselves from their shackles, their fists defiantly held forward. 'Warshavianka', danced to a song of the 1905 uprising and echoing Duncan's 'Marseillaise', shows the relentless march of the red flag; the first bearer (or bearers) rushes across the stage and is felled, another takes up the banner (imagined, not real) and is also felled, and so on until, at the end when the last one is down, the first manages to rise and urges the others to follow suit. The song continues throughout and by the close all are standing and still singing.

In these, Duncan's last completed works, she was no doubt influenced by the artistic ferment in the young Soviet state. She drew on distinct proletarian iconography – movement associated with labour and the clenched fist – and took their gesture further toward what would become key elements of modern dance, the tense body and architectural composition. Their sculptural quality suits their functionality, and they have a poise and a tempo that, allied to the regular beat of the tunes, makes them declamatory rather than aggressive. Three of these dances – 'The Blacksmith', 'Dubinushka' and 'Warshavianka' – are considered among her most important, yet at a memorial organised by her family the year after her death, none was included and the existence of the Soviet school was ignored.

Their impact did not die with her, nevertheless. When her pupils danced them in Paris in 1929, the poet Fernand Divoire described their effect as overwhelming. They were also widely seen in the US in the late 1920s and influenced, among others, Martha Graham, Doris Humphrey, Helen Tamiris, Hanya Holm and José Limón as well as radical movements such as the Workers' Dance League and the socially aware work of the New Deal Dance Project.

FURORE ABROAD

The Revolution, however, did not deliver for Duncan. The Bolshoi Theatre was not available for the one night a week she had hoped for; more importantly, she could not raise sufficient funds for her school in the Soviet Union and once again had to trawl in the West. Accompanying Duncan on her first trip abroad was the leading Soviet poet Sergei Esenin, with whom she had a destructive, violent and passionate relationship. Since meeting in 1921, neither, it appears, could live with or without the other. Eighteen years his senior, Duncan had married Esenin in 1922 to protect him while they were away from Russia – marriage was not contractual or financial in the Soviet Union and either partner could dissolve it without penalty or loss. Although the Soviets still regarded her as an American, her marriage had annulled her US citizenship and the Americans regarded her as a Soviet. By marrying Esenin, she had made herself stateless outside Soviet borders and the handful of countries that recognised the new regime.

The plan was to travel across Europe and then tour the US with pupils from the Moscow school to show her homeland the truth of Soviet achievement, but the children did not make the trip, possibly because of reluctance by the authorities in both Russia and America. Duncan and Esenin proceeded with their European itinerary and arrived in the US in October 1922, leaving in their wake the aftermath of scandalous behaviour by the poet, which he claimed was publicity for the Revolution. Their arrival in New York came against a national backdrop of lynching, race riots and a sharp rise in 'Russiaphobia', triggered by the first of many 'red scare' episodes in which trades unionists and left-wingers were rounded up as dangerous subversives, with many subsequently deported.

It was perhaps not surprising, although to Duncan completely unexpected and outrageous, that she and Esenin were prevented from landing. Not only was she seen as an alien ideologically, she had now become an alien literally. In a statement Duncan had prepared before docking, she preached conciliation between the land of her birth and her adopted country: she and Esenin were 'representatives of young Russia' but were not mixing in politics.[41] The message was greeted with enmity, however, and the two of them were viewed as agents of the revolutionary atheistic state. Her manager Sol Hurok, a Russian who had become a naturalised American, was allowed on board, but on leaving he was strip-searched by immigration officers. They also subjected the couple to an intrusively thorough inspection. Material in Russian was confiscated, and both Duncan and Esenin were taken to Ellis Island for interrogation before being released.

The furore helped the box office but not her reception. To many Americans, her red views were those of a traitor. She had even dyed her white hair red like her politics and her tunic. Yet she had no connection to the fledgling American Communist Party, which had been driven underground, and, in one speech, she defined her Communism as nothing more threatening than 'everybody singing and dancing together'.[42] Her libertarianism, however, was now seen as anti-American and a danger to the state.

Her speeches caused uproar, and the critics savaged her. Sections of the press that had denounced her since she had gone to Soviet Russia dogged her every move, and the chief attacker – the Hearst press – even offered a coded call for her execution, using the Mata Hari spy case as a precedent. Such was the price of Duncan's political idealism. Her celebrity had thrust her into the limelight, but it had made her more vulnerable and afforded no protection.

In Boston, an old puritan town with some of the severest censorship in the US, Esenin stirred additional trouble by hanging a red flag from Symphony Hall, an act that was banned in many states. It was in this volatile context that Duncan gave what has become a notorious and iconic performance. Reports vary but it seems that after finishing 'Pathétique' she attacked the repressive character of New England whilst waving a red scarf. 'This is red. So am I,' she proclaimed. 'It is the colour of life and vigour . . . you were once wild here! Don't let them tame you!'

While calling out, 'You don't know what beauty is. This is beauty', she tore her tunic to bare a breast and hysteria broke out.[43] Although she denied deliberately 'mismanaging' her garments, the mayor banned her from reappearing in the city. Three federal departments began investigating her alleged Bolshevik connections with a view to deporting her, and cancellations ensued elsewhere. But in those towns where she did still appear, such as Kansas City, Milwaukee and Memphis, ticket sales for her concerts rocketed.

Hurok forbade her to make any more statements, but at her next performance, in Chicago, she announced to the audience: 'My manager tells me that if I make any more speeches the tour is dead. Very well, the tour is dead. I will go back to Moscow where there is vodka, music, poetry and dancing. Oh, yes, and Freedom.'[44] The tour continued, however, though scarred by drunken and anti-Semitic outbursts from Esenin. The press had a field day. One mayor impounded her red tunics in order to stop her performing revolutionary dances while another insisted that policemen be in attendance to ensure she kept her costume on and to arrest her if not.

Duncan was vocal in her counter-attack, deploring Prohibition, which from 1920 had prevented the manufacture or

sale of alcohol, and, as a consequence, had forced her and
Esenin to acquire bootleg liquor. (She blamed some of the
much publicised incidents, including a concert she gave when
inebriated, on the effects of this potent illegal drink.) In an
interview for a Hearst paper, *American Weekly*, she castigated
materialistic America as 'stupid, penurious, ignorant'. She was
quoted as saying, 'You feed your children here canned peas
and canned art, and wonder why they are not beautiful . . . It's
the smugness, the sanctimonious righteousness . . . that crushes
my soul.'[45]As her manager said, she supplied her enemies with
plenty of ammunition.

The tour lost money but ended with a full house at Carnegie Hall, New York, in January 1923. Duncan's departure
from the US, this time apparently waving a red scarf from the
boat, marked her farewell to the land of her birth. The American press, however, went on reporting her exploits abroad,
mostly in a sensationalist and censorious manner.

Neither she nor Esenin had been good ambassadors for the
Bolsheviks. Their relationship was fracturing, and their return
across Europe continued the litany of Esenin's destructive
conduct, fuelled by alcohol, homesickness, resentment at his
treatment in the West and an acute sense of the incongruity of
the whole trip. In the clash of celebrity, Esenin did not like being seen as the appendage to Duncan, and the fact that neither
spoke the other's language added to mutual frustrations.

While Duncan had been away, state support for her school
had stopped altogether, and the staff had been whittled down
to twenty. It had moved for the summer to Litivino, some fifty
miles outside Moscow, and was in the care of Irma Duncan,
a long-standing student of Duncan's and an adopted daughter, who was the only one of the pupils to come with her to
Russia. The two Duncans left for a tour of the Caucasus without Esenin, who had in fact decided to break from Isadora.
Although they never divorced, their union was over. It had
been exhausting, and she took the break-up badly.

Duncan continued her work, touring to publicise and
present her dance and to earn money for the school, the cost
of which was steadily rising. In Kislovodsk in the north
Caucasus, she was reminded of her American trip and the
close attention of the law when the local Cheka, the feared

secret police, were tipped off that she was performing 'God save the Tsar'. This snatch from 'Marche Slave', which had caused problems before, now led to her being told she could not dance the counter-revolutionary anthem. At the theatre, with police in the wings, she defied the ban to huge cheers. The police decided to arrest her secretary rather than her, but Duncan sent a letter to Trotsky, the Minister of War, who happened to have a dacha nearby; he ordered the secretary's release.

During her absences, the pupils at her school continued to give dancing lessons to the children of Moscow workers, and when she returned to her house in the capital in August 1924 she was greeted by several hundred children and pupils dancing and singing the 'Internationale'. This display inspired her to create her seven last compositions, most of which she presented for the first time that September when she gave a series of concerts at the Kamerny Theatre in Moscow before leaving on a fund-raising tour of Germany. She offered several different programmes, but she began the revolutionary one acknowledging an ancestral political heritage by dancing to 'The Wearing of the Green', which the children followed by a jig and a reel. In the French section she danced 'La Marseillaise' and the children performed a carmagnole, a popular song and dance that became part of the revolutionary tradition at the time of the Jacobins. The Hungarian 'Rakoczy March' was followed by her Russian repertoire of late dances and the 'Internationale'.

After the final performance, an impressed Mrs Kalinin, the wife of the Soviet president, asked what she could do to help. Duncan said she wanted to show the work of her school to Communist leaders in order to win their support. The next night a concert for party officials was duly given at the Bolshoi Theatre, and it included a stirring tribute to Duncan by Lunacharsky as well as a rapturous ovation. Unfortunately, she had to leave for Berlin the following day without having the time to exploit this favourable opportunity.

As if acknowledging that her crusade was already doomed, she had told the American Communist paper, the *Daily Worker*, that 'my dream of a school devoted to the expression of life in terms of the dance came true in Russia. Unfortunately, the catastrophe of these last years, especially the famine, have ended the dream.'[46] In addition, she had received a foretaste of the reaction she was going to meet as she crossed Europe pleading for funds when three of her pupils renounced her political views in the expectation of agreeing an American tour. In Germany, and subsequently in France too, she ran into visa problems because she was seen as a Communist. Her political association also allowed managers, who had often exploited her, to treat her badly with impunity. She wrote to Irma Duncan in March 1925, 'Any reports that I have spoken against the Soviet government are *absolutely* false and unfounded. On the contrary, it is because I speak only well of them that I meet with *universal persecution.*'[47]

In Paris, she had meetings with the Soviet ambassador and French Communist Party at which they discussed three topics: support for her Soviet school; a plan to bring her Moscow pupils to France, which had been sanctioned by the Soviet authorities; and the creation of a French school in association with the Soviet one. The talks, however, were as unproductive as her general fund-raising efforts, where her Soviet association counted against her. Marooned in Europe, approaching fifty, subject to bouts of illness and in a desperate financial state, she responded to requests to write her memoirs as her only way of making money. Exhausted by her fruitless time away from her school, denied even the solace of teaching, the news of Esenin's suicide in December 1925 shattered her, despite their estrangement. She never saw the Soviet Union again.

Her debts were mounting, credit was being denied, she felt helpless. A suicide attempt in Nice only made it harder for her to secure backing. Six months later, in July 1927, she did manage to give a concert in Paris. It comprised dances to Franck, Schubert and Wagner, but no revolutionary pieces and no speech afterwards. It turned out to be her last performance.

My Life appeared in September that year. She was ashamed at having written for money, but having already spent the advance, she had to finish the book to earn more. The memoir bears the marks of haste as well as her own desire for heightened sensation and wish to control her own story. This was partly owing to an understandable and common craving for self-determination and partly owing to a lack of concern for the vagaries of memory and the status of official documents, several of which relating to her early life were lost in the 1906 San Francisco earthquake.

She ends the book at the point just before her adventure in the Soviet Union, which she describes as the culmination of a longstanding artistic and political dream. This may be an over-statement written with hindsight (although she had announced such a plan in 1917) and it may have been designed to disturb her bourgeois readers, but it carries some weight and was never repudiated. Indeed, she planned to write a sequel, *My Two Years in Bolshevik Russia*, and she would have become very popular and very rich if she had denounced the Soviet regime. She told her Paris agent that if she had written about her time in the Soviet Union, she feared the book would have been banned in America.

The Soviet experience had been very hard for Duncan and very inspiring at the same time. She was deflated at not having realised her 'big idea on a big scale' and disenchanted with the lack of official support for her school. She prophetically said the effigy of Lenin kept in a glass case in Red Square sym-bolised the embalming of the Revolution. Yet, despite her dis-illusionment and the agony of the ordinary people she had witnessed, she said in a letter that the Soviet experiment was the 'greatest miracle that has happened to humanity for two thousand years' and told a Berlin audience she had found in Moscow 'the song of the world'.[48]

At the close of *My Life*, she sums up the hope engendered in her by the Soviet Union, employing a familiar mix of uto-pian and mystical philosophy:

> The dream that had been conceived in the head of Buddha; the dream that had resounded through the words of Christ; the dream that has been the ultimate hope of all great artists; the dream that Lenin had by great magic turned to reality. I was entering now into this dream that my work and life might become a part of its glorious promise.[49]

The final words of the book follow: 'Adieu Old World! I would hail a New World.'

Shortly before her death, in an interview in Nice, where she had a studio, she was asked what had been the greatest and happiest period of her life. She answered, 'Russia, Russia, only Russia. My three years in Russia, with all their sufferings, were worth everything in my life taken together.'[50] She said she wanted to return to the Soviet Union but never did. (The Soviet school survived until the 1940s, and in Moscow a studio and studio theatre were also named after her.)

LAST YEARS

She lived her last years shuttling between Paris and Nice, socialising with the rich and famous, and having affairs with both men and women, but for all that she was poor and very lonely. The anomalies that had marked her life persisted, especially in relation to being American. She had pride in her birthright and joined the massive crowds who welcomed her compatriot Charles Lindbergh when he arrived in Paris after flying direct from New York on the first non-stop solo flight across the Atlantic. Yet in an interview, she complained that America had rejected her and her desire to have free schools and a free theatre. The reason? 'There they still have child labour, and only the rich can see opera and beauty is commercialised . . . All they want is money, money, money.'[51]

She supported the Italian-born American anarchists Sacco and Vanzetti when, on very flimsy evidence, they were found guilty of killing two men in a payroll attack. The appeal process took more than six years and was accompanied by a huge support campaign across America and Europe. They were finally executed in 1927 in Massachusetts. In France, Duncan hosted meetings on the case and attended protests. She kept on her mantelpiece a photograph of the Massachusetts governor, on which she had written in lipstick 'Down with the Philistines!'

Although she was still technically a Soviet citizen when she died in September 1927, she had the Stars and Stripes laid on her coffin along with the robe she wore when she danced her tragedies. There was also a sheaf of red gladioli bearing a red ribbon with the inscription in gold letters, 'The Heart of Russia Weeps for Isadora.' By chance, the procession of her hearse through Paris coincided with an American Legion parade celebrating the tenth anniversary of US involvement in World War I. A detachment of French mounted police sent to protect the American Legion from Sacco and Vanzetti supporters lowered their tricolours in salute as they passed her coffin. US papers reported that few attended her funeral and downplayed the story in relation to their panting coverage of the parading compatriots. If the journalists had gone to Père Lachaise cemetery instead of only watching the cortège pass by in the street, they would have seen a crowd estimated to be 10,000 strong.

The manner of her death cemented her celebrity myth. Aged fifty, she died an iconic death in Nice when the fringes of her red shawl caught in the back wheel of a sports car. Her neck was snapped and her body dragged 30 metres along the sea's rim. According to Jean Cocteau, it was the perfect end.

THE REVOLUTIONIST

The ideas we have of Duncan come from a variety of sources and offer highly conflicting accounts. She continually refashioned herself through her own contributions, at one moment the gossamer offspring of nature, her Hellenic dancing the expression of an ethereal transcendence, at another the scion of pioneer stock, her American dance born of the frontier spirit and the Irish jigs her grandmother so enjoyed.

To become a celebrity, she raised her flag as a 'revolutionist'. 'All geniuses worthy of the name are,' she said, adding pointedly: 'Every artist has to be one to make a mark in the world today.'[52] She defined and defended that 'mark' through her off-stage life, through her performances and through her publications – autobiography, diary, pamphlets, essays, articles, letters, interviews, speeches. She was mindful of the dilemma of celebrity. She not only recognised the necessity of fame, without which her pioneering dance would not have been seen and reported, but also the need to assert her own views against the very reports which derived from and fuelled that requisite quality. Most of these reports, unsurprisingly, were interested in her as a personality rather than as an artist and preferred to ignore her generosity, wit, courage and integrity in favour of her selfish, brutish carelessness and reckless abandon. The subsequent slew of biographies and articles by lovers, friends and acquaintances on the one hand and scholars and critics on the other has confirmed her celebrity as well as her disputed status. Along with surviving artefacts and memorabilia of her life, in addition to the reconstructions of her dances, they provide a mass of material from which later commentators have built their own idea of her.

Most of our images of Isadora Duncan come through the testimony of others. She is celebrated at the Théâtre des Champs Elysées in Paris, completed in 1913, in the bas-relief fresco on the theatre façade and murals inside. There are also a number of drawings and still photographs of her but no moving shots. She did eventually agree to be filmed but it was not to be. She had wanted to lose weight first but instead lost her life, and maybe that is how she would have preferred it. She had refused to appear in films written specially for her because she could not trust either what the filmmakers would do with the images or how she would come across on screen; the young technology still produced flickering results and she did not want to appear ridiculous. She was also aware that this absence would feed her myth.

For every dismissive account of her, there are serried ranks of admirers. The two opposing views of her – bizarre 'sacred monster' versus humane, compelling pioneer – are represented in later fictional recreations of her: the former in Ken Russell's television film *Isadora Duncan: The Biggest Dancer in the World* (1966) and Kenneth MacMillan's ballet *Isadora* (1981), the latter in Karel Reisz's film *Isadora* (1968) and Martin Sherman's play *When She Danced* (1985).

Auguste Rodin described her as 'the greatest woman I have ever known. Sometimes I think she is the greatest woman the world has ever known.' Konstantin Stanislavsky called her a 'galvanic inspiration'. Dorothy Parker, who dubbed her 'Duncan Disorderly', nonetheless honoured her as 'a magnificent, generous, gallant, reckless and fated fool of a woman . . . She ran ahead, where there were no paths.'[53]

However assessed, Isadora Duncan's celebrity was undeniably conspicuous; the media coverage attests to this. She performed before royalty and the heads of state of Europe and the USA. The influential columnist Janet Flanner wrote eight months before Duncan's death that, Charlie Chaplin and Douglas Fairbanks aside, Duncan was the best-known American in Europe, which is a considerable tribute since the two men achieved their fame through the mass medium of cinema whereas Duncan's dancing was only ever seen in person.

The battle over her myth has been intense within the dance world. She was outcast from its record for many years and her rehabilitation came only towards the end of the twentieth century, yet her development of what might be termed the protest dance (notwithstanding the reductionist tendency of such labels) was historic. She risked her reputation and her art for her idealism, suffering most in her homeland where she was vilified for her association with the young Soviet experiment.

Her commitment to articulating social and political meaning in her dance challenged the core vocabulary and categories of performance and posed deep questions for aesthetics and politics that reverberate still. She sketched a new idea of acting as much as dancing through her attempts to fuse the mind and the body, through her emphasis on the corporeality of expression and through her focus on simplicity and the abandonment of the decorative. She replaced virtuosity with emotional, imaginative statement, making her impact through lambent minimalism.

In striving for an impassioned yet impersonal simplicity, she bridged romanticism and modernism. Her emotionalism appealed to Romantics, who saw an inner self being given compelling and authentic outer expression, while modernists liked her stress on form and structure. Her desire to relate metaphorically to the social world beyond her dance kept her in the Romantic camp, and her own view of modernism in dance at the time was dismissive. When she saw the Ballets Russes, she admired its leading individuals like Nijinsky and Pavlova but thought the company decadent. 'If that is Art,' she said, 'I prefer Aviation.'[54]

She was trapped within but journeyed beyond the limits of representation determined by factors such as gender, race, nationality, age and history. She made a physical reality of the contradictions she wished to supersede, coexisting in the present, the 'other' to which she aspired experienced in the palpable here and now. She could be a dancer and not a dancer, an individual and not an individual, a private person and not a private person, a woman and not a woman, an American and not an American, a revolutionary and not a revolutionary. Her single figure could become the multitudinous world.

In modern dance, which was pioneered by women, this contribution to the politics of representation and identity has been significant, even if sometimes it has developed through contrary influence. Dance commentators have seen Martha Graham's early absence of emotion as a feminist reaction to Duncan. They have also seen in male modern dance an affirmation of a gay sensibility that contradicts both Duncan's universal aspiration – the solo female standing for all – and her insistence on opening up the inner space, preferring to defend it as private.[55] Furthermore, her individual radicalism, however ill defined or partially directed, gave an egalitarian impetus to modern dance, especially in the US.

BEYOND DANCE

She was also influential beyond dance, in education (and the role of dance in it), on dress fashion, social behaviour and morality. These have not traditionally been seen as part of politics, yet Duncan, with little understanding of politics in the conventional sense, embraced them, like life, as political. She subverted distinctions between inner experience and outer behaviour, art and life, the public and the private. Whilst she maintained a biological essentialist view of woman as Mother Nature, she also presented a vibrant and active image of women and contributed to feminism in her dancing and her non-dancing life by challenging and redefining women's role and place in society and what was considered acceptable gesture, comportment and behaviour for women.

The massiveness of her mission, in dance and in life, fed both her idealism and the contradictions of her idealism. She believed in the indivisibility of life and art while living a different reality. Her belief led towards involuntary dance, the ultimate sanction of the impulsive, and allowed her to continue to be committed in the face of, and without having to adjust to, contrary realities. She mixed the science of Darwin with the mysticism of mesmerism, the sacred with the profane. She acknowledged 'the magic power of money' yet was frequently dismissive of, or at least ambivalent towards, wealth.[56] She did not become rich as a celebrity yet, without her celebrity, she would not have attracted the rich patrons who supported her. Whenever she did earn big sums, she spent the money either on immediate pleasures or on her school, or she gave it away. Although needing money, she emptied her bag in Russia at her last performance, scattering her cash across the Bolshoi stage, and, when even more impoverished, she refused to take Esenin's inheritance after his death. At what turned out to be the end of her life, she decided she hated poverty and wished she had kept all the money that had come her way.

Whether in America or the Soviet Union, she was an exemplar of contrarian individuality at the dawning of the epoch of mass culture. Through her Romantic doctrine of 'be yourself', she challenged patriarchal rationalist definitions of politics yet made a fetish of spontaneity and replaced sustained political activity with political gesture. The emphasis on feeling, on liberating the individual as a response to the homogeneity of both the ruling elite and the collective idea of 'the people', was an assertion of human agency in the face of establishment views of history defined by the deeds of 'great men'. It was also a democratisation of that agency and a counter to instrumentalist views of politics, which upset both the right and the left.

Duncan's focus on the individual fed accusations of arrogance and compromised the activist aspirations of her politics. The 'self' she wished to be was complex and contradictory and it changed, or the dominant and highlighted aspects changed, and this changing 'self' had an unstable relationship to factors such as class solidarity or political movements that are indispensable to the political realisation of those aspirations. Max Eastman believed she corrupted the notion of the radical by identifying it with irrelevance to fact and rationality and by making a cult of impracticality, rapture and abandon. In this, she was a forerunner of major elements in the 1960s revolt among middle-class western youth (often characterised as 'hippies'). She shared with them utopianism and ethical stridency, features that were common to much left politics of her time and are generally familiar in radical activism still (what W.B. Yeats calls the 'delirium of the brave' and the 'vertigo of self-sacrifice').[57]

This tension in her politics and her dance – expressed in her constant spiritual longing – came from her way of opening up the private in the public through her insistence that she was the ultimate source of authority. She hid her technique behind the label *natural* as a way of defending her 'self' and the integrity of her 'self' as this private source of authority. Yet her desire to reach beyond her 'self' led her towards the social and the political, with which she merged as the source as well as the destination. Her committed dance, however, was rarely left to speak for itself, as if implicitly acknowledging there was another source; and in her speeches and writings, she recognized the importance of context and of explanation as an act of identification with this other source.

Yet for Duncan, the social and the political were idealised and exclusive. She danced the valiant, sacrificial soldier or the heroic, noble worker not the killer, the coward or the consumer. She danced her comradeship with universal humanity or with the poor and downtrodden but her embrace did not include 'uncivilised' or 'primitive' American Indians or African Americans, whose emotional release, unlike her own, she considered dangerous. She danced a 'real' America as mythical as the one she opposed, celebrating the white pioneers who wiped out the indigenous population, as well as lauding the country's democratic traditions and energetic individualism, which, however vibrant, nevertheless saw huge numbers of its citizens impoverished and disenfranchised.

She appealed to the bohemian and briefly the revolutionary left as a bourgeois radical and, despite her exhilarating vision of an organic, primal communism, she also managed to appeal to some on the right because of her aestheticism. She had no examples to follow beyond the Romantics like Shelley and Whitman; she searched for but rarely found other artists who were striving to create new art forms for their new world in this spirit. She did try to replace her elitist patronage network with a more popular and left-oriented one but perhaps

Podvoysky was right: she had arrived a century too soon. In other respects, however, her time had already passed.

She could have pursued a celebrity career as a solo dancer but that option never interested her. She believed the whole culture of the body was social – for instance, that movement, gesture, clothing and related public constraints were shaped by and in turn shaped social factors – so that, in one sense, all her work was political and required political commitment. She sacrificed a peaceful, luxurious life for her ideals, and, most notably through her three years in the young Soviet state, risked her art and her reputation in order to pursue those ideals in uncharted and intensely political territory. What she did achieve came in spite of many obstacles, political, financial, social and artistic. She was mocked, she was ignored, and the energy required to maintain her commitment exacted a heavy emotional price, as was to be the case with later female pioneers like Billie Holiday and Janis Joplin. Duncan expended her energy on sustaining her defiance, which became her way of life and inevitably meant continually biting the hands that fed her.

The pallor of the imitations of Duncan's dance might suggest that her character was the defining force of her creativity. Clearly, this was crucial, as it is with any performer, but to focus primarily on that, as some critics have done, would be to limit her significance unjustly. Her dances exist independently of her, although, as with Brecht, her legacy in technical terms has dated quickly. Her contribution goes beyond her personality and her dances. She was a celebrity, but she was more than that. However inconsistent were the politics for which she suffered, she fused performance and politics in a unique and historic way. Politics for her, the necessary iconoclast, was not a means to an end but an inspiration for the performer to question ceaselessly.

NOTES

1. Quoted in Ann Daly, *Done Into Dance: Isadora in America*, Bloomington and Indianapolis, Indiana University Press, 1995, p. 6.

2. Isadora Duncan, *My Life*, New York, Award Books, 1966, p. 9.

3. *ibid.*, p. 9.

4. The opening line of Walt Whitman's 'Song of Myself'. The poem first appeared (untitled) in 1855 in his collection of twelve poems called *Leaves of Grass*.

5. Quoted in Peter Kurth, *Isadora: A Sensational Life*, London, Abacus, 2003, p. 21. The next quotation, *ibid.*, p. 5.

6. *ibid.*, p. 79.

7. *ibid.*, p. 27, quoted from an autobiographical sketch Duncan wrote in 1905 for programme notes.

8. *ibid.*, p. 50.

9. Quoted in Victor Seroff, *The Real Isadora*, London, Hutchinson, 1972, p. 47.

10. Duncan (1966), p. 26.

11. Daly, p. 35.

12. Quoted in Frederika Blair, *Isadora: Portrait of the Artist as a Woman*, Wellingborough, Northants, Equation, 1987, p. 69.

13. Duncan (1966), p. 72.

14. Quoted in Walter Terry, *Isadora Duncan: Her Life, Her Art, Her Legacy*, New York, Dodd, Mead & Co., 1963, p. 41. She told one accompanist, George Copeland, who could not understand why she had not rehearsed with him: 'It's the *music* which is important. Play as if I were not there, as if you were simply playing a recital alone, and it will be all right. You see, I can't dance without the *music*.' (Blair, p. 249.)

15. See Marc Franko, *Dancing Modernism/ Performing Politics*, Bloomington and Indianapolis, Indiana University Press, 1995, p. 11.

16. Duncan (1966), p. 98.

17. *ibid.*, p. 148.

18. The Soviet Union, or the Union of Soviet Socialist Republics as it was formally known, was established in 1922 during Duncan's time there.

19. Quoted in Kurth, p. 190.

20. Duncan (1966), p. 243.

21. *ibid.*, p. 226.

22. *ibid.*, p. 226.

23. Quoted in Daly, p. 16.

24. Quoted in Kurth, p. 267.

25. Duncan (1966), pp. 289–290.

26. *ibid.*, p. 304. The racial bias in her dislike of jazz was shared by others in the modern dance movement, such as Ted Shawn.

27. *ibid.*, p. 169.

28. *ibid.*, p. 221.

29. Carl van Vechten, quoted in Blair, pp. 256–258.

30. Quoted in Seroff, p. 221.

31. *ibid.*, p. 226.

32. Kurth, p. 389.

33. Quoted anonymously (from 'Isadora Duncan Dances the Marseillaise', *Current Literature*, January 1917) in Daly, pp. 188–193.

34. Carl van Vechten, quoted in Blair, p. 289.

35. Ernest Newman, quoted in Kurth, p. 457; Ellen Terry is quoted in Seroff, p 226.

36. Quoted anonymously (from 'Music and Musicians: Isadora Duncan Dances World Struggle with "Star Spangled Banner" Climax', *New York Sun*, 7 March 1917) in Daly, p. 187.

37. Quoted in Seroff, p. 216.

38. Quoted from Isadora Duncan programme in Kurth, p. 437.

39. *ibid.*, p. 408.

40. Duncan and Lunacharsky quoted in Irma Duncan and Allan Ross Macdougall, *Isadora Duncan's Russian Days and Her Last Years in France*, New York, Covici-Friede, 1929, pp. 12–13.

41. Quoted in Kurth, p. 513.

42. *ibid.*, p. 524.

43. Quoted in Duncan and Macdougall, pp. 152–153. Eighty years on and bared breasts are still causing consternation, as the Janet Jackson incident at the 2004 Superbowl showed.

44. *ibid.*, p. 159.

45. Kurth, p. 528.

46. Quoted in Daly, p. 198.

47. Quoted in Duncan and Macdougall, p. 298.

48. Letter quoted in Gordon McVay, *Isadora and Esenin*, Ann Arbor, Michigan, Ardis Publications, 1980, p. 39; quotation to friend in Blair, p. 370.

49. Duncan (1966), pp. 318–319.

50. Quoted in Ilya Ilyich Schneider, *Isadora Duncan: The Russian Years*, New York, Da Capo Press, 1968, p. 213.

51. Quoted in Daly, p. 197.

52. Quoted in Seroff, p. 331.

53. Rodin quoted in Kurth, p. 354; Stanislavsky quoted, *ibid.*, p. 253; Parker, quoted from her review of *My Life*, 'Poor, Immortal Isadora', *The New Yorker*, 26 January 1928.

54. Quoted in Kurth, p. 281.

55. See, for example, Franko (1995).

56. Duncan (1966), p. 293.

57. With reference to the issue of individualism and the radical soloist, the example of Edith Segal (1902–1997), an American dancer, teacher and writer, has been cited as a contrast to Duncan. Segal's work

in dance was always closely allied to her political activism. In the 1920s and '30s, she directed the Nature Friends Dance Group, the Red Dancers and the Dance Group of the Needle Trades Workers Industrial Union. She was also the Social Director at Unity House, the vacation resort of the International Ladies' Garment Workers' Union. She remained active in the arts and political communities until her death in 1997. (Biographical details taken from http://digilib.nypl.org/dynaweb/ead/nypl/dansegal.) See Lynn Conner, 'What the Modern Dance Should be: Socialist Agendas in the Modern Dance, 1930–34' in J. Reinelt (ed.), *Crucibles of Crisis: Performing Social Change*, pp. 231–248; and Mark Franko, *The Work of Dance: Labor, Movement, Identity in the 1930s*, Middletown, Ct., Wesleyan University Press, 2002. Another example might be Katherine Dunham, founder of the Ballet Nègre in 1930 and director of the Negro Unit of the Chicago branch of the Federal Theatre Project, who was a renowned dancer, choreographer and social activist. See Vèvè A. Clark and Sara E. Johnson (eds.), *Kaiso! Writings by and about Katherine Dunham*, Wisconsin, University of Wisconsin Press, 2005. The first Yeats quotation is taken from the poem 'September 1913' and the second from a letter to his sister Lolly, describing Patrick Pearse, one of the leaders of the Easter 1916 Rising.

CHARLIE CHAPLIN: CITIZEN OF THE WORLD

'You'll never find rainbows if you're looking at the ground'
from a song by Charlie Chaplin[1]

Like Isadora Duncan, Charlie Chaplin shaped his chosen art form. As an Englishman working in America, he was himself an outsider who would create in the little Tramp another outsider who became the seminal film icon of the period, predating by nearly half a century the iconic tramps of Samuel Beckett.

For much of Chaplin's film career, he owned the studios where he made his films and controlled every aspect of the filmmaking process. He was an innovator in screen story-telling and performing, an emblematic international star who did as much if not more than anyone to make cinema not only accepted as an art form but the dominant art form of its era.

As probably the single most influential artist in the history of cinema, his influence is impossible to quantify; it reaches from the easily traceable and acknowledged – the surrealists, Sergei Eisenstein, Léonide Massine or the French cinéastes, for example – to the myriad untraceable imprints in everyday life. In addition, he is possibly the cinema figure about whom the most has been written.

UNPRECEDENTED CELEBRITY

Thanks to the newness and great reach of the medium and, at its outset, the transnational appeal of its wordless mimesis, the dimensions of his celebrity were unprecedented. As a consequence, the distance Chaplin had to plummet was always going to be greater than for any other performer. While moral issues played a central role in his eventual downfall in America, to what extent was the underlying cause political? And what was the nature of his own political opinions?

Chaplin's fame gave him the security from which he could enter the political arena and offer the public socially committed art, but his fame could not shield him from, and indeed was critical in, the American public's disillusionment with probably the most popular performer of the twentieth century.

Uniquely among the trio of Chaplin, Duncan and Robeson, Chaplin's rehabilitation occurred during his lifetime, marked by a special Oscar awarded on his seventy-third birthday and an even later knighthood from the country of his birth. As with Duncan but unlike Robeson, Chaplin did not espouse a consistent political position. He was interested in ideas, which led him to have many political acquaintances, but he did not describe himself as a political artist and was certainly not a political activist, although in wartime he did campaign for causes he felt were vital. As an artist, he was an individualist who eschewed propaganda and didacticism, but that does not render him or his films apolitical.

There is in his films a discernible pattern of growing social engagement. It broadly follows a curve in the political consciousness of America from World War I through the Depression and the rise and defeat of fascism to the beginning of the Cold War. At a crucial moment, it also coincides with the single most important technological change in film, the introduction of sound, when Chaplin was approaching forty and had made more than seventy Tramp pictures. This change marked a sharper challenge in Chaplin's films, as he buried the Tramp, and a loosening of his control over his off-screen image, a process in which the journalistic media were able to play an increasing and increasingly hostile role in the reception of his films and the public's attitude towards him.

ROOTS

Born in 1889 in a poor part of south London, Chaplin was unsure of his roots and was not certain who his father was, believing at times that he was Jewish or even possibly African American. Chaplin on occasion claimed to have been born in France; sometimes he acknowledged his partial Romany heritage and sometimes he denied it.

Chaplin and his older half-brother Sydney had a disturbed and fragmented upbringing; a younger half-brother was taken from the household when Charlie was only six months old, and Sydney left home when Charlie was seven to undergo training on a ship for service at sea. Despite erratic schooling, Chaplin loved reading and always retained his great curiosity and enjoyment of ideas, not in an abstract sense but as a means to understand the world and counter the power of those who controlled knowledge. He followed his mother and presumed father into music hall in 1894 when he was five. He took a variety of jobs from the age of eleven, including the one he cherished most, that of professional entertainer, at first with a clog-dancing troupe, the Eight Lancashire Lads, then as an actor and most importantly with one of Fred Karno's music hall companies. This brought him his passport to America. After his second Karno tour there in 1912, Chaplin stayed in the New World where the new and mass art form of cinema was in its infancy.

Chaplin did not relish live public performance. The screen allowed him the distance he needed in order to be prodigiously creative, and in the silent era, being a foreigner made no difference as long as you were white. Furthermore, the particular requirements of the silent screen allowed his creativity to overcome the separation from his audience and make unprecedented contact with them, which became the platform for his political interventions.

Elements of social comment are evident in the creation of the Tramp at Max Sennett's Keystone Studio in January 1914 for Chaplin's second film, *Mabel's Strange Predicament*. Chaplin revealed that the Tramp's genesis lay in his own upbringing. He drew on memories of a destitute figure he had seen and imitated as a child, and on features of the class-conscious culture of the English music hall, which gave him as well the sentimental aspect, the constant, hapless search for happiness and 'true' love.

Also from the music hall and its celebration of the absurdities of ordinary life came the Tramp's incongruous physical elements. Chaplin borrowed them from different sources (as befits a tramp), and chose them to make him look silly – the oversize trousers for matchstick legs, and the large boots for small, tired feet along with the too small bowler and too tight coat as well as a trimmed moustache that was inappropriately dapper and the mischievous cane with a will of its own. 'I wanted everything a contradiction,' Chaplin wrote.[2] He said the costume determined the character. The Tramp was the nimble, graceful clod, whose awkward comic walk belied the superbly agile skills he was given by his creator; he was the sad funny man, socially a scruffy outcast but with aspirations to the ethos of a true gentleman, self-mockingly fastidious and refined. He looked pasty and feeble, but had the bearing associated with wealth and power.

Chaplin's Tramp brought early and rapid rewards. He became widely popular very quickly. There was a dance named after him, songs were written about him, and his image was used as a mass marketing tool. In 1916, only two years after the Tramp's debut, Chaplin became the first actor to have a comic strip devoted to him, and a year later he was reported to be the first actor to enjoy a million-dollar contract. His remarkable wealth and celebrity meant he could overcome the usual anxiety of the film performer in relation to the director, the camera and the editing process by exercising a degree of independence and control over his means of production not seen before or since. In 1919, with Douglas Fairbanks, Mary Pickford and D.W. Griffith, he became owner of his own production company, United Artists, which they formed to avoid the inevitable outcome of a move by the main film companies to control the stars as well as their rewards.

Like Henry Irving, the leading English actor of the late nineteenth century whose funeral he attended, Chaplin became the chief creator in all the projects with which he was involved, and, like Irving, he even directed by showing the other actors how he wanted all the parts to be played. From the mid-1910s Chaplin wrote, directed, produced, scored and starred in all his movies (with the exception of *A Woman in Paris*, 1923, and his final film *A Countess From Hong Kong*, 1967, in both of which he gave himself only a cameo).

MODERN ARCHETYPE

With this leverage, Chaplin, an ambitious but shy stranger, created in the Tramp a modern archetype (and, for the time, it had to be male as well as white).[3] Chaplin's Tramp is an almost androgynous figure who appealed to both men and women. He has no history and seems most himself when alone or unrecognised, yet he is very much a creature of a particular modern industrial world, and engages in the commonplace struggles of existence that were recognisable to his audiences as the kind they habitually had to face. The Tramp as the 'little guy' becomes 'everyman' in the social milieu of minimum subsistence that chimes with the lived experience of his audience.

He represents an urban version of the disruptive outcast who is threatening only to those in power. However mischievous, he is on the side of 'good' against 'evil', of the poor against the rich and their lackeys. The ethical underpinning of this world of parable may be simple, yet the underdog does not stand for the victory of 'good' but for its enduring resilience in a system where social rule favours the 'evil'. Despite his brushes with danger, the Tramp remains indestructible and maintains an apparent innocence, which may contrast with the obviously mechanical nature of the new art form but which helps him be seen as universal. The Tramp is symbolic *and* social. This, in turn, helps the audience themselves feel both individual and at the same time part of humanity in general.

While the Tramp fulfils the traditional clown role of challenging the system and its customs, it is a role that is also traditionally made safe when the chaos is reordered. In much of Chaplin's output, this aspect of accommodation is absorbed by what the critic C.L.R. James calls the 'blithe quality' of the films, but Chaplin raises the tension derived from the impulse to challenge, particularly in his most overtly political films, to a point at which transgression destroys this buoyancy.[4]

Chaplin's Tramp is not like other silent film characters who appear to talk but cannot be heard. Often he does not speak because he expresses himself and his feelings in other ways, through movement and gesture, which are very precise. This physical creation of character, also derived from music hall, gave the Tramp a directness that was enhanced by the way

Chaplin as an actor acknowledged the audience, through glances or chuckles or looking straight to camera, and the way Chaplin as a director showed the audience all of himself, from top to toe. Such openness, and the ease and pleasure with which he moves, made the Tramp instantly understandable and accessible: this very popularity was political, even though Chaplin's main concern was to earn a reasonable living.

As with popular theatre forms like music hall or commedia dell'arte, Chaplin's audience gained pleasure from recognition of characters, situations and conventions, and delighted in the performer's ability to improvise and show variation within the refuge of the familiar. The Tramp becomes anything he chooses, from lover to thief, but always within the persona of the Tramp and compelled by the situation. In this respect, Chaplin embraced realism, but not in representational terms – his Tramp films are mostly not peopled with individualised characters, and he delights in using cartoon devices such as huge bullies to emphasise his tiny stature. Instead, he achieved for his audience an imaginative authenticity through performance, and, as such, he was always socially aware. Without the situation, the comedy would not work, and the misfortune, even cruelty, at its centre would be distasteful.

Chaplin's contextualised and plot-driven 'business', often executed seemingly without effort and in an instant, was the outcome of much hard work and experiment. His superlative agility and physical inventiveness as he manipulates and transforms commonplace objects allow the audience to enjoy, and to be astonished by, the playful aspects of his performance, in which he is defined not by what he says but by what he does. He is the epitome of one of the two principal strands of modern acting, known in shorthand as 'outside in' (as opposed to the other, 'inside out', when an actor works from something internal to find the character).

His talent was to work within as well as against the dominant Hollywood aesthetic. Whilst his early films use broad effects, in *A Woman of Paris* he counters the prevailing fashion and bravely understates the emotions. As the Tramp, he both celebrates and undermines the American dream, emphasising the uniqueness of the plucky individual fighting against the odds and dreaming of but never achieving lasting happiness.

Reality always undercuts the dream. Far from being god-fearing and upright, the figure he presents is amoral though dignified. Without directly challenging the heterosexual ideal of romantic love until his 1947 film *Monsieur Verdoux*, Chaplin constantly undermines it. The Tramp subverts the norms of masculinity by being quick-witted and dexterous rather than muscle-bound and WASP handsome. He flirts, and, despite his self-evidently impecunious state, sees himself as a fetching 'catch' (a role reinforced by Chaplin's personal affairs), but he remains ultimately unsuccessful in 'love'.

AMERICAN DREAM

Chaplin's position as an independent producer not only allowed his perfectionism full rein but also gave him unparalleled control over his image, both on and off screen. There was a private and intensely complex Chaplin as well as the celebrity Charlie (who was) the Tramp. Chaplin was careful to protect the way his image was exploited and expected his press representatives to police the media assertively. He was aware of the isolated world in which celebrities lived and, when he was visiting Europe in 1931 and receiving unprecedented adulation, he expressed his concern at the power of stardom. Speaking to the novelist, essayist and fellow south Londoner, Thomas Burke, Chaplin asked: 'what kind of a filthy world is this – that makes people lead such wretched lives that if anybody makes 'em laugh they want to kneel down and touch his overcoat, as though he were Jesus Christ raising 'em from the dead?'[5]

The interplay between performer and 'character' also became crucial in Chaplin's reception, especially when his socially pointed films became as much about him as his role in them. The most basic contradiction – that the indigent, ill-fated Tramp was in his off-screen life fantastically wealthy and, within the film industry, tremendously powerful – seemed to enhance the myth not undermine it. Chaplin was living proof of the 'rags to riches' American dream. He promoted the myth himself, and was equally fearful of what eventually befell him, a rapid fall from grace.

What the Tramp did over his twenty years on film that preceded this fall changed considerably, despite for much of the time the externals remaining constant. At first, Chaplin was worried that the Tramp was not funny, and then that his slapstick was too crude – he even took to telling the press to call him Mr Charles Chaplin instead of Charlie because he wanted to be treated seriously. Later, the concerns centred on the political realm the Tramp had entered.

It seems Chaplin made his libertarian views known from the outset and was not fearful of the possible effect on his future employment. According to his biographer David Robinson, a cameraman at the Keystone studio recalled him as 'a bit off-colour in politics'.[6] His first major political scandal came in World War I. His loyalty to his homeland was questioned when it was discovered that the terms of his film contract barred him from returning to Britain for the duration of the war. Spurred, it seems, by having lost the chance to syndicate a dubious biography of Chaplin, newspaper mogul Lord Northcliffe led a campaign in Britain denouncing Chaplin as a millionaire 'slacker' and coward. It hurt Chaplin badly. He had registered for the draft in the US but was turned down by the recruiting office for being underweight. Nevertheless, he continued to receive white feathers and other slurs on his willingness to fight. It was reported that his alleged lack of courage also cost him a knighthood on the explicit instructions of Queen Mary.[7]

The issue of loyalty would return to dog him later when opinion in the US turned against him. In and to America, he described himself as a paying visitor and praised the country's youthful élan, which he believed was a beacon for the future. At the time of World War I, he bought war loans and was active in the liberty bond campaign (he made a propaganda short called *The Bond*). He was not opposed to the war like most of the left, although he became anti-war later in the 1930s and believed militarism led people to accept authoritarian rule, as happened under Hitler. He answered the British campaign against him in his film *Shoulder Arms*, with Charlie fighting for democracy on the front-line in the trenches. It was made in 1918 when it was publicly acceptable in America because the US had by then joined the war. In its mix of comedy and tragedy and its appeal to common humanity that cuts across the national divisions of war, the film looks forward to *The Great Dictator* twenty years later.

Along with the rich and famous, Chaplin mixed eclectically with the left. He became friendly with the left-leaning bohemian intelligentsia, comprising captivating figures like Max Eastman and the writer Frank Harris, and he also met Upton Sinclair, an active Socialist whose novel *The Jungle* (1906), an exposé of the meat packing industry in Chicago, was seen as a metaphor of the capitalist system. Rob Wagner, a leading member of the Socialist Party who had become a habitué of Chaplin's inner circle by 1917, gave him a copy of the book, which was required reading on the left. Chaplin says in his autobiography that his interest in Socialism stemmed from his acquaintance with Sinclair.

Early on Chaplin saw the difficulties that could be encountered because of expressing dissident views. His friend, the actress Florence Deshon, who was having an affair with Eastman, lost employment after she refused to stand for the national anthem at a film première, declaring she was an internationalist. Chaplin gave a small sum towards Eastman's magazine *The Liberator*, and at one of his parties was impressed by a former Industrial Workers of the World (IWW) activist. Also in New York, Chaplin met the fabled Irish trade-union leader Jim Larkin and the Jamaican-born Socialist poet Claude McKay. Eastman, who later became right-wing after living in the Soviet Union and who testified as a 'friendly' witness during the McCarthy period, said in the 1950s that Chaplin liked radical ideas but not paying the price. Chaplin, however, did not turn to the right and he certainly paid a price for his stand.

Following the Bolshevik Revolution and attempts by western powers to curtail it, Chaplin attended a 'Hands off Russia' campaign meeting with Eastman. Chaplin had already become interested in that country and, like many another radical, was inspired by the promise of a better future. He told a journalist, 'Wealth has allowed me to think. I used to be afraid to have ideas' – a position he was to reinforce later in his life when it came to espousing unpopular political views on and off screen. He also told the journalist of his admiration for Lenin because he 'trims his sails and modifies his ideas to meet the changes of each day'.[8] Asked in 1918 if he was a Bolshevik, he replied, 'I am an artist, not a politician', and to the question whether he believed Lenin or Lloyd George the greater man: 'One works, the other plays.'[9] On another occasion when posed a similar comparison, he retorted that this 'desire to compare everything and anyone to something or someone else is one of the platitudes of mass thinking'.[10] He also admitted that he had once shown off his radical opinions largely for the pleasure of shocking his cousin.

That did not mean, however, that he did not hold such opinions. Indeed, he made them public during his European tour of 1921, and his views on economics were reported in the financial pages of the *New York Times*. He met the British Socialists H.G. Wells and Rebecca West on this trip. In Paris, the expatriate writer Waldo Frank, who had praised Chaplin in his book on politics, *Our America* (1919), introduced him to left-wing thinkers and artists. In Berlin Chaplin met again the IWW activist from Eastman's party, who had become the European purchasing agent for the Soviet Union.

Chaplin saw the politically repressive atmosphere of America intensify in the immediate post-war period against a background of rising labour militancy, the wave of violent white attacks on black people in 1919 (dubbed the 'red summer' because of the blood spilt) and the series of raids against the left launched by the infamous Attorney-General, A. Mitchell Palmer, who initiated the country's first 'red scare'. In 1922, Chaplin hosted a fund-raising party at his studios for labour activist and Communist William Z. Foster, a fact noted by an agent of the Bureau of Investigation (BI), forerunner to the FBI, which opened a file on Chaplin that year.[11] The BI had infiltrated the Severance Club in Los Angeles, a dining and debating society, which Chaplin had joined and which discussed issues such as censorship, the unions and progressive cinema. Chaplin was alleged to have donated to the Communist Party and to have been visited by a Communist organiser of the Garment Workers' Union. There was no proof and his surveillance was lifted, despite the dislike of Chaplin by J. Edgar Hoover, Palmer's special assistant before becoming head of the FBI. Hoover found Chaplin's films dangerous because they portrayed the 'lower depths' of society at a time of social instability.

Social criticism and sympathy for the dispossessed are evident in many Chaplin films from *Work* (1915), *The Immigrant*

(1917), *A Dog's Life* (1918) and his first full-length film, *The Kid* (1921), through to *The Gold Rush* (1925) and *City Lights* (1931). *Work*, like other early Chaplin short films, owes something to music hall. But, according to David Robinson, its anarchic portrayal of decorators in a middle-class home could also be said to reveal the influence of left-wing ideas in its view of labour as 'exploitation and humiliation . . . the reverse of the Victorian ideal . . . '[12] He also points out that *Work* looks forward to avant-garde Soviet films of the Eisenstein era.

MORE THAN A CLOWN

Chaplin was clear that his films were not political, though it is equally clear they are not ideologically innocent either. The artist and writer Clare Sheridan, whom the Soviet government had commissioned to sculpt busts of Lenin and Trotsky, warned Chaplin not to let his films become propaganda. Chaplin was adamant that his films were not, and, in reply to Sheridan, who had been ostracised for publishing a book about and lecturing on Soviet Russia, said presciently, 'Why enter the political arena? You are bound to get hurt.'[13] Even after *Modern Times*, his 1936 film that was interpreted as a critique of industrial society, he said that, 'I am always suspicious of a picture with a message.'[14] Yet Chaplin wanted to be seen as more than a clown, and the resulting tension between aesthetics and ideology is apparent throughout his major work.

The Kid in particular earned him respect as artist, and its reception allayed his concerns about the taste and crudity of his work. His reputation but not his popularity was further enhanced after making *A Woman of Paris*, his first film for United Artists and therefore made under his complete control. A serious drama and one very close to his heart, it was a departure for Chaplin in that it did not star him. He was aware that his treatment of the melodramatic story concerning a young woman who elopes with her lover but ends up the mistress of an unscrupulous rich man might cause problems for his audience. Chaplin had trouble with the ending, in which the woman is reconciled with her lover's mother after her lover has killed himself. Together they raise orphans in the country, a resolution criticised for pandering to popular taste but which Chaplin intended to be low key and ironic. After showing the woman in a hay cart with the orphans, the final shot is of the rich man's car speeding by. Asked by his secretary what happened to his mistress, the rich man shrugs.

The film had to be cut to satisfy the censors by making the characters behave in an acceptable fashion. In a programme note for the New York première, Chaplin wrote about his struggle for realism, and said he was 'showing it with as much truth as I am allowed.'[15] In an uncanny forewarning of things to come, he inserted a written title after the cast list, which reads: 'The ignorant condemn our mistakes . . . But the wise pity them.'[16] *A Woman of Paris* was critically well received but it failed with the public. This hurt Chaplin so much that he prevented the film from being distributed for many years. The failure also returned him to the Tramp: *The Gold Rush* was released in 1925, the year he became the first actor to appear on the cover of *Time* magazine.

The problems of 'acceptable behaviour' and morality he encountered with *A Woman in Paris* signalled a new atmosphere of restraint and censorship in Hollywood. In his previous film, *The Pilgrim* (1922), he had softened the satire but nevertheless ran into difficulties with local censors and church dignitaries because of its portrayal of an escaped convict who steals the clothes and identity of a minister. That same year, Republican Will Hays, a former Postmaster General, established the self-regulatory Motion Picture Producers and Distributors of America, Inc., which was to become notorious for its control of Hollywood film content through its imposition of the 'Hays Code'. Chaplin opposed Hays' censorship role and boycotted Hollywood's 'Welcome, Will Hays' celebration.

Chaplin also hated the hypocrisy, venality and scandal-mongering that fuelled Hollywood at the same time as it was instituting the Hays controls. Chaplin was caught up in several such scandals, which were integral to the myth as well as the reality of film celebrity. He was connected, for instance, with an important unsolved mystery, the death of producer Thomas Harper Ince, shot aboard the yacht the *Oneida* in 1924. But it was Chaplin's sexual 'liberalness' that brought scandal closest to him. His (dangerous) predilection for younger women, which on occasion crossed the legal boundary, can be seen in his four marriages. His first wife was sixteen when Chaplin was twenty-nine, the second was also sixteen when he was thirty-five (some believe the story of this marriage to Lita Grey, a.k.a. Lillita McMurray, inspired Nabokov's *Lolita*), the third was twenty-five when Chaplin was forty-seven and the fourth was eighteen when he was fifty-four.[17]

Much about his private life – tales of unconventional sexual activity and abortions, for example – spawned damaging publicity. His second divorce (1927), around which particularly colourful rumours swirled, coincided with the arrival of tax problems, which were to recur throughout his time in America. Chaplin faced bankruptcy, jail and deportation for tax evasion but struck a deal with the tax authorities. There was suspicion among his intimates that he was being targeted because of his politics, and he certainly felt persecuted. The episode foreshadowed his later harassment by state agencies when his political stance was more overt and his own sense of maltreatment even more acute.

World politics and technology combined to take Chaplin in a new creative direction, which altered the politics of his films. He was not keen to embrace sound, and made excuses that the equipment would be too large to fit into his studio. In fact, having to cope with sound would disrupt the pace and tempo of filmmaking he had learned to control through years of experiment and, more importantly, it would destroy his pantomimic world, of which he was emperor. Chaplin's controlling position and ownership of the means of production allowed him to delay his surrender to technological advance and prolong the life of the largely silent Tramp (he was in his mid-forties when he made *Modern Times*, the final Tramp film).

For *The Circus*, begun in 1925 and released in January 1928 just after *The Jazz Singer* had heralded the transition to sound by demonstrating voice synchronisation, Chaplin worked with a composer to produce a special score. The film, made during the troubled Lita Grey divorce, regained public affection for Chaplin, and he won a special Oscar at the first Academy Awards ceremony in 1929 for his 'versatility and genius' in acting, writing, directing and producing it.

When he came to make *City Lights*, he considered the idea of producing a 'talkie' but rejected it. The film has sound effects and a musical score (by Chaplin), but also, in its opening scene, manages to depict the inequality of contemporary society whilst attacking the use of sound, as if to say 'I can make compelling cinema my way without succumbing to the latest fashion.' The scene shows a large crowd gathered for the unveiling of a civic monument to 'Peace and Prosperity'. As the unveiling takes place, the audience sees the Tramp asleep on the statue. Inevitably, he is commanded to come down but as he does so, his trousers catch on the Sword of Peace. As the national anthem plays, he dangles forlornly, trying his best to stand to attention. Chaplin makes fun of the 'talkies' too by having the political speeches of the local dignitaries represented by incomprehensible screeching.

The film's story of the Tramp wandering a metropolitan jungle and meeting a blind flower girl as well as a millionaire who treats him well when drunk but badly when sober captures the chaotic madness of urban life under capitalism. It offers a critique of the role of money and the ideology of the ideal, recognising both the need for the imaginary and its limitations. Chaplin began the film in late 1927 and released it in early 1931, thereby straddling the Wall Street crash and appearing two-and-a-half years after the first all-talking movie, *Lights of New York*, had come out.

Chaplin did shoot some dialogue for his next film, *Modern Times*, but did not use the footage. Begun in 1933 and released in 1936, it only has a minor sound track, with one scene in which for the first and last time the Tramp has a voice. And for this momentous occasion he sings nonsense. The scene comes at the end of the film when the Tramp is employed as a singing waiter, who entertains the customers as well as serving them at table. His waif companion writes the words of a 'naughty' song on his shirt cuff but during his introduction, the cuff flies off. The gamine mouths, 'Never mind the words', and the Tramp extemporises in his private language. Allied to the film's attack on the use of machinery, Chaplin's attitude to sound led some of the Communist left to criticise him as a Luddite. When Chaplin finally capitulated to the 'talkies', with *The Great Dictator* which was released in 1940, the delay had an effect on the film and its reception. The public had become used to sound, and Chaplin's tardiness emphasised his difference from Hollywood, which was reinforced by his political views.

WORLD TOUR

Between *City Lights* and *Modern Times* Chaplin undertook what turned out to be a sixteen-month world tour (February 1931–June 1932) during which he delved deeper into and commented more on economics and politics. Popular film stars were not expected to express such views, and he was offended that they were not being given proper consideration, whether in the US or abroad. His quandary is summed up in the *New York Times* headline of the time: 'Chuckles follow Chaplin in France – comedian is unable to avoid humor, no matter how serious he is.'[18]

He recounted the conversations he had with politicians and leading figures on his trip and offered his own solutions to topical problems, some of which he hoped to put before the League of Nations. He had political discussions with a range of renowned intellectuals, from Aldous Huxley to Albert Einstein and J.M. Keynes. He disagreed with George Bernard Shaw on the role of art – Shaw believed in the propaganda value of art whereas Chaplin believed art should 'intensify feeling, colour or sound'.[19] He became friends with John Strachey, a former Labour Party MP who was moving towards Communism. Strachey's 1932 book, *The Coming Struggle for Power*, which sees the world polarised between fascism and Communism as capitalism enters its final convulsion, influenced Chaplin and made him consider the necessity of taking a stand. They later worked on a Napoleon film scenario together, which was never filmed.

Chaplin also exchanged views with politicians such as the British Prime Minister Ramsay MacDonald and Winston Churchill, at whose house he reproved another guest by saying, 'The Gandhis and the Lenins do not start revolutions. They are forced up by the masses and usually voice the want of the people.' To Churchill's rejoinder, 'You should run for parliament,' Chaplin replied: 'I prefer to be a motion picture actor,' and added, 'we should go with evolution to avoid revolution.'[20] Chaplin met Gandhi, who was visiting Britain, and, before he explored the subject in *Modern Times*, found himself debating the merits of advancing industrialisation and machine progress.

He told a journalist: 'Machinery should benefit mankind. It should not spell tragedy and throw it out of work.' He knew there were those who were comfortable and wished the present state of affairs to remain but insisted 'there must be some radical change' otherwise 'bolshevistic' and 'communistic' ideas might become prevalent.[21] His solution: shorter hours and a minimum wage that would guarantee a decent life.

His economic thinking was influenced by Major C.H. Douglas' 1924 book *Social Credit*, which, following Marx, says all value is derived from labour and explains unemployment in relationship to the failure of profit and capital. The book prompted Chaplin to convert his stocks and bonds into 'liquid capital' and thereby survive the Wall Street crash; it also led Chaplin to believe unemployment was America's greatest ill.

He tussled with big ideas and their contradictions without becoming intensely intellectual. He believed in world trade and private enterprise as long as it did not run counter to the well-being of the majority, just as he believed in smaller government but also in controls on prices, interest and profit. He was critical of patriotism, in the sense of narrow nationalism, 'as the greatest insanity the world has ever suffered'; having toured all over Europe, he percipiently said it 'is rampant everywhere, and the result is going to be another war'.[22]

Following the tour, Chaplin's politics became more deeply entwined with his films. His next three films, which span almost two decades of filmmaking, move on from his concern with a particular aesthetic and an emphasis on romance and pathos to bring into focus the social issues that had always been present in his work.

POLITICAL FILMS

These films – *Modern Times*, *The Great Dictator* and *Monsieur Verdoux* – are key to the debate about Chaplin's politics. During this period, he did consider making other, less obviously political films, but he shelved those plans. In the trio he did make, earlier traces of political sensibilities coalesce. In a changed historical context for politics, society and the film industry, Chaplin abandons his earlier lack of direct engagement with the society he is criticising, and declares his colours in a way that allows no retreat. This leads to moments of self-consciousness and over-statement, and the films do not achieve the internal consistency of some of the earlier work, but they demonstrate rare foresight as well as a defining courage. The identification of Chaplin the person with Chaplin the film persona becomes a dangerous liaison. Whatever his precise political beliefs, in this period he was seen as being political and making political films. His potency lay in the unusual fact that he was both taken seriously as an artist by the international intelligentsia and was hugely popular to mass audiences in the US and abroad.

During this period, America overcame the Depression with Roosevelt's New Deal, fought in World War II and unleashed the first 'hot' war of swift and enormous destruction before turning in on itself as the 'cold' war ensued. Chaplin was inspired by Roosevelt and felt that under him the best attributes of America were on display. In 1933 when Roosevelt was elected, Chaplin made a broadcast in support of the National Industrial Recovery Act and began making *Modern Times*;[23] it was released in 1936, the year Roosevelt was re-elected. Chaplin began work on *The Great Dictator* before Britain declared war on Germany and issued it during the war before America had joined. Production started on *Monsieur Verdoux* in 1946 after America had dropped the first A-bombs on Japan and Churchill had made his 'iron curtain' speech; the film was released a year later after the founding of the International Monetary Fund and the proclamation of the Truman Doctrine to stem the spread of Communism.

The strong cosmopolitan character of the film industry brought European politics to the fore in Hollywood, especially with the influx of Jewish refugees from the old Austro-Hungarian empire who were fleeing Nazism. After New York, Hollywood had become probably the most politically aware place in America, with growing trade union and Communist activity. The Soviet Union had altered its view on alliances and had adopted a more inclusive approach, which culminated in the Popular Front concept that was officially agreed by the international Communist movement in 1935. As one commentator put it, this led in the US to a shift on the left from an emphasis on Marx, Engels and Lenin to Paine, Jefferson and Lincoln.[24] For the rest of the decade, solidarity with Republican Spain was a focal point of activism. Chaplin, a committed antifascist, wrote a short story and private poem that show his deep sympathy for the Republican cause, and he refused to visit Spain while Franco was alive even though his daughter Geraldine was living there.

In 1935, a journalist said it had long been known that Chaplin was a 'parlour pink' but also that he was not particularly serious about politics. His friend Rob Wagner described Chaplin as an entertainer whose 'Red stuff leaks out, helps the cause, and doesn't crab his profession'. If, however, Chaplin were to align himself publicly, judged Wagner, 'he'd lose half his audience.'[25] Chaplin had been conscious of this dilemma before; when he backed Upton Sinclair's 'End Poverty in California' campaign for the state governorship in 1934, he asked for his name to be kept secret. The 'pink' accusation against Chaplin soon turned red, although in his politics he showed independence from the Communists. The Communist Party, for example, opposed the Sinclair campaign (which Chaplin supported) and Chaplin never went to Moscow, unlike Pickford and Fairbanks, who had visited the Soviet capital in 1926. He was wooed by the Soviets, later than might have seemed likely, yet he refused to grant Amkino, the Soviet film distribution agency in the US, the rights to his films and insisted he was paid in hard currency when his films were shown in the Soviet Union. Nevertheless, Martin Dies, chair of the House Committee on Un-American Activities, cited Chaplin in the late 1930s as a Communist sympathiser. The charge led nowhere but it reinforced the idea generated by Chaplin's own views and films of the period that he was political and on the left.

The first of the films to elicit this interpretation was *Modern Times*, which shows in its preparation, production, publicity and public reception the complex nature of Chaplin's commitment and how it was perceived. Chaplin's interest reflected the dissatisfaction with capitalism that had given the working class a new sense of itself as a class and as a radical force, a situation that was not to last long. The idea for the film was prompted, he said, by a remark a reporter had made to him about the factory-belt system in Detroit, which lured healthy young men off the farms and then, after several years, turned them into nervous wrecks. Chaplin went through various scenarios; at one time, it was to be a film about the 1886 Haymarket riots in Chicago and the subsequent victimisation of protesters. Early notes call it a drama of Communism, and possible titles included *Commonwealth* and *The Masses*. At its core, the film follows on from an earlier statement of Chaplin's that 'Something is wrong. Things have been badly managed if five million men are out of work in the richest country in the world.'[26]

The film can be seen as an attack on the Fordist system of mass production by using its own iconography in a way that chimes with the new representation of work in left culture, especially in Living Newspapers and dance. The left recognised the necessity of labour and elevated it to heroic status but criticised its alienation under capitalism. As with the left, Chaplin sees positive and negative in the machine. He also shows workers as active historical agents and presents work as worthy of artistic attention. Indeed, his portrayal of work (which is work itself) gives his critique its edge, as he reveals mass production to be a form of social choreography.

Chaplin's own relationship to technology is ambivalent, as can be seen from his attitude to sound in film, and he uses ambiguity to deal with the social world in *Modern Times*, a world which is more directly represented than in previous films. Workers are shown both as passive and assertive. They are literally portrayed as sheep in recognition of the reality of their factory experience, but they also protest. The Tramp gathers up a misplaced red flag not to celebrate its militant symbolism but in order to return it, and only by accident comes to be at the head of a demonstration. Yet he validates the symbolism of the flag when the police break up the march violently. Chaplin once again lampoons the American Dream but also yearns for it, as if to say it should be possible – even if not in contemporary conditions. Paradoxically, the insistence of his anarchic individuality becomes an emblem of the potential he still sees in the system he is criticising.

Despite the film's echoes of New Deal politics, *Modern Times* represented a bold risk for an artist of Chaplin's status given the popular, mass nature of the cinema world within which he was operating. As if wary of the political Pandora's Box he knew he had opened, Chaplin said he did not see the Tramp and the waif whom he befriends either as rebels or victims but as free spirits in a world of robots, representatives of humanity crusading for happiness. At the end of the film, freedom, however, is shown to be a dream, as the Tramp and the waif set off toward the far horizon.

A Soviet visitor to whom Chaplin had shown a rough cut subsequently wrote up his experience in *Pravda*, the official organ of the Soviet Communist Party, and this was reported in the *New York Times* by way of the American Communist papers *New Masses* and the *Daily Worker*. Such publicity bothered Chaplin, particularly as the article claimed the visitor had influenced the film's ending. Even if true, it showed poor judgement to associate Chaplin with Soviet intervention and was guaranteed to upset a filmmaker whose control of material was legendary. The publicity for the film countered the red image and, consequently, played down its politics. Nevertheless, and unsurprisingly, those politics were noticed and commented upon with great eagerness.

Generally, the more conservative critics questioned the film's humour as well as its politics, while the left was divided. The agitprop portraits of the boss and of factory production driving the Tramp mad were applauded, but differences arose over interpretation of the Tramp, who was seen as being as much of an anarchist as a Bolshevik, and by some as even a capitalist utopian. The left saw the film's politics as fragmented and unclear but insisted it was a political film and that, roughly speaking and despite its problems, its politics were on their side.

Modern Times was not as successful at the box office as Chaplin's previous three films and did not cover its production costs until it went into foreign distribution. It is difficult to assess to what extent its reception was affected by the film still being silent ten years after the introduction of sound and to what extent by being political.

THE GREAT DICTATOR

Chaplin was not daunted; he accelerated his movement towards more overt politics in his films by deciding to make a sound picture. The Tramp could no longer survive as a silent figure, but that left him with the question he had been avoiding: what voice should he give the Tramp? Chaplin toyed with abandoning the Tramp altogether, but rejected the idea of filming either a 'costume' romance or the tale of an American millionaire in love with a white Russian Countess who had become a 'taxi-girl'. The reason was political: he wanted to address the threat posed by Adolf Hitler. The result, a satire called *The Great Dictator*, far removed from Hollywood convention in length, style and attitude, represented an enormous financial, personal and artistic gamble.

Conceived in 1938 as *The Dictator* before the Munich appeasement of Hitler, the film met resistance from within and without the industry. Jewish producers asked him not to proceed with it, both to avoid adding to the plight of European Jews and to maintain lucrative European outlets. The British government, also concerned not to antagonise Hitler but for different reasons, said it would ban the film, which would be Chaplin's most costly yet.

By its very title, *Modern Times* had announced an affinity with the contemporary world, a signal of topicality that had been absent since *Shoulder Arms*, which was made during the previous world war. It was an association Chaplin would repeat with *The Great Dictator*, but this film posed the predicament of evoking a contemporary political figure while events involving him were still unfolding.

Opinion polls suggested most Americans supported neutrality, a position backed both by Hollywood and by commanding elements in corporate America like Ford, which kept factories in Nazi Germany until December 1941 producing vehicles for war use. On the left, some believed the conditions were ripe for a kind of fascism to arise in the US, citing factors from corporate dominance, the interest in eugenics and pervasive anti-Semitism to the existence of fascist militias and the four-million-strong Ku Klux Klan in a still segregated and racist society.

Despite the Jewish presence in Hollywood, American cinema had played down Jewish themes and refrained from attacking the Nazis. Chaplin, who knew many Jewish exiles in Hollywood, showed concern for the situation of Jewish refugees. In 1939 he told United Artists to pay his future share of European rentals earned by *The Great Dictator* to a Viennese Jewish organisation aiding Jewish emigration (which did not happen because the organisation no longer existed by the time the film was released). In 1940, Chaplin contributed to a fund in Italy that helped emigrating Austrian Jews. During the making of the film, he attended Anti-Nazi League meetings and those of the committee to Defend America by Aiding the Allies.

The Nazis, who had banned *The Gold Rush*, were angry at the euphoric welcome Chaplin had received in Berlin in 1931. They hated him as a dissenter and, erroneously, a Jew. Chaplin never contradicted those who called him Jewish, and of *The Great Dictator* said, 'I did this film for the Jews of the world.'[27]

It was to be the final venture of Chaplin's tramp figure, no longer Charlie the Tramp but on this occasion transmuted into the double role of a Jewish barber and a dictator called Adenoid Hynkel, whom the barber resembles (a physical likeness that allows comic reversal when the barber replaces the tyrant). Hitler's rise had coincided with, and shaped, Chaplin's desire to make a political film, and Chaplin exploited another coincidence – the physical similarities between the Tramp and the Nazi tyrant. (Mussolini's chauffeur once claimed Hitler had trimmed his moustache to make it look like that of the most famous comic character in the world.) Several accounts say Chaplin's decision to make the film was prompted by a press cutting that reported Hitler had banned Chaplin's films because the two men looked so much alike. There were other coincidences. Chaplin thought Hitler a great actor, and was angry that he borrowed film techniques successfully. Hitler, like Chaplin, had known poverty in childhood and had even been a tramp in Vienna. Extraordinarily, Chaplin and Hitler were also born in the same week of the same month of the same year.

Chaplin started shooting in September 1939, a few days after the British declaration of war. Most of the filming was completed by March 1940, but the final shots were taken as late as October 1940. By the time the film had entered the editing stage, the Nazis had swept through France, Denmark, Norway, Belgium and Holland, and Britain was being bombarded with the Blitz. Chaplin considered abandoning the film but instead concentrated on changes to the film's ending, when the question of 'what voice' the Tramp would adopt became inescapable. Clearly, there could be no utopian exit over the far horizon, and Chaplin was not satisfied with a pacifist montage, which he could not make work. He replaced it with a direct appeal in which Chaplin himself emerges from the character of the barber to address the audience. As he described it – reflecting his desire to be taken seriously – 'the clown turns into the prophet'.[28]

At work Chaplin was himself a dictator, but, although proud and stubborn, he did heed advice in the reworking of the film's finale. In deciding how to deal with real dictators, inevitably he came up against politics; he had parted company with one collaborator, who sued him for plagiarism, and hired a young Communist, Dan James, to work on the script instead. As Chaplin gathered his team around him he added another Communist, Robert Melzer. James described Chaplin as an anarchist and a libertarian fascinated by people on the left who were in revolt against wealth and conservatism. Chaplin regarded Stalin as another dictator and he was horrified at the Nazi-Soviet pact, which had undermined the Popular Front anti-fascist campaigns. Indeed, the American Communist Party, following Stalin's line, was now against the war. Chaplin had to be dissuaded by James and Melzer from including Stalin in the film's long last speech. When Chaplin finally came to shoot the speech, however, he barred them from the set.

The speech lasts six minutes – unprecedented in a Hollywood film – and was attacked for naivety and cliché. It remains a simple statement to the world about its future, which holds its point still:

> The way of life can be free and beautiful, but we have lost the way. Greed has poisoned men's souls – has barricaded the world with hate – has goose-stepped us into misery and bloodshed . . . Machinery that gives abun-

dance has left us in want. Our knowledge has made us cynical; our cleverness, hard and unkind. We think too much and feel too little. More than machinery we need humanity. More than cleverness we need kindness and gentleness. Without these qualities, life will be violent and all will be lost.[29]

The ending remains the most controversial part of the film and it cost Chaplin much public support. Although American opinion had shifted towards intervention, there was a mixed reaction to the film. Chaplin had not appeared on screen for seven years and the film's pre-publicity had laid the ground for the 'talkie' to carry a message, but many found the film to be in bad taste. Chaplin justified making a comedy out of a serious issue by declaring people needed laughter at this time more than ever. Later, however, he said, perhaps defensively, he would not have – could not have – made the film if he had known then of the horrors of the concentration camps. Critics on the right denounced the film, particularly the ending, for being red and, as such, pro-appeasement because its appeals to liberty and democracy were accompanied by a warning to soldiers not to be used as cannon fodder. The Communist Party of Great Britain endorsed the speech by publishing it as a pamphlet, while other Communist parties criticised it as sentimental.

The Great Dictator breaks with Hollywood convention not only by explicitly addressing a topical political issue but also in its aesthetics, by the daring of its humour and, in its switch from pantomime to monologue, its refusal to offer a neat resolution. Although Chaplin himself was not announcing that he had become a political artist, he felt a duty to engage with political events with this film, which verges on the didactic and overtly affirms the social function of art.

Despite the initially uneven response, in terms of box office and media coverage the film was Chaplin's most successful yet. It gained five Academy Award nominations, though – unsurprisingly perhaps, given the political context – it won none (Best Picture went to Alfred Hitchcock's *Rebecca*). In 1942 it was listed as the third most successful moneymaking film of the previous five years. British audiences loved the equation of Hitler and the world's greatest comedian and, unlike the Americans, warmed to the film's humour and derision. The neutral US government met diplomatic problems over the showing of the film in Latin American countries with sizeable German populations, and the film was banned across Europe where the Nazis ruled as well as in neutral Ireland. The Nazi invasion of the Soviet Union brought the Soviets into the war and allowed Chaplin to be lionised there. The film was shown in Rome shortly after liberation from the fascists, and audiences apparently left subdued and stunned.

The Great Dictator has been described as the first mainstream anti-fascist film, and, for some, it stands as a badge of honour that could only have been made by a filmmaker in complete control of his material and at the height of his fame.

For Chaplin, however, the film also marked the beginning of a decline in his huge American popularity. The Senate Subcommittee on War Propaganda called him to appear in order to explain why he made the film, but the hearing was cancelled because of the Japanese attack on Pearl Harbor, which precipitated America into the war and both his sons into armed service.

AMERICA AT WAR

Chaplin made his own contribution to the war effort and was at his most politically active in the early 1940s. He was alarmed at the extent of pro-Nazi ideology in the US, revealed to him by the hate mail he received from American Nazis and Nazi sympathisers, and he was angered at the anti-Soviet feeling on display, which even saluted growing Soviet casualties in anticipation of the Nazis and the Communists annihilating each other. His response was to join several American-Soviet friendship associations.

His dislike of live performance extended to public speaking, ironic for the most famous actor in the world and the man who had just made the most famous political speech on film, yet he made many political speeches at this time. Charles J. Marland suggests this release came because Chaplin had something important to say, and because the Tramp was to be no more. Chaplin used his celebrity in public free of the need to protect the image of the Tramp but also free of the protection the Tramp afforded him.

He read the film's final speech for a national radio broadcast and spoke at meetings of the Artists' Front to Win the War. Some of his critics contrasted his willingness to make speeches with his alleged unwillingness to entertain American troops (a reluctance that derived from his dislike of live performance and the fact that his talent lay in film). Sections of the right believed his speeches exposed him as dangerously pro-Soviet. This view was given credence not long after America joined the war when Chaplin made a speech to a meeting organised by the American Committee for Russian War Relief in May 1942. In an echo of the moment in *Modern Times* when the Tramp innocently picks up the red flag, he was a last minute replacement for the US Ambassador to the Soviet Union, who was ill. Addressing perhaps 10,000 people, Chaplin used the term 'comrades' and went much further than previous speakers in his support of the Soviet Union. 'I am not a Communist,' he said, but they 'are no different from anyone else'.[30] He did not endorse or criticise the Soviet system; he simply said the Soviets were vital to defeating Hitler. Chaplin felt he had become carried away and was concerned that he might have overstepped the mark, a feeling corroborated by the later comment from the actor John Garfield: 'You have a lot of courage.'[31] Subsequently Chaplin would identify that speech as marking the beginning of his troubles.

Whatever his disquiet, Chaplin's admiration of the Soviet Union and its role fighting fascism both in Spain and now on its own soil led him to campaign for the opening of the Second Front. This activity included his addressing by radio-telephone a 60,00-strong, New York mass meeting organised by the Council of the Congress of Industrial Organisations, a speech in Chicago to 'Salute Our Russian Ally', a broadcast to Britain and the recording of an address that would be broadcast in the Soviet Union. Former friends began to snub him and press attacks mounted. He continued to campaign and to address rallies as 'Comrades' – 'Yes, I mean comrades' – and, unusually for him, he even justified the Stalin purges as having liquidated quislings.[32] He was guest of honour at an 'Arts for Russia' banquet, to which Dmitri Shostakovich and Ilya

Ehrenburg sent supportive telegrams. This prompted an FBI investigation and a syndicated columnist, Westbrook Pegler, to accuse him of being 'decidedly partial to Communism', anti-American and having no concern for US troops.[33] Pegler also questioned why he had not been deported, that being a favourite means of the American right-wing to quell dissent.

The dangerous mix of morality and politics hastened the rapid decline in his popularity. The trigger was a paternity suit filed in June 1943 by a twenty-two-year-old woman called Joan Barry. Although her affair with Chaplin had ended, she still believed they would marry; he refused and married Eugene O'Neill's daughter, Oona, instead. Barry and her mother used two right-wing columnists, Hedda Hopper and Florabel Muir, to exact revenge. The FBI, which believed Chaplin might escape to the Soviet Union, widened its investigations to include allegations of his procurement of two illegal abortions for Barry, his abuse of Barry's civil rights and his transportation of her across state lines for illicit sexual purposes. The indictments on these accounts he faced in 1944 could have led to years in prison and substantial fines. When he was acquitted on the first two counts, J. Edgar Hoover feared Chaplin would be exonerated, would make the FBI look incompetent and vindictive, and would become a martyr. To prevent this, the FBI blackmailed the judge, who had once dated Barry; the rest of the case against Chaplin never came to trial.

The paternity suit, however, was heard later that year. Blood tests showed Chaplin could not have been the father but they were then not admissible in California. The trial jury reached stalemate, the majority in Chaplin's favour; a second jury found against and, despite an appeal, Chaplin had to pay support until the child reached majority, although the sum was less than Barry had claimed.

Media coverage was generally antagonistic to Chaplin. It was led by Hopper, an isolationist and would-be Republican politician, who attacked Chaplin's politics and highlighted his status as a guest of the US, not a citizen. Mass circulation papers gave the Barry case great publicity and, interspersed with jibes at his political stance, began to undermine Chaplin's standing with the public and within the industry.

Understandably, Chaplin's involvement in political activity diminished during the Barry case. Already socially restricted by his fame and abandoned by many in Hollywood, he found solace among friends on the domestic left and in the political exile community. His circle included several prominent writers such as Ella Winter and Donald Ogden Stewart, who co-founded the Hollywood Anti-Nazi League, John Howard Lawson, a leading local Communist who became one of the Hollywood Ten, Clifford Odets and Theodore Dreiser, whom Chaplin met at the Soviet consulate in Los Angeles. Chaplin read Dreiser's poem 'The Road I Came' at Dreiser's funeral in 1946, only a few months after Dreiser had joined the Communist Party.

Among the exile community, Chaplin was particularly friendly with Berthold and Salka Viertel, who hosted the cultural salons that were the hub of left-wing émigré social life, the writer Lion Feuchtwanger, Bertolt Brecht and the composer Hanns Eisler, with whom he struck up a particular rapport. While Chaplin apparently found Brecht's theorising about art and politics too much to take on occasion, he warmed more to Eisler's sense of humour. Echoes of Brecht's mordant wit, however, can be found in Chaplin's next film, *Monsieur Verdoux*, for which Eisler was asked to be musical adviser. Eisler also began a septet based on music from *The Circus* but did not finish it because of his deportation in 1948. Chaplin played a prominent part in the unsuccessful campaign to prevent Eisler's expulsion, and he stood by Brecht during his tribulations with the House Committee on Un-American Activities (HUAC). Such solidarity may have revealed the disdain in which he held sections of right-wing America, but it also cost him friendship and support within liberal America.

Since the Barry case, the FBI had increased its political investigations of Chaplin. Hoover was preparing to place him on the Security Index as a potential danger to national security. The FBI not only kept a watch on him, it scrutinised published material on him and interviewed his associates and staff. It provided right-wing columnists like Ed Sullivan with information to feed an insidious public propaganda campaign against Chaplin, and, in return, the Bureau received information from them about him. It accumulated a mass of supposed evidence linking Chaplin to Communism, including such 'revolutionary' activities as attending a film showing and party on board a Soviet ship. Eventually the FBI placed him on the Index in November 1948.

MONSIEUR VERDOUX

The immediate post-war years saw a decline in the anti-capitalist ideas of the post-Depression Popular Front period. Despite the Soviet and Communist role in winning the war, Communism was no longer an ally – indeed, many denied it had ever been an ally – but the chief enemy. Its supposed associates were in the front line of attack along with the card-carrying party members themselves. Congress debated deporting Chaplin, and when HUAC chose to investigate Communist influence in Hollywood, Chaplin, it was reported, would be among its first witnesses.

It was in this hostile atmosphere that Chaplin made *Monsieur Verdoux*, which was based on an idea by Orson Welles. The first film of Chaplin's after the Barry affair represented a continuation – and a sharpening – of his political interests but a radical change in all other respects. The critical difference was the absence of the Tramp or comparable 'little man' figure. Here, its central character, played by Chaplin as a dapper, finicky gentleman, cannot be easily interpreted as sympathetic because he is a Bluebeard figure who kills women for money. Chaplin portrays him, nonetheless, as a victim of a society that puts profit before people.

The office that enforced the film industry's moral code initially found the whole script unacceptable but subsequently overlooked the 'anti-social' elements, which indicted the current social system, and concentrated instead on complaints about sexual innuendo and Verdoux's conversation with a priest. Chaplin acceded to minor changes but none that prevented him from defying Hollywood conventions once again.

Gone is the world of Chaplin's earlier morality stories, although not of their two-dimensional sense of good and evil. There are few visual 'gags'; the comedy is ironic. Romance becomes a mask for murder, and, far from sentiment, the film veers sardonically towards misogyny (attributed by some to the bitterness Chaplin felt over the Barry case). There is no temporary escape into fantasy from the strife of modern living, no 'happy ending' or even courageous individualism in the face of overwhelming odds. Verdoux does not skip off into the sunset but is led away to be executed, showing no remorse.

In the Tramp films, Chaplin had played with the tension between social contradictions and their imaginary or desired resolutions, often resorting to pathos to hold the tension in place. He had raised the tension between the two in *Modern Times* and, with the final speech of *The Great Dictator*, had broken away completely into new territory. In *Monsieur Verdoux* he went further still by incorporating this departure within the aesthetic of the whole film; as a snub to critics of the ending of *The Great Dictator*, he delivered yet another speech with a message, this time in character but also clearly as himself.

Although set in France between the two World Wars, audiences took the film, as intended, to be about contemporary America, especially in Verdoux's trial speech when he says he was simply following the logic of capitalist society. For thirty years he had used his brains honestly in a bank, but after the Depression when he lost his job no employer wanted to use his brains any more. 'So I was forced to go into business for myself.'[34] That business was murdering rich widows and investing their money. When he meets an attractive young woman working as a whore, who tells him her sad story, instead of testing a poison on her as he originally planned, he persuades her that life is worth living. By the time he meets her again, another world war is about to erupt and, while his investments have been destroyed by a stock market crash, she has become the mistress of a thriving armaments manufacturer.

Verdoux suggests to the judge that the world encourages mass murder. 'Has it not blown unsuspecting women and children to pieces, and done it very scientifically?' By comparison, he is only an amateur. 'Killing is the enterprise by which your System prospers,' he says. He reinforces this view as he awaits execution when he observes that his way is 'the history of many a big business. One murder makes a villain . . . millions a hero. Numbers sanctify . . .'[35]

Chaplin cultivated a sense of mystery in his pre-publicity for the film, which by major movie standards began late. This may have been because of his awareness of the problematic content or his relish at annoying his critics, who attributed arrogance to this strategy. After bad reviews (as well as disconcerting hissing) greeted the New York opening and he suffered a disastrous press conference, which United Artists had advised him to avoid but which he said he could handle, Chaplin, in an unprecedented move for him, withdrew the film.

His decision to open the doomed press conference with the words, 'Proceed with the butchery', was in keeping with his Verdoux persona of victim and his personal sense of persecution. The media interrogation was intimidating and antagonistic, mostly focusing on his views and whether or not he was a Communist sympathiser. He replied: 'If you step off the curb with your left foot, they accuse you of being a Communist. But I have no political persuasion whatsoever.'[36] This did not satisfy the journalists, especially those on the right from organisations like the Catholic War Veterans, who persisted and then turned to questioning his loyalty. In the process, neither film nor Chaplin's own opinions were properly promoted. One later detractor, Joyce Milton, believes Chaplin's strategy was very clever. In one-to-one interviews, which would have been more pointed, it would have been harder for Chaplin to be evasive; faced with the inevitable media scrum, it was easier for him to cast himself as the injured party denied a fair hearing.

In this ultra-conservative context, *Monsieur Verdoux* was guaranteed to upset because it attacked American capitalism and linked it to war. The American Communist Party, however, was also critical of the film, finding the morals of Verdoux at odds with Chaplin's political message. Interpretations have continued to polarise, from those who regard it as an unalloyed, Kremlin-inspired attack on America's atomic-led, international peace-keeping role to those who wish it were tougher and could, indeed, be seen as the powerful denunciation of Uncle Sam's global cowboy tactics that its critics claim it to be.

In whichever many ways the critics interpreted the film, there were plenty who believed they knew exactly the message Chaplin was sending. A month after the film first appeared, more than 300 Ohio cinema owners called for a national boycott, and the relaunch was postponed after the campaign was intensified by veterans' organisations, which urged exhibitors not to book the film, using as ammunition the fact that Chaplin was not an American citizen. The Memphis censorship board went as far as to ban *Monsieur Verdoux*.

New publicity was issued exploiting both the film's controversial reception and the historic absence of the Tramp. The slogan was: 'Chaplin changes – can you?' The publicity also exploited the fact that HUAC was likely to call Chaplin, who sent a telegram to committee members inviting them to the opening. This ploy to advertise the film worked in Washington DC, the home of HUAC, but not elsewhere. Screenings dwindled and *Monsieur Verdoux* was buried barely four months after its relaunch. It did receive, however, an Oscar nomination for Best Screenplay, but it was United Artists' worst performing film of 1947 and, with the exception of *A Woman of Paris* in which Chaplin had not starred, it was his first US box-office failure. It fared better in Europe, where Chaplin had told a journalist, 'Hollywood is dying,' and that he planned to leave the US. Echoing Isadora Duncan, he said: 'I think, objectively, that it is time to take a new road – so that money shall no longer be the all-powerful god of a decaying community.'[37]

HUAC postponed calling Chaplin, possibly because the committee was frightened that Chaplin might turn the tables on them. Whilst support for non-cooperative witnesses waned among the leading film stars who had initially rallied to the resisters' cause, Chaplin's backing remained, and he was denounced in Congress.[38] His livelihood was as much under threat as that of the celebrities who had backed off, but he continued to stand by those caught in the anti-Communist witch-hunt. During the campaign to prevent Hanns Eisler's deportation, Chaplin wired Picasso (whom he did not know), urging him to lead a committee of artists to protest to the US embassy in Paris. Picasso declined, but the telegram appeared in left-wing publications in France. This caused a stir in the US because Chaplin was a non-citizen trying to organise an anti-US protest in a foreign country, and it led to more calls for his removal.

Chaplin's name occurs frequently in HUAC proceedings, usually as someone exploited by the Communist Party or its associates. He sent the committee a telegram saying he was not a Communist but 'a peacemonger' and that he had never joined a political party.[39] His own appearance was postponed twice more and then HUAC decided not to call him, thereby depriving him of the chance to confront them as the Tramp and subject them to the same ridicule as he had meted out to Hitler. 'I almost wish I could have testified,' he is quoted as saying by biographer David Robinson. 'If I had, the whole Un-American Activities thing would have been laughed out of existence in front of the millions of viewers who watched the interrogations on TV.'[40] Robinson comments that Chaplin's closest friends doubted he would have proceeded with such a display, but if he had, it could have been his greatest performance.

HARASSMENT

The campaign against Chaplin did not stop. His isolation grew and he increasingly became the subject of harassment by government forces as well as by influential voluntary groups like the American Legion, whose members stepped up their demands for his deportation. Unsurprisingly, he protested at the dangerous effect of such a coalition of forces when, following threats from war veterans, vigilantes aided by the state police attacked the Paul Robeson Peekskill concerts in 1949.

Unable to mount a case to deport Chaplin, his enemies tried other manoeuvres designed to handle his dissent by exclusion. When he applied for a re-entry permit in advance of a trip to England he planned to make in 1948, he was unexpectedly subjected to a four-hour interrogation by an immigration officer and an FBI special agent.[41] Chaplin had to answer a long list of personal and political questions. The full transcript, only made available in the 1970s, represents a rich source for Chaplin's views, albeit filtered for officials. He says he is not a Socialist or a Communist but admits to being 'liberal' (which in the US is code for progressive or even left-wing) and to backing Henry Wallace's Progressive Party. He does not renounce his views or denounce the Soviet Union, but acknowledges the role the Communists played in World War II. He says he knows nothing of their way of life and is not interested in their ideology. 'I am interested to the point where – they say they want peace, and I don't see why we can't have peace here.' He thinks a trading relationship would help, a view that was years later to become government policy.

He presents himself as non-ideological and politically non-affiliated. He supports 'people's unionism' and raising the standard of living. He is surprised if such views have led people to consider him a Communist. 'I don't like revolution,' he says. 'I just want to see everybody pretty well happy and satisfied.'[42] Clearly irritated by the citizenship jibes, which were never directed at other famous non-citizens such as Mary Pickford, he proclaims himself an internationalist and 'a citizen of the world'. This is why, he says, he has never applied to become a US citizen. He answers those who claim he should have because the US is where he earns his money by pointing out that 75 per cent of his revenue comes from outside the US whereas the US receives 100 per cent of his tax.

Chaplin was told he would be granted the re-entry permit but he was suspicious, given the virulence of the campaign for his removal. The Inland Revenue Service also became involved, claiming a huge tax sum and demanding an even greater amount in a bond if he were to leave. He abandoned plans to shoot some of his next film, *Limelight*, in London. He was right to be wary. Despite the interview and the fact that the FBI had found nothing conclusive, it placed him on the Security Index that year. Chaplin had even filed a suit in response to a television broadcast that had called him a Communist, but to the FBI, his circle – not just the left-wing and Communist intellectuals he knew but the likes of the Communist trade-union leader Harry Bridges – was evidence enough; the Bureau was desperate to make something stick.

In April 1949 Hoover requested an update of Chaplin's security file, yet the response was mostly a transcript of the earlier four-hour interrogation. The 1950 testimony of a former managing editor of the *Daily Worker* kept Chaplin's file open because he said Chaplin was a 'concealed' Communist. Chaplin was not intimidated and did not desist from political activity as the temperature of the Cold War rose – NATO was formed, the Communists took power in China, and the Soviet Union exploded an A-bomb. In 1949, Chaplin supported the Waldorf Astoria peace conference and the Paris meeting of the pro-Communist umbrella organisation, the World Peace Congress. In 1950, he endorsed the Mexico City meeting of another pro-Communist body, the American Continental Congress on World Peace, and in 1952 he protested against the travel ban imposed on Paul Robeson by the removal of his passport.

Chaplin was not, however, an uncritical supporter of everything on the left, and wished to keep his films free of direct political taint. He refused, for example, to allow a Communist paper to show *The Circus* as a fund-raiser. In turn, he was criticised by the puritanical Communist left for his morals, self-centredness and alleged lack of assistance to those suffering the blacklist. Yet one of its most famous victims, Zero Mostel, not a man to forgive those who betrayed him during that period, led the cheering at the gala in 1972 following Chaplin's award of a special Oscar.

Anti-red hysteria intensified against the backdrop of the Korean War and Communist spy mania. Chaplin's son, Charles Jr, looking back to that time, wrote about the social cost his father paid for his defiance: 'It must not be supposed that my father's fight for his convictions was made without sacrifice . . . I was saddened to see the effect his stand had had on his own life. It was no longer considered a privilege to be a guest at the home of Charlie Chaplin. Many people were actually afraid to be seen there lest they, too, should become suspect . . . I think my father must have been the loneliest man in Hollywood in those days.'[43]

Chaplin privately seethed at his treatment in America, and wrote to the playwright Clifford Odets in 1951 that the country had been taken over by homegrown fascists. Publicly, Chaplin tapped into the strand of support that remembered and celebrated him as the Tramp, apparently floating free of politics and controversy. As if to remind the public himself, in 1950 he re-released *City Lights* and it proved popular. His dilemma was common in Hollywood during these years and all the starker for his prominence: how to remain a popular performer and remain true to his views? His response in *Limelight* (1952) showed that he was not ideologically besotted, but neither did it represent a political retreat.

He was nearly sixty when he began working on the film, which acknowledged his farewell to the Tramp was final. *Limelight* was the next best thing to reconnect himself to Charlie and memories of past glory. He took nearly four years writing the screenplay, the longest time he spent on any of his film scripts, and it was written first as a novel, imbued with the London of Chaplin's youth. The link to the silent era is underpinned by the appearance of Buster Keaton, who, with Chaplin, had dominated silent film. *Limelight* also represents a return to comedy and romance, with a clearly autobiographical appeal – it has two of his sons in the cast and is the story of a once great music-hall performer, Calvero, who has lost his self-confidence, the very fate Chaplin had always feared. As Calvero acquires both dignity and isolation, there are clear parallels with Chaplin's loss of public acclaim, and the melancholia that pervades the film can be seen as his coming to terms with this.

Chaplin said it was to be his final movie, and, although he made two more, it turned out to be his farewell to Hollywood, which he had been threatening to leave for some years. *Limelight* was not released in America until after Chaplin had left for Europe to attend the film's world première in London – a fitting choice given the film's location as well as a rebuff to his American critics. He was granted a re-entry visa to the US, but was told it could be revoked by the Justice Department at any time. Two days after setting sail for Britain, he heard on board via the ship's radio that the Attorney-General, James McGranery, had revoked the visa and that, before he could re-enter the US, he would have to answer questions regarding his political views and moral behaviour.

This decision followed a month of discussion between the Justice Department and the Immigration and Naturalization Service, which had insufficient grounds to bar Chaplin and feared such a move could backfire if Chaplin sought to return. President Truman, who was keen to demonstrate that he was not 'soft on Communism', had recently appointed the Attorney-General, and there was a presidential election coming just after *Limelight* opened in Europe. The FBI had handed the Attorney-General the files from the Barry episode because of the weakness of the security case against Chaplin and had enlisted the CIA in its manoeuvres.

Both Hoover and the Attorney-General saw Chaplin's European trip as an opportunity to keep Chaplin out of America. Chaplin, who was aware of this possibility, nevertheless decided to proceed with the trip; perhaps he was testing the state or was so tired of the aggravation in the US that he wanted to bring things to a head. When he arrived in London he repeated, 'I've never been political. I have no political convictions. I'm an individualist and I believe in liberty.'[44]

EXILE

Although *Limelight* was not a political film, the actions of the Attorney-General had sustained the politicised image of Chaplin, which cast its shadow over the reception of his portrayal of an ageing artist searching for a new identity. In Cherbourg, Chaplin told the press: 'This is not the day of great artists. This is the day of politics.'[45] In the US, not all the press was hostile to Chaplin. While on the left (by now divided more clearly into those who broadly followed a Soviet approach and those who distanced themselves from the Soviets) there were the expected differences, in general, a sharply right-wing view prevailed, spearheaded by Hopper, who wrote of the banished Chaplin, 'Good riddance to bad rubbish.'[46]

A US campaign to boycott *Limelight*, which included rioting in Iowa, began before the film was released, and ostensibly was to run until Chaplin's political and moral fitness to return was cleared up. The American Legion led the campaign, supported by the major distribution chains. *Limelight* was quite well received in New York, where it opened on the same day as in London, but the boycott proved effective elsewhere and the film was little seen, reinforcing the new public image of Chaplin as the undesirable alien. The US ambassador to France joined in by missing the film's première in Paris. *Limelight* was not shown in Los Angeles and therefore did not qualify for an Academy Award nomination yet uniquely won one twenty years later – for Best Original Dramatic Score (by Chaplin) – when it was first screened there after Chaplin's rehabilitation.

Distribution of his films in the US became problematic after the campaign against *Limelight,* while in Europe he was celebrated as a heroic figure. Already decorated by the French government for his outstanding work as a filmmaker, he was elevated to Officer of the Legion of Honour in 1952, following his exclusion by the US authorities. Despite the urging of British politicians, their government was noticeable in its official silence, concerned not to upset its American allies.

Chaplin's subsequent public utterances were uncontroversial, emphasising his belief in freedom and his earlier image of the spirited individual surviving in the face of an oppressive social apparatus. In early 1953, Oona Chaplin removed their belongings from America, and in April, upon receiving another huge US tax bill, he handed in his re-entry permit at the US embassy in Switzerland. His explanation: 'I have been the object of lies and vicious propaganda by powerful reactionary groups who, by their influence and by the aid of America's yellow press, have created an unhealthy atmosphere in which liberal-minded individuals can be singled out and persecuted.'[47]

Perhaps he could not face the humiliating accommodation that would have been required to return and the debilitating process of having to justify himself? This time, the response in the US was primarily political rather than moral, and the victors gloated. Some who had supported him over the revocation of his permit – for example, the *New York Times* – argued that handing it back was a form of surrender that aided the proponents of cultural cauterisation. In 1954, Oona Chaplin renounced her US citizenship, an act that carried important symbolism, as she was the daughter of America's first towering playwright, Eugene O'Neill. By 1955, Chaplin had sold off all his business interests in the US and by 1958 he had settled all US claims for back taxes.

Chaplin's own bitterness and continuing boldness can be judged by his thinly disguised attack on HUAC and his ridiculing of American society in the ironically titled *A King in New York* ('The King' was his mother's nickname for him). It was the first of the two films he made in exile – the second being the unsuccessful *A Countess from Hong Kong* (1967, based on one of the ideas he had abandoned in order to make *The Great Dictator* and which he regarded after its release with unease as 'a little heavy-handed').[48]*A King in New York*, released in 1957 but not seen in the US until 1976, was certainly not a film designed to woo America back in love with Chaplin, and he banned the American press from its world première.

It was impossible for such a huge public figure not to be implicated in the ideological aspect of the Cold War when it suited both sides to define politics in relation to their own positions and to limit or deny space to critical thought.[49] Both sides for their own and different reasons made more of him than he intended. Both, however, wanted him to be 'red'; his meetings in the mid-1950s with Communist leaders Chou En-Lai, Nikita Khrushchev and Nikolai Bulganin and his acceptance of the Peace Prize from the World Peace Council fed this dual desire. There were also those who wished to ignore the politics of his films altogether and promote an image of the loveable little fellow who moves audiences to laughter and tears as well as those who did identify and recognise the challenge of his films but outside the crude political labels that dominated the debate.

Chaplin was still critical of the cliques he saw running the US and generally upheld the Soviet foreign policy line. He supported unilateral disarmament and remained sympathetic to the Soviet Union after its suppression of the Hungarian uprising but he refused to visit Moscow and was angry that the Communist-led countries wanted his films at cheap rates and were pressing him to speak out more like Robeson. His son Charles wrote that after the war his father discovered how badly the Soviet government treated its artists, but Chaplin Senior kept quiet about this.[50]

The American campaign against Chaplin continued throughout the 1950s. The FBI maintained its file, which came to number more than 1,900 pages, and he was excluded from the Hollywood Walk of Fame when it was first planned in 1958. His rehabilitation gathered momentum during the 1960s without his compromising his opinions. He published *My Autobiography* in 1964, and in 1969 he wrote new scores for a number of his films (e.g. *The Kid*, *The Circus*), which he was to re-release. From the late 1960s on, now that his era, and the McCarthy period that punished him, was in the past, he was increasingly seen as he had seen himself – a victim of repressive times – and he was gradually granted the status of cinema's outstanding creative genius, who had produced a genre of films all his own.

He returned triumphantly to the US in 1972 to receive an honorary Oscar, but he remained bitter about his treatment in America and noted in his illustrated autobiography, *My Life in Pictures*, published in 1974, that there was 'a certain irony' about the award.[51] The British authorities had denied him in 1956 both a knighthood and the award of Companion of Honour for fear of upsetting the US at the time of Suez and because of continuing concerns over his morals. The government finally caught up once the Americans had cleared the way and honoured Britain's own unique performer with a knighthood in 1975, two years before he died in his sleep at his home in Switzerland, having withdrawn from public life and been confined to a wheelchair. He was also honoured in 1994 on a set of US stamps commemorating silent screen stars and again in 1998 in the 'Celebrate the Century' stamp series.

A mass of books and essays about Chaplin, festivals dedicated to him, statues, plaques, artefacts featuring him, the 1992 film *Chaplin* and the release of his own work on television, video and DVD have ensured his endurance. The image of Charlie the Tramp is one of the most globally familiar of any from the twentieth century, as readily identifiable as that of Mickey Mouse, and, not surprisingly, it has become an enormously valuable commodity. IBM used the Tramp in its advertisements (1981–87), showing that, if not as extreme an appropriation as that of Che Guevara's image, icons can be used to sell and promote a bewildering range of goods and events irrespective of any association they may once have held.

During most of his working life, Chaplin was remarkably successful at controlling his image – what Chaplin the person and Chaplin the performer stood for – even if for many years after the war he failed to do so in America. Chaplin was the Tramp, but his off-screen persona was markedly different from his on-screen image, though the political aspects began to merge in the 1930s and '40s. Chaplin controlled this distance by his invention and his pretence, which, within the singular figure of the Tramp, created the dynamism and potency of his performances. Although the main physical picture of the Tramp seems not to have altered, what it and its creator represented did change with changing circumstance, from the endearing comic figure of the early silent movies to the socially conscious artist of his maturity. Yet, at root, all his work casts the defining struggle of his era as that between the rich and the poor.

DEBATE ON CHAPLIN

Autobiographies of colleagues, friends and lovers and critical reappraisals have added to the debate about what Chaplin represents, and tend to divide into two camps, which, as one writer put it, vilify Chaplin as villain or venerate him as victim.[52] Luis Buñuel in his memoirs, for instance, accuses Chaplin of selling out, of becoming an icon of the down-trodden as well as of American capitalism. That judgement is true, and a necessary result of Chaplin's popular appeal, but it ignores the intricacies of some of Chaplin's films and, within the popular arena, his unprecedented, abrasive exploi-tation of paradox. Fernand Léger's early 1920s cubist picture of Chaplin captures this complexity and anticipates the multi-plicity of meanings in films like *Modern Times*.

Contradictions are woven into his films, and his attempts to allow their co-existence or to resolve them through make-believe and myth give his work its social and political richness beyond the brilliant versatility of his physical performance. The deference of the silent film era may have disappeared but the unpredictability and insecurity of life – and the fear of that – have not, and this helps give his films their continuing pur-chase. His later films may be more uneven than the earlier pic-tures because their politics are more prominent, but Chaplin's critique of mass production in *Modern Times* and his message at the end of *The Great Dictator*, though both are now commonplace, have lost none of their force, and his associ-ation of corporate business and war in *Monsieur Verdoux* has been vindicated by subsequent US foreign policy.

The understanding of contradiction he demonstrates in his films mirrors the contradictions in his own life, which could be as sharp as his mood swings. 'I have no design for living,' he wrote. 'I vacillate with inconsistencies; at times small things will annoy me and catastrophes will leave me indifferent.'[53] Chaplin was a sexual libertarian from a masculine perspective and father of nine children who, nevertheless, became a devoted husband for more than three decades of his life. He enjoyed the company of powerful right-wing friends, such as the press magnate William Randolph Hearst, as much as of militant Communists. In fact, Chaplin's friends were drawn from across the political spectrum, regardless of their opinions. He was conservative in his tastes (for example, he disliked abstract painting and Shakespeare productions in modern dress), yet he was radical in political opinion. He did not, however, associate with the avant-garde or with the left-wing film movement and did not agitate to transform the film industry. He did not see himself as a leader, spokesman or cause célèbre.

Thomas Burke wrote that Chaplin 'likes to enjoy the best of the current social system, while at heart he is the reddest of Reds.'[54] If pressed on his politics, he would protest that he was just an actor or a clown, yet he wanted to alter people's minds and be regarded as a serious, influential figure, and was upset if not treated in this light.

Whereas Paul Robeson was criticised for the coherence in his politics, Chaplin, like Isadora Duncan, was – and is – belittled for the contradictions in theirs, implying implausibly that middle-of-the-road consistency is the norm. Such patronising dismissals are often covert attacks on the presumption of artists and performers in holding political views at all, as if politics were the exclusive province of a separate professional class. If Chaplin was out of his depth politically, then that could be said to have generally been the case in such highly politicised and polarised times. He could support New Deal economic intervention and be a risk-taking capitalist who disliked state regulation. He could be an internationalist who detested the puritanism of his adopted home yet who could value America's energy, promise of freedom and emphasis on the importance of the individual. He could defend freedom and protest against attempts to limit it while choosing not to criticise Soviet repression. He could be a pacifist and support the opening of a Second Front or be critical of nationalism and praise Soviet patriotism, but none of this disqualifies those opinions or signifies he did not hold them sincerely.

Although he did back the Progressive Party presidential candidate Henry Wallace after the war and was said by his one-time assistant Alistair Cooke to be sympathetic to the British Labour Party, he was not party political or in the narrow sense ideological. His biographer David Robinson judges him to be more anarchistic than anarchist, which brings him closer to Duncan than to Robeson. He could be partisan but not politically practical or acute, and showed little interest in political detail. Yet, when he had at last found stability in his private life with Oona O'Neill, he displayed great courage in the 1940s and early 1950s in the face of the professional and political dangers facing him.

He did not spend the resulting exile from Hollywood and America in his homeland, about which he was ambivalent (as were Robeson and Duncan about their native countries). The British campaign against Chaplin during World War I continued to rankle, as did the lack of honours from Britain. Despite his love of England, he told a reporter (unguardedly) during his visit there in 1931: 'They say I have a duty to England. I wonder just what that duty is? No one wanted me or cared for me in England seventeen years ago. I had to go to America for my chance and I got it there.'[55] He remained faithful to America, until that, too, spurned him, and he chose to live his last years in Switzerland, the symbolic country of neutrality.

The courage Chaplin displayed was not motivated by politics but by his non-conformism and independent character. His son Charles, who believed the 'red' label that was stuck on his father adversely affected his own screen career, has attested to the personal cost of this courage, which must have influenced Chaplin's decision not to return to the US. He may have been politically naive – and, indeed, he always retained a childlike quality – but he knew the risks he was taking and presumably believed solidarity was more important than celebrity. He was always aware of the dilemma of celebrity – the trapped world of those who are massively adulated offers enormous influence as well as gigantic distortion of, and distance from, society – and his fame proved to be no shield when he needed it; in fact, it fuelled calls for his punishment. As he was always scared of losing his appeal, which for a time was unparalleled, the stand for which he paid his price becomes the more notable.

Chaplin believed important art came from popular forms, and he saw himself in that tradition. This made him political because he used the cinema to put the relationship of the 'ordinary' individual to society at the heart of his films and to have this seen by a truly mass audience, which was historically exceptional. He used his celebrity to make the kinds of films he wanted, which were enormously popular but set apart from the system that determined and dominated the popular cinema of his day. As an independent producer who built and owned his own studios, he exercised complete artistic control that allowed him the time for painstaking preparation and selection, always striving for unattainable perfection. The summation of his character, he said in an interview in 1966, is that 'I care about my work . . . If I could do something else better, I would do it, but I can't.'[56] In this work, commitment to his craft as a performer is central; his skills in other departments – directing, writing, composing, producing – were focused on and channelled through (and have been overshadowed by) his ability to perform. As Thomas Burke noted in his marvellously illuminating portrait published in 1932: 'He is first and last an actor.'[57] But, however private as a person, he was a public actor with a sharp political awareness and definite worldview, which he expressed in his films.

A reticent man anxious about appearing in public, Chaplin found in the seclusion of the non-live art form to which he dedicated his life the sustenance to create for the public his lively, liberating view of life's anarchy in films that have proved their popularity across continents and generations. He saw his films as a way to comment on what it means to be human at a time when, as he wrote, 'Our living sense has been blunted by profit, power and monopoly.'[58] He described his art as apolitical because he wanted to avoid making propaganda, not because there were no politics in his work; his view was: 'I'm loading the dice for something more important than politics – the affirmation of the man [sic].'[59] He wanted to avoid having his art limited by the political label, yet he knew politics in a broad sense were essential to life-affirmation, but only if they expressed and responded to the complexities of human existence. This understanding imbues many of his films with a crusading as well as a lyrical spirit, which, along with his supreme artistry, lifts them beyond the commonplace into a class of their own.

NOTES

1. The first line of 'Swing, Little Girl', the opening song to the 1968 re-issue of the film *The Circus*, written and sung by Charlie Chaplin.

2. Charles Chaplin, *My Autobiography*, London, Bodley Head, 1964, p. 154.

3. Outstanding African American vaudeville artist Bert Williams had developed on stage his own archetypal figure, Mr Nobody, before Chaplin created the Tramp on film. Williams first appeared on screen in *Darktown Jubilee* (1914) but his performance without blackface was greeted by a riot. Given creative control by the Biograph film company, he produced, directed and starred in the short comedies *Fish* (1916) and *Natural Born Gambler* (1916) but, unhappy with what he could achieve in film, he returned to the stage.

4. C.L.R. James, 'Popular Arts and Modern Society' in *The Struggle for Happiness and American Civilization*, Oxford, Blackwell, 1993, p. 134.

5. Quoted in Thomas Burke, 'A Comedian' in *City of Encounters: A London Divertissement*, London, Constable & Co, 1932, p. 150.

6. David Robinson, *Chaplin, His Life and Art*, London, Penguin, 2001, p. 135.

7. Queen Mary was reported to have resisted Chaplin's knighthood in order to prevent the monarchy becoming a party to a publicity stunt for a film comedian, yet later records reveal only the influence of the Northcliffe campaign (Robinson, p. 454).

8. Joyce Milton, *Tramp: The Life of Charlie Chaplin*, New York, Da Capo Press, 1998, pp. 188–9.

9. Robinson, p. 294.

10. Milton, p. 189.

11. FBI files on Chaplin (2,063 pages) are available online at http://www.fadetoblack.com/foi/charliechaplin but not from the FBI website.

12. Robinson, p. 150.

13. Chaplin (1964), p. 312.

14. Robinson, p. 487.

15. *ibid.*, p. 337.

16. *A Woman of Paris*, DVD, Warner Brothers, Z1 37976, 2003. When the film was reissued in 1977 Chaplin had made a few changes, one of which was to drop this written title.

17. The date of Chaplin's third marriage (to Paulette Goddard) is disputed and may have happened when she had just turned twenty-six.

18. Milton, pp. 319–20.

19. Quoted in Charles J. Marland, *Chaplin and American Culture: the Evolution of a Star Image*, New Jersey, Princeton University Press, 1989, p. 131.

20. Quoted in Milton, p. 312.

21. Quoted in Robinson, pp. 485–6.

22. *ibid.*, p. 464.

23. The National Industrial Recovery Act was an ambitious programme initiated by Roosevelt during his first one hundred days in office. Under the Act, the federal government took a leading role in cooperating with and managing business, primarily through the creation of the National Recovery Administration (NRA). The NRA controversially established codes to regulate trade, prices and labour practices, which were successfully challenged in the Supreme Court as abuse of federal power.

24. Marland, p. 160.

25. Quoted in Milton, p. 338.

26. Quoted in Robinson, p. 486.

27. *ibid.*, p. 161.

28. *ibid.*, p. 526.

29. Chaplin (1964), p. 433.

30. Quoted in Robinson, p. 554.

31. Chaplin (1964), p. 444.

32. Quoted in Charles J Marland (ed. and intro.), ' "Are You Now, Or Have You Ever Been . . . ?": The INS Interview with Charles Chaplin', *Cineaste*, vol. xiv, no. 4, 1986, New York, p. 13.

33. Milton, p. 403.

34. Robinson, p. 574.

35. *ibid.*, p. 575.

36. Both press conference quotations, *ibid.*, p. 583.

37. *Reynold's News*, 7 December 1947.

38. HUAC's so-called 'unfriendly witnesses' were supported initially by an ad hoc Committee on the First Amendment that boasted several stars like Lauren Bacall, Humphrey Bogart, Judy Garland, Danny Kaye, Gene Kelly, Groucho Marx and Frank Sinatra. This support soon evaporated. Two months later, after Congress had cited ten of the 'unfriendly

witnesses' for contempt, the president of the film producers' association announced that these ten – who became known as the Hollywood Ten – would be banned from working in the industry. The blacklist had begun. See later, in 'Would-be Gaolers of the Imagination: Contexts of Coercion and Control'.

39. Milton, p. 467.

40. Robinson, p. 591.

41. The interview involved a senior officer from the Immigration and Naturalization Service, an FBI special agent and a stenographer. Accounts differ on certain minor details; Robinson (p. 594) says it lasted four hours whereas Chaplin (1964, p. 496), who seems to mistake the year it occurred, says four people not three came, and the interview lasted three instead of four hours.

42. Interview quotations in Marland (1986), pp. 14–15.

43. Charles Chaplin Jr, *My Father, Charlie Chaplin*, London, Longmans, 1960, p. 352.

44. Robinson, p. 624.

45. Milton, p. 487.

46. Quoted in Robinson, p. 632.

47. *ibid.*, p. 640.

48. Charles Chaplin, *My Life in Pictures*, London, Bodley Head, 1974 (no page numbers).

49. For example, Spencer Golub, in 'Charlie Chaplin, Soviet Icon' in Sue-Ellen Case and Janelle Reinelt (eds.), *The Performance of Power: Theatrical Discourse and Politics*, shows how Soviet reception changed in relation to changing ideological needs of the Soviet Communist Party.

50. See Chaplin Jr, p. 340.

51. Chaplin (1974, no page numbers).

52. Marland (1989), p. 372.

53. Chaplin (1964), p. 528.

54. Quoted in Burke, p. 139.

55. Quoted in Robinson, p. 464.

56. From an interview with Richard Meryman, 'The Tramp was something in me', reprinted in the *Guardian*, 11 January 2003, as an edited extract from the full interview, which appears as an appendix in Jeffrey Vance (ed.), *Chaplin: Genius of the Cinema*, New York, Harry N. Abrams, 2003.

57. Burke, p. 130.

58. Chaplin (1964), p. 506.

59. Quoted in Robinson, p. 649.

PART TWO

WOULD-BE GAOLERS OF THE IMAGINATION: CONTEXTS OF COERCION AND CONTROL

'Open your window, let the sun
Bring light into every corner of your house'
from a song by Victor Jara,
written after the Popular Unity victory in Chile, 1970 [1]

Rebel performers are inevitably defined by what they challenge. The specific elements of the social, cultural and political context in which they perform, or seek to perform, shape both the performances they make and the political commitment that lies behind their proclamations of resistance. Context comprises many factors, and these change and differ according to period and place.

The response of those challenged also varies. It may involve incorporation, marginalisation, censure, censorship or outright proscription. Much of the reaction is based on the fear that watching a representation of an act is the same as watching the act itself, as if there were no distinction between representation and that which is being represented. This continuum of complicity further suggests that to explore, let alone explain, is to condone, and to condone is to support; prohibition, therefore, is in order. When censorship is invoked, it is frequently carried out in the name of a better future; the political vision justifies turning the art of the present, and by extension its performers, into servants of a supposedly forward-looking ideology.

Censorship takes many forms, and usually combines 'hard' and 'soft' power. In certain circumstances, censors seek to control all aspects of performance, its production, distribution and reception, even if control may not be exerted equally over all these aspects. In less overt situations, control is exercised through a more complex apparatus of persuasion and self-regulation.

For the most part the link between prohibition and performance lies in the perceived content of the material being performed, although in some instances the type or manner in which, and place, it is performed may be critical. In other cases, particular individuals are targeted regardless of the material they perform because of their views or even who they are, and this proscription may embrace an entire category of performer, for example when women are forbidden from appearing on stage.

The invention and advance of mechanical reproductive technology, such as sound recording, cinema and the internet, has added to the censor's woes and extended performance far beyond live exchange. Nevertheless, the political potency of live communication – the very social nature of which, for instance, led England's seventeenth-century Puritans to close all theatres – still means that a politically committed performer is likely to seek live public outlets, and this is usually easier for authority to limit or prevent than it is to control printed matter or recorded material. Human ingenuity, however, has a long and inspiring history of circumventing its would-be gaolers. In the twentieth century, the Polish director Tadeusz Kantor recalled staging secret drama under Nazi occupation in Warsaw; concentration camp survivors told of covert cabaret performances in Dachau; and in Czechoslovakia, after the Soviet invasion, subversive clandestine theatre took place in people's flats.

Social systems and their ruling authorities clearly play a central part in defining political performance, through their promotion of what is deemed politically acceptable or their suppression of what is deemed unacceptable. This does not mean that political intention or meaning, let alone artistic value, can be read in an easy way from a performer's relationship to authority or from simple notions of victim and oppressor, especially as into the category of what is permitted falls much critical art, or art used critically, that evades or defies the censor through coded meanings.

Crisis is often said to be productive of, if not necessary to, the creation of significant art but that assertion merely reflects the historic omnipresence of acute social strain as well as a particularly modern and western view of art. Yet, in certain historical circumstances, the existence of censorship, paradoxically, has provided an edge and focus to art – even to a more distinct definition of political effect – and its removal can leave art momentarily stranded. This is not to provide a rationale for the imposition or continuation of censorship, more a reflection of the importance of context.

WAR

War represents a special context for censorship and authoritarian control, be it in legislation, economics or art. In wartime, there is pressure from above and often below to reinforce or create grand myths of national endeavour. War involves action against internal opposition as well as external aggression; censorship and oppression are used to fight both.

Not long before war was declared in 1939, for example, the British censor prevented the performance of the play *Pastor Niemöller* by Ernst Toller because it might offend Herr Hitler. During the war, the BBC exerted strict control of the radio airwaves. The writer J.B. Priestley's popular wartime broadcasts were halted in 1942 after he attacked the concept of private property. The same year the BBC banned crooners for fear they would weaken the moral fibre of the nation. In 1943 the BBC excluded Noël Coward's song 'Don't Let's Be Beastly to the Germans' because it was regarded as being too nice to the Nazis rather than a satire on the situation after Britain had won the war. In addition, the BBC – with help from MI5 – carefully but secretly monitored Communists or their close associates who might be appearing on or contributing to its programmes. The Corporation briefly banned twelve artists, including the actor Michael Redgrave, because they had signed and refused to withdraw their support from the Communist-led People's Convention (calling for a People's Government). Redgrave, who was associated with the Communist-backed Workers' Music Association and Unity Theatre, was included along with Charlie Chaplin (and thirty-three others who were not performers), in George Orwell's 1949 list of people he believed were 'crypto-communists, fellow travellers or inclined that way', a list he wrote for a friend in the Information Research Department of the Foreign Office.[2]

The BBC maintained its MI5 monitoring procedures in the post-war decades and, unsurprisingly, continued to proscribe during subsequent wars. During Northern Ireland's Troubles, for example, it banned Paul and Linda McCartney's relatively gentle 'Give Ireland Back to the Irish', and during the Falklands War its censorship extended to the Gang of Four's song 'I Love a Man in Uniform'.

War also throws up many examples of heroism by performers as well as of capitulation, resulting in cases that remain controversial or subject to sharp debate years after that conflict has ended. War can also stimulate particular and distinct responses by performers, who become swept up in a general mood of increased social responsibility. This can be seen, for instance, in international reaction to the Spanish Civil War, the Vietnam War or to the 2003 invasion of Iraq, as well as by the following individual examples, which stand for a multitude of similar acts of defiance.

As part of an assault on the West Bank town of Beit Jala in 2000, Israeli tanks shelled the Inad Theatre, but this did not stop the Palestinian company performing (Inad means stubborn). During the Bosnian war, the 1993 production of *Waiting for Godot*, directed by Susan Sontag in besieged Sarajevo using local actors, became a symbol of courage and resistance. The Catalan cellist Pablo Casals fled Spain when the Republic fell and helped distribute food and clothing to refugees across the border in France. He refused to play in Spain while the dictator General Franco remained in power. In protest against the Japanese occupation of China in 1937, the Beijing opera actor Mei Lanfang ceased to perform until the Japanese had been defeated. (Those who did perform were later blacklisted.) On the other hand, exceptional actors, such as Jean-Louis Barrault of France, responded to the occupation of their countries during World War II by continuing to perform in their homelands. In 1940, in a prisoner-of-war camp, Stalag VIII at Görlitz in Silesia, Olivier Messiaen and three other inmates performed his *Quartet for the End of Time*, which he had composed there for the instruments that were available – piano, violin, clarinet and cello. The quartet has become an emblem of the spirit of human struggle.

All social systems are to a degree built on war (even in countries that have enjoyed passages of peace, the war industries are critical to the economy and political culture), and many political processes are predicated on the possible resort to force. Throughout one such major confrontation, the four decades of the Cold War, performers in music, drama and dance (as well as in sport) were commandeered by the intelligence services on both sides to spy on their opponents as well as more obviously to act as propagandists.

REPRESSION

For dissenting performers, survival under totalitarian and repressive regimes, whether at war or not, is similarly problematic. It can mean negotiating a difficult compromise, balancing a necessary obligation to authority against a duty to art. Failure to strike the right balance can result in the absence of employment, incarceration, exile or, at worse, execution.

The Nazis promoted Aryan culture and banned many performers – Romany, Jewish and those with African roots – because of their 'degenerate' and 'inferior' ancestry or, in the case of homosexuals, their sexual preference. Political opponents, like the Communists and Socialists, were also banned, as were suspect artistic forms, like modernism, which Nazi ideologues associated with Communism and Judaism. Prohibition was accompanied by extermination, and many performers who did not flee Germany died in prisons and in the camps.

Others stayed and worked for or with the Nazis. Soprano Elisabeth Schwarzkopf, in her memoirs, says she joined the Nazi Party for 'administrative' reasons, and several performers, like the opera singer Hans Hotter, although not party members, were favourites of Hitler.[3] The actor Emil Jannings, who was an international celebrity when the Nazis came to power – he had featured in the 1930 film *The Blue Angel* as the professor in thrall to Marlene Dietrich's nightclub singer – performed on stage and on screen under the Nazis. Although 'denazified' in 1946, he was denied work in the US film industry because of his Nazi links and never made another film.

The performer who came to epitomise collaboration was the actor Gustaf Gründgens. Despite his Communist associations in the 1920s, he was appointed head of all the theatres in Prussia the year Hitler became Chancellor, and from 1934–1944 was manager of the Staatstheater, Berlin, reputedly the best theatre in Germany. At the end of the war Gründgens was interned but following rehabilitation became director of the Düsseldorf Schauspielhaus and went on to run the Hamburg Schauspielhaus. He committed suicide in 1963. He became known outside Germany after his death through the play and film versions of Klaus Mann's 1936 novel *Mephisto*, which follows the different fortunes of a group of actors who start out together in a left-wing cabaret. Mann attacks the key figure, based on Gründgens, who makes his pact with the contemporary devil and flourishes under the Nazis playing an acclaimed Mephistopheles, unlike another in the group, based on the Communist actor Hans Otto, who is murdered. Otto, an organiser for the workers' theatre union, was arrested in 1933 by the Sturm Abteilung (SA), the Nazi paramilitaries known as 'brownshirts', who tortured him and beat him to death.

In the Soviet Union, where art was also thoroughly politicised, the regime came to stand for the worst excesses of censorship, having been one of the major stimulators of creativity across the world. Soviet performers had to ride the vicissitudes of a volatile history, from the initial upsurge in energy and experiment, the Stalin purges of the 1930s and the imposition of strict artistic guidelines that devastated cultural life, to the war years of national survival and the post-Stalin thaw, followed by retrenchment and collapse. Of the many performers who were killed by the state, the best known are the actress Zinaida Raikh, her husband, the actor and director Vsevolod Meyerhold, and the leading Jewish actor Solomon Mikhoels.

Raikh was the leading actress in the 1920s and '30s at Moscow's Meyerhold Theatre, the chief experimental theatre in the Soviet Union, which was closed in 1938 because of its alleged anti-Soviet tone. In 1939 Stalin's secret police arrested and imprisoned Meyerhold and then sent assassins to Raikh's flat. They broke in and brutally assaulted her. She died of numerous stab wounds, at least two of them through the eyes. Six months later Meyerhold was shot dead in prison. Mikhoels was one of the main actors, as well as the director, of Moscow's Jewish State Theatre. As part of a post-war anti-Semitic drive, Stalin closed all Jewish theatres in 1948. That year Mikhoels died in mysterious circumstances when a lorry 'accidentally' hit him and mutilated his body. It later turned out that Stalin had personally ordered the murder.

In the post-Stalin period, Vladimir Vysotsky, poet, song-writer, actor and the seminal Russian Hamlet of his era, became the voice of the repressed through thousands of tapes that circulated underground. He was harassed and censored. When he died of a heart attack aged 42 in 1980, the authorities would not allow his body to be buried in Moscow's best-known cemetery as his family wished. A commemoration of his life was banned, although, following appeals to Communist leaders, an invitation-only event was grudgingly permitted.

In the Soviet 'satellite' states, culture was treated likewise as an arm of state policy, and, consequently, performers were tightly controlled. The German Democratic Republic, for example, banned the singer/songwriter Wolf Biermann in the mid-1960s from making public appearances and publishing books or records. Biermann (whose father was a Communist who had died in Auschwitz) supported the Czech experiment of 'Socialism with a human face', which preceded the Soviet invasion. In 1976, following a concert Biermann gave in West Germany, he was deprived of his nationality and forbidden from returning. He eventually went back to East Berlin in 1989 after the collapse of the regime.

Performers were at the forefront of resistance in neighbouring Czechoslovakia after the Soviet invasion in 1968 when many of them were prevented from working. They became central to the movement that challenged the puppet state and gave rise to the 'velvet revolution' of 1989. Playwright and future post-Communist president Václav Havel organised a protest in 1976 at the imprisonment of four members of The Plastic People of the Universe, a rock music group (inspired by The Velvet Underground) which had continued playing after being banned. The protest eventually gave rise to the founding of the human rights campaign Charter 77, one of whose spokespersons was the singer Marta Kubišová. The first copies to enter the public domain of the document that gave its name to the campaign were seized by the police from a car driven by an internationally known actor, Pavel Landovsky.

He and other banned performers were also involved in the clandestine Living Room Theatre, which opened in 1978 with a seventy-five minute version of *Macbeth* (in honour of which Tom Stoppard wrote *Cahoot's Macbeth*). To see a perform-ance, one had to telephone a number and five people with a suitcase would later turn up at your home. The group in-cluded the celebrated actress Vlasta Chramostová and its founder, the playwright Pavel Kohout. With Landovsky, he was subsequently exiled. Chramostová, though banned, re-mained in Czechoslovakia and became a major symbol of defiance.

The Chinese Communist Party broke with the Soviets in political interpretation but not in control of culture. Its ideo-logical retraining programme included performers, and its revision of traditional operas led in 1964 to their being banned altogether and replaced by model revolutionary ones. The Cultural Revolution (1965–68) that followed took the perse-cution of performers and the prohibition of 'bourgeois' culture to new depths.

REBEL MOVEMENTS

While the Chinese did not allow the existence of a campaign like Charter 77, in many repressive regimes rebel performers were likely to be associated with an opposition movement, which might have both a political and a cultural strand but with the latter operating more openly. The dictatorships in the 1970s and '80s of central and south America were opposed by a 'nueva cancion' or new song movement as well as by various left-wing parties. Although distinctive in each country, each was a movement for political change that respected indige-nous art forms and rebuffed the cultural imperialism of its north American neighbour as well as its European colonial conquerors.

Brazil, under military rule from 1964 until 1985, had the brief but influential Tropicália movement, which stemmed from music that combined African rhythms, bossa nova, samba and electric, urban sounds with satire and humour, and embraced visual art, cinema and theatre too. Although the Tropicálistas were not allied to the left, in 1968 the military raided a Tropi-cália production of singer/songwriter Chico Buarque's scath-ing play *Roda Viva*, and many were beaten and imprisoned.

Buarque soon went into exile. Later that year fellow musicians and the movement's founders, Caetano Veloso and Gilberto Gil, were imprisoned and subsequently released only in order to perform a fund-raising concert for their air fare to exile in London. Gil became Brazil's Minister of Culture in 2002 in President Lula da Silva's popular left government.

In Bolivia, which also came under a military dictatorship in 1964, singer/songwriter Benjo Cruz swapped his guitar for a gun in 1970 and died of exposure in the jungle, and singer/songwriter Nilo Soruco was forced into exile, too. In Uruguay, which suffered a dictatorship from 1973–1984, singer/songwriter Hector Numa Moraes was banned and went into exile in 1972, the same year that singer/songwriter Daniel Viglietti was gaoled; he subsequently was also banished abroad. In Argentina, the military took charge in 1976 and banned the music of Mercedes Sosa and Victor Heredia, leaders of the Argentine New Song Movement. In 1978, Sosa was arrested during a performance and ordered to leave the country. Heredia was unable to perform, and those who did were often punished, like rock musician Charly Garcia, who was gaoled. The pianist Miguel Angel Estrella, who was abducted and tortured, went into exile and in 1982 set up in Paris the organisation Musique Espérance to involve musicians in human rights and peace activities, a movement which had echoes in the 1990s' 'pianos for Cuba' campaign to improve that beleaguered country's musical stock.

The brutality of the South American regimes as well as the role of the 'nueva cancion' in opposing them is symbolised by the murder of the Chilean singer/songwriter Victor Jara. Born into a family of rural labourers in Loquen, a small town not far from Santiago, he studied at the University of Chile's Theatre School but became increasingly interested in the musical folk heritage of his country and a central figure in the new song movement. He joined the Communist Party and, through his singing, supported the party's campaigns, including the presidential election bid of the Socialist Salvador Allende. The victorious Allende appeared under a banner that read 'You can't have a revolution without songs'. On 11 September 1973, the first day of the US-abetted military coup that assassinated the President, Jara was trapped at work by tanks.

He was eventually taken to the Chile Stadium where he had sung for Allende. This time, guards beat Jara savagely, broke his hands and machine-gunned him to death. The junta, led by General Pinochet, wished to erase Jara by destroying all his recordings. Although it succeeded in wiping out his original 'master' copies, songs he recorded on vinyl, reel-to-reel tapes and cassettes survived. Repression of performers continued throughout the junta's rule. It banned artists of the new song movement and declared indigenous instruments subversive. Exile groups like Inti-Illimani and Quilapayun, prevented from returning, carried on the struggle abroad in association with solidarity groups. Inside Chile, punk-rock trio *Los Prisioneros* campaigned against Pinochet in a 1988 plebiscite on his continuation in power. Pinochet lost, and the way became clear for a return to civilian government two years later.

In South Africa, the movement against apartheid, which similarly linked internal and external opposition, had performance at the heart of the struggle for a democratic state. Under apartheid, culture suffered both suppression and segregation. Police routinely beat up performers and closed down their shows. Even the innocuous entertainer George Formby was banned just after the Second World War when he insisted on performing to black audiences. The anti-apartheid movement targeted culture along with sport and trade in its boycott. The cultural boycott divided opinion, as such boycotts do; some argued for the power of exchange and communication while others argued for isolation. Those performers, like the singers and musicians Hugh Masakela, Miriam Makeba and Abdulla Ibrahim, who went into exile, fought the regime abroad and were joined there by artists, black and white, from across the disciplines and genres. It was an astonishing array: in music alone, the range stretched from Stevie Wonder, Peter Gabriel and Paul Simon (who broke the UN sanctions to record *Graceland*, which, he argued, supported indigenous black performers) to Miles Davis and Jerry Dammers. In 1988, despite a right-wing campaign to prevent it, the BBC broadcast the Nelson Mandela birthday concert live from London and copies of the programme were smuggled into South Africa.

With playwright Athol Fugard, the actors Winston Nshoni and John Kani, who had themselves been gaoled, created the play *The Island* (1973), a reference to Robben Island where Mandela and other anti-apartheid leaders were incarcerated. The play has become an emblem around the world of resistance to apartheid and, more generally, of the struggle for human emancipation. Pieter-Dirk Uys, a white, gay, Jewish Afrikaner, was never arrested but when the censors banned his plays, he became a stand-up satirist, who developed his own stage persona Evita Bezuidenhout. As a performer, Uys again ran into trouble (often deliberately) with the censors, who were baffled by a man in a dress attacking liberals as well as racists. The authorities harassed his relatives and Uys left for London; Mandela saw videos of his performances on Robben Island. The arrival of democratic, post-apartheid government did not blunt his theatrical attacks, and he has lacerated Mandela's successor Thabo Mbeki, whom Uys once admired, for his ostrich-like views on HIV and AIDS, which have denied millions the medication they need and thereby condemned so many compatriots to death.

RELIGION AND MORALITY

In many parts of the world, in the Middle East and Arab countries or South-East Asia, for example, religious censorship plays a central role in underpinning political control of performance. In Iran, the ayatollahs' regime closed the prestigious international Shiraz theatre festival and banned the singer Faegheh Atashin (known to her audiences as Googoosh), while in Afghanistan, Farida Mahwash, whom the pro-Soviet regime had banned from singing in support of the guerrilla resistance, had to flee the country in 1991 when the Taliban took over. They banned not only television, cassette players and video recorders but musical instruments as well.

In Israel, there was once a ban on performing Michael Tippett's 1944 opera, *A Child of Our Time*, because it contained references to Jesus. The longer-lasting unofficial but strictly enforced Israeli ban on performing the music of Richard Wagner began in the Palestine Protectorate in 1938 as a direct response to Kristallnacht, the particularly barbarous pogrom which saw one thousand synagogues destroyed in a day.[4] The prohibition widened and included the music of Richard Strauss and Carl Orff, yet the work of other anti-Semitic composers, such as Modest Mussorgsky and Alexander Borodin, was permitted. Perhaps in this context the direct link with the German culture that was centrally important to the perpetrators of the Jewish Holocaust became decisive.

The Wagner ban was challenged by Zubin Mehta in 1981 when he conducted the Israel Philharmonic Orchestra in the prelude from *Tristan und Isolde* played as an encore. The audience erupted in indignation and surprise and, although some left, Mehta finished the piece but concluded the time was not yet right to lift the ban. In 2000, another attempt was made to challenge the ban when the Rishon LeTzion Symphony performed the *Siegfried Idyll* conducted by Mendy Rodan, a 71-year-old Holocaust survivor. One newspaper reported that the conductor saw the performance as revenge on the Nazis. Daniel Barenboim, himself a Jew, having been persuaded to drop an extract of *Die Walküre* from his series of concerts, repeated Mehta's experiment in 2001 by offering the *Tristan* prelude after the last encore of the last concert. Protests ensued but he did play through to the end.

The ban, in a state that has a democratic system of government on the western model, attests to the potency of performance. Wagner, once the favourite of progressive Jews because of his role in modernising music, still has a place in Israeli cultural life (however awkward and intermittent), in books and on TV and radio; the prohibition is social, on live public performance.

Religious intolerance of performers crosses the boundaries of politics and geography.[5] Fundamentalist Christians forced the banning in Uganda of Eve Ensler's *The Vagina Monologues*, while in Britain, although protests against the alleged blasphemy of *Jerry Springer – The Opera* failed to stop performances and a television broadcast, an evangelical Christian group threatened the show's charity work and picketed its regional tour. The group had been spurred by the success of elements within the Birmingham Sikh community in forcing the cancellation of performances of *Behzti* ('Dishonour'), a play by Gurpreet Kaur Bhatti set in a gurdwara, a Sikh temple. Pressure from within sections of the Jewish community had previously compelled the Royal Court Theatre, the focus of the fight to end theatrical censorship in Britain two decades before, to cancel (in 1987) the run of Jim Allen's *Perdition*, a play which explores the collaboration of Hungarian Zionists with the Nazis in the deportation of Jews.

In many instances, moral prejudice becomes the driving force, often subsuming a political intention, as Charlie Chaplin and Lenny Bruce believed happened to them. Bruce rose from the club circuit to gain a national reputation as a comedian in the US through recordings and TV appearances. His presentation of the often painful confrontations we experience with the paradoxes of life had an intensity that combined his background in Yiddish performance and the spontaneity of African-American jazz. His ethical compulsion pushed him beyond joke-based stand-up comedy, and he exploited autobiography, using sexual and scatological language as a shock exposure of the hypocrisies of the society he lived in. (His prominent sexual libertarianism, although forceful for its day, was trapped, however, in the narrow world of unfettered masculine desire.) Bruce's insistent repetition of taboo words to demonstrate how they lose their power once the taboo has been broken did not convince all his audiences or the police and press. He was booed when he appeared at the Establishment, a London club run by the satirist Peter Cook, and was barred from re-entering Britain as an undesirable alien, even when invited by the Earl of Harewood to an International Drama Conference at the Edinburgh Festival. Bruce was also banned from Australia, for blasphemy.

In 1961 Bruce was arrested on a narcotics charge but acquitted; the first of his obscenity arrests followed in 1962, and he spent the rest of his short life battling the US legal system as it relentlessly indicted him for drugs and obscenity violations. By the time his autobiography, *How to Talk Dirty and Influence People*, was published in 1965 and he was declared a bankrupt pauper, he reckoned he had been arrested nineteen times. He died of a morphine overdose in 1966, aged 40. He had contracted hepatitis as a teenager, which had led to health problems in later life; he suffered from staphylococcus septicaemia and pleurisy; he took methedrine for lethargy and depression, and carried a doctor's confirmation of this, yet the media, in collusion with the police, said he had died of a heroin overdose, in keeping with the 'sick' label that had been applied to his act. This image had been carefully created by his opponents. The police, following US custom, would invite the media whenever he was arrested so that on his death the photographs and reports concluded a story they had already set up. 'I'm not sick,' Bruce would say. 'The world is sick and I'm the doctor.'[6] He never saw himself as a saint, but he was canonised as a martyr by the likes of Bob Dylan, Jim Morrison and John Lennon. As an icon, he inspired subsequent generations of iconoclastic comedians.

DEMOCRACY

Within the democratic tradition, the workings of censorship outside explicit legislation and times of war are very complex. Mostly, there is a high degree of self-censorship – a phenomenon for which theatre activist Augusto Boal has coined the term 'cop in the head', in which the ideological landscape is seen as a multifaceted apparatus of discriminations and repressions that needs to be confronted by the individual. This area is necessarily much harder to analyse than that of physical compulsion and is, therefore, less visible (though no less important) in the political domain.

In the combination of consensus and coercion that typifies democracies, the political process itself can still generate a resort to physical clashes. During national elections in India in 1989, for example, thugs connected to the ruling party attacked a performance given in support of the local Communist Party of India (Marxist) candidate by Janam ('new birth') people's theatre in Jhandapur, just outside Delhi. The play, *Halla Bol* ('Attack'), dealt with, among other things, the right to perform in the face of oppression. A political worker, Ram Bahadur, and Safdar Hashmi, one of the group's founders, were killed. Hashmi was bludgeoned to death with iron rods as he tried to help others escape. In Jamaica, the left-wing Prime Minister asked Bob Marley and the Wailers in 1976 to perform at a 'Smile Jamaica' festival; they agreed, and later Manley called a general election, thereby politicising the concert. The group received death threats and gunmen attacked them at Marley's home.[7] Although shot, Marley survived, as did the others. Two days later, he performed at the festival without being able to play the guitar, and he spent the next eighteen months abroad.

In Britain, the history of political and social activism among performers in many disciplines – both amateur and professional, individually and collectively – has involved physical confrontations at certain moments yet not often with the state, although some of the causes to which performers were linked, such as female emancipation at the beginning of the twentieth century, proved to be exceptions. (The UK did much of its fighting abroad during its imperial period.)

In the 1930s, the state did take an interest in the 'red' culture that came under the hegemony of the Communist Party, and MI5 kept cultural groups and individual activists under surveillance. Police would clear agitprop performances off the streets – for example, sketches by the Salford Red Megaphones in support of a Lancashire weavers' strike in 1932 – and in 1938, in response to Unity Theatre's satirical pantomime *Babes in the Wood*, which lampooned the Prime Minister and attacked the Munich appeasement of Hitler, questions were asked in the House of Commons (to no avail) about the possibility of forcing the theatre to shut. After the war, Unity was fined for a minor breach of its membership rules in another attempt to close it, but the ploy backfired when the campaign to raise the fine gained Unity more money than required and increased its levels of support. Two Unity members were moved from their jobs in the Ministry of Supply because of their association with the theatre, and other Unity members found travel to the US blocked. Bill Rowbotham, a central figure at Unity who was known in the acting profession as Bill Owen, said he needed the intervention of Katharine Hepburn to gain entry to the US in 1950 to act alongside her on Broadway as Touchstone in *As You Like It*. There was even a 'red' scare in the actors' union Equity, which led to three leading lights, Peggy Ashcroft and two former union presidents, Beatrix Lehmann and Lewis Casson, being removed from the executive council in 1949. In the 1970s, during a wave of widespread radicalism, some actors like Corin Redgrave suffered professionally because of their political activities.

While people in community theatre and interventionist, political theatre often have had to negotiate with authorities in order to receive grants or to perform in certain spaces, only rarely have their personnel faced serious risk. (Warfare in Northern Ireland inevitably affected performers there, regardless of persuasion.) While a group like Portable Theatre did have trouble finding venues for a show about Ireland, Gay Sweatshop faced the additional problem of physical attacks. Generally, those British political companies such as Belt and Braces that sought to present themselves as popular entertainment were greeted by nothing less hostile than indifference or barracking, unlike Dario Fo, the Italian writer/performer and one of their major inspirations. He and Franca Rame, his wife, who challenged the establishment in various guises, whether the Communist Party, the Italian government or the Pope, suffered censorship, beatings, harassment and detention. They were denied entry to the US for several years long before Fo won the Nobel Prize for literature in 1997.

Until 1968, political theatre, as with all theatre in Britain, was subject to pre-performance text censorship. This did afford immunity from prosecution to managers who gained a licence, although transgressive ad-libbing occasionally led to punishment. In 1966, the loophole by which unlicensed plays could be performed in club conditions was closed when the Royal Court was convicted for performances of Edward Bond's *Saved*. The repeal of the Lord Chamberlain's censorship powers, however, did not remove theatre from obligations regarding incitement to racial hatred, the presentation of obscenity or provoking breaches of the peace. In 1981, a simulated homosexual rape in Howard Brenton's *The Romans in Britain* was the subject of a private prosecution for procurement, which was withdrawn mid-trial.

In the post-9/11 world, the government proposed legislation on religious hatred and the glorification of terrorism that, while not aimed at performance, could be used to restrict it. Such moves, and the examples of religious and moral pressure cited earlier, show that, despite the absence of overt state censorship, other strategies to control dissident performance have not disappeared. *The Times* even launched a brief but bullish campaign in 2004 against David Hare's touring play *The Permanent Way* about botched rail privatisation. The media, along with pressure groups, can play a role in censorship by also seeking to influence the distribution of private and state funding. The monetarist reliance on private support increases self-censorship because potential applicants will try to avoid offending commercial sponsors or powerful interest groups, while the state sector is vulnerable to economic and political inconsistency and can require artists to meet non-artistic criteria in order to qualify for subvention. The restriction of public funds in the 1980s and '90s, which saw the demise of activist groups like 7:84 England and Gay Sweatshop, the decimation of Theatre-in-Education and the continued under-representation of black and Asian theatre, was possibly a tacit acknowledgement that, by being linked to broader social and political movements, these strands were having a cultural and political effect.

POPULAR MUSIC

In contrast, the politics of popular music, which by definition is more closely linked to the lives of its audiences than forms like political theatre, have been less clear cut – but who is to say less effective? Any number of pop songs, from The Who's 'My Generation' to David Bowie's 'Rebel Rebel', are susceptible to political interpretation and may, indeed, have had great influence. Yet, to what extent is content sufficient to qualify as political, or does connection to the audience become decisive as opposed to audience reach? Rock music during the Vietnam War, for example, fed into a loosely defined but palpable counter-cultural movement that crossed from film to photography and fiction to fashion. Performers and their songs, however, have to be seen within the international production system of pop music that neutralises political consequences where it can through the enormous control exerted by recording companies and by radio and television broadcasting. Local reactions like punk were a response to this multinational conformist culture and allowed the possibility of more direct political effects, as had been the case with the folk tradition in a previous era.

With punk, an alternative lifestyle was created that constructed its own identity, as happened among Communists in
the 'red' 1930s, albeit with a very different purpose. The
names of the bands (e.g. The Clash instead of The Heart-
drops), the adopted names of the performers (e.g. Johnny
Rotten), the nature of the acts (from the aggressive lyrics to
activities such as guitar smashing), the venues, the behaviour
and dress of the audience, and the self-produced fanzines all
cohered to comprise a platform for political performance. The
Sex Pistols were banned by the BBC, sacked by their first two
record labels and harassed by the police on grounds of taste.
In the context of the Silver Jubilee celebrations in 1977 their
screaming, sneering anthem 'God Save the Queen' was a
political act, and when they sailed down the River Thames on
jubilee day singing 'Anarchy in the UK' across the water from
the Houses of Parliament, that too was an act of political
performance, but still a commodified one. Yet, with the existence of a strong local punk scene that spread to other music,
and groups like The Sex Pistols, The Clash, The Jam and The
Specials recording important albums within a few years of
each other, it is arguable that a significant political effect was
achieved, although not in the traditional sense.

Jerry Dammers, the leader of The Specials, a band that
comprised black and white musicians, was a leading figure
in the late 1970s umbrella movement Rock Against Racism.
The Specials and other bands were targeted by the resurgent
neo-fascist National Front (NF) and vicious skirmishes ensued at various concerts as a result. The Specials' 'Ghost
Town', released in 1981 against a background of rising unemployment and the destruction of traditional industry, pre-
figured a wave of race-related riots across England that year;
in Southall, west London, local Asian youths confronted
visiting NF 'Oi' skinhead bands and torched the pub they
were using.

By the end of the twentieth century it was no longer hard
to find politically motivated music made in Britain, whether
from Sting, Scritti Politti, Manic Street Preachers, The Flying
Pickets, Marianne Faithfull, Elvis Costello, The Group of Four,
Robert Wyatt, Billy Bragg, Crass, Radiohead or Chumba-
wamba, which engaged with its antecedents by releasing the

self-explanatory album *English Rebel Songs 1381–1914* in 1988. Some even used politics itself as material – MC Daylight's Remix of London Mayor Ken Livingstone's anti-war speech in Hyde Park in 2003 was followed by an album of speeches by left-wing politician Tony Benn set to ambient grooves by producer Charles Bailey.

But this very profusion brought its own problems of political accommodation. Politicians of all hues have taken to courting outspoken musicians to improve their credentials and using pop music to marshal their campaigns. Performers are looking for ways to resist this and other means of incorporation; when Coldplay's album *A Rush of Blood to the Head* was released in 2002, lead singer Chris Martin insisted fair trade was discussed in any interviews with him, and buyers of the album were directed to activist websites. He was, predictably, criticised for 'showboating'.

The internet, which is helping democratise the politics of resistance, has offered an alternative to the conventional music industry. A visit to the online Peace Jukebox affords the listener hours of free anti-war music from hip hop, rock, punk, acoustic and classical music as well as the spoken word. In 2004, the site claimed to reflect the most prolific period in protest song-writing history, and said it had received more than 500 anti-war songs from different kinds of musicians, all available to anyone with access to the net.

AMERICA

The Peace Jukebox was symptomatic of reactions to the post-9/11 wars in Afghanistan and Iraq and their consequences, which triggered a wave of protest performances across art forms. The 2004 US presidential election was a particular magnet for those on both sides of the argument. During the campaign, in an echo of the 1930s when the League of Nations impotently watched fascism take hold in Europe and lead the world to war, singer/songwriter Rickie Lee Jones said it would be a sin not to speak out, and many performers seemed to agree. Michael Moore's agitprop film *Fahrenheit 9/11*, accompanied by an album of music that inspired it, became a political event as a tribune for a wider movement that was anti-war but also concerned at the attempts by corporate America to smother independent expression.

The particular experience of American democracy figures prominently in this book, which is both a tribute to the country's promethean dynamism as well as a recognition of its history of internal contestation and crises, in which different strands of thought have struggled to define and even to appropriate the identity of the nation.

Underlying the political crises in the lives of Paul Robeson, Isadora Duncan and Charlie Chaplin, for example, was a central ideological battle around Communism that lasted for nearly three-quarters of the twentieth century. As well as reflecting the more obvious differences in economic beliefs, anti-Communism in the US was a fundamental defence of a distinctly American way of doing things and an expression of fear of the outsider, which can be found in different forms in most societies. It reached a pitch of paranoia in the 1950s, known by the shorthand of McCarthyism, but it was alive from the moment the Bolsheviks gained power, and it led immediately to attacks on left-wing radicalism in general, regardless of actual affiliation.

As far as performers were concerned, the focus of this attack was the House Committee on Un-American Activities (HUAC), which was separate from, although related to and reinforcing, the work of Senator Joseph McCarthy and his associates on various state and federal committees. HUAC instigated 'witch-hunts', as did the Senate Permanent Sub-committee on Investigations, which McCarthy chaired; both organisations, in the drama of their trial settings as well as in the way their publicity was organised, represented a type of theatricalised politics. The HUAC proceedings were themselves dramatised by Eric Bentley under the title of its infamous question concerning Communist Party affiliation, *Are You Now Or Have You Ever Been?*

From its origins, a social and political element can be found in American theatre, whether promoting the revolutionary democratic values of the new country or, in the nineteenth century, arguing against slavery. The notion of theatre as an active political weapon, however, came most sharply alive, as it did elsewhere, following the establishment of the Soviet

Union, and, by the 1930s, America had a raft of left-wing theatre groups, amateur and professional (for instance, the League of Workers' Theatre, New Theatre League, Theatre Union, Labor Stage, the Group Theatre). There was also a strong political dance movement, involved in mass dance and pageants (to be found, for example, in the Workers Dance League, New Dance Group, Theatre Union Dance Group, the Modern Negro Dance Group, the New Duncan Dancers). Such vibrant activity made for an extraordinary decade of cultural commitment and creativity.

Both strands came together in 1935 in the Federal Theatre Project, part of the government's New Deal response to the ravages of the Depression. The Project did not survive the decade. It folded for several reasons, including financial cutbacks and its own inefficiency, but the end was hastened when HUAC's predecessor, the House Special Committee on Un-American Activities, set up in 1938 as much in response to American fascist activity as Communist, immediately attacked it. Newspaper coverage of the attacks spread the idea that the Project harboured a nest of 'reds'. The committee's report in fact carried only one paragraph on the Project, in which it stated that many of its employees, performers included, were members of or sympathetic to the Communist Party. In the atmosphere of the time, that was enough to kill the Project.

Potential 'trouble-makers' continued to be closely monitored, for example those in the folk movement like Woody Guthrie and Pete Seeger; in 1940 Conlon Nancarrow, a pianist, jazz trumpeter and composer, was exiled for having fought against Franco during the Spanish Civil War. The major showdown, however, was to come in 'tinsel town'.

The onset of the Depression had coincided with the introduction of sound to films and the consequent influx to Hollywood of those with the necessary new skills, particularly writers. Many were refugees, or children of refugees, from pogroms in Europe, their ranks swelled in the 1930s by escapees from Nazi Germany. They came from a European Jewish background that was animated by political and cultural ideas, and this provided a dynamo for the local Communist Party. Many members and their friends looked favourably to the Soviet Union, which was not to them a foreign land in the grip of an alien ideology. Its social activism, vision of a better world and constitutional commitment to equality attracted them, particularly during the Popular Front years when Communists engaged in broad campaigns and found favour through their fight against fascism. America itself was still seen as an idealistic country of youthful energy, which the left sought to harness in patriotic spirit to improve the democratic dispensation.

In the 1940s, Hollywood was riven by a series of fierce strikes; in 1945 a critical one began. The moguls, who dominated the film industry, saw it as a 'red' attempt to seize control of the studios. Although Communist influence in the content of films was overstated and amounted to little more than treating equally and as equally interesting all people regardless of class or race, there was reason for the bosses to be anxious. Party membership in California was estimated to be around 10,000, second only to that of New York.

The moguls were suffering economically at the hands of competition from television and believed defeating the strike was essential if the 'dream factory' were to survive as the profitable powerhouse it had been before the war. They won after imposing a lockout, in which they used the mafia and gained the support of a large section of the Screen Actors' Guild, led by Ronald Reagan. Many actors broke the strike – Clark Gable, Esther Williams, Greer Garson and Mickey Rooney among them.

Divisions among actors were accentuated when HUAC swung into action behind the studios to investigate Communist Party membership in the Screen Writers Guild and the incorporation of subversive or pro-Soviet propaganda in films. The studios had always operated their own internal, private blacklist, related to personal whim, sexual behaviour and race. Now, after previous attempts by other anti-Communist investigators had failed to make any impact, HUAC became the focal point of several anti-union and anti-Communist initiatives – governmental, voluntary and ideological – and it helped institutionalise the practice of blacklisting.

HUAC moved on Hollywood in 1947, the year Congress passed the Taft-Hartley Act (overruling President Truman's veto), which ended the closed shop, forbade unions to contribute funds to political campaigns and required union leaderships to affirm they did not support Communism. Ironically, HUAC's assault was aided by a change in the Party's approach, prompted by Moscow, which saw the CP abandon its broad front policies in the name of a return to Marxism-Leninism. This conjunction of state repression and ideological narrowing isolated the American Party, which remained one of the most ferociously loyal to its Soviet counterpart.

In 1947, HUAC drew up in closed session lists of those the committee wished to interview. Of the forty-one named, twenty-two were deemed 'friendly', and they came first; they included the actors Gary Cooper, Adolphe Menjou, Robert Montgomery, George Murphy, Ronald Reagan and Robert Taylor. Nineteen were classified as 'unfriendly', having declared they would not cooperate. Of the nineteen, most were writers but there was one actor, Larry Parks, who was the best known of the group, having starred in the film *The Jolson Story*. Eventually, only eleven were called, including Bertolt Brecht, who left the country immediately after his appearance. Congress cited the remaining ten for contempt. Two days later fifty senior studio executives inaugurated a secret blacklist by agreeing to ban the ten, who received prison sentences of up to one year. The studios, however, denied the existence of the blacklist.

NAMING NAMES

HUAC was able to resume its 'red hunting' in 1951 after the case of the Hollywood Ten, as they became known, had worked its way through the courts. By this time, events both abroad (for instance, the Soviet blockade of Berlin and the Korean War) and at home (such as the outbreak of spy mania in the Alger Hiss, Klaus Fuchs and Rosenbergs cases) had helped create an even more rabid atmosphere in which the likes of Senator McCarthy and HUAC could flourish.

Fuelling this aggressive mood was the publication in 1950 of *Red Channels*, which listed the names of 151 writers, directors and performers alleged by the authors (a former FBI agent and a right-wing television producer) to have been members of subversive organisations who had not yet been banned. All were blacklisted until and unless they appeared before HUAC and informed. Even if they did 'name names', however, they were not guaranteed absolution, as was seen when its first witness – Larry Parks – also became HUAC's first 'informer' but to no advantage. He offered the committee the names of other former members of the Communist Party yet he was still blacklisted. Later, he asked to appear before HUAC again, in an attempt to get back into films, but the boycott of Parks continued.

Bans were applied regardless of actual party membership or association and could be triggered not only by involvement with HUAC but by appearing before other committees, like the Senate Internal Security Sub-committee, or by being named by organisations like the American Legion, which organised pickets of theatres and cinemas and lobbied TV companies and their sponsors. Many 'blacklistees' were condemned to a form of internal exile, especially if their passports were revoked or denied; some went to Mexico, which did not require a US passport. Others, who retained their passports, went further abroad, to Europe.

Nearly 400 people were blacklisted, not just in film but in TV, radio and other branches of entertainment. About one-fifth of those summoned and a quarter of those who were blacklisted were actors, among them: Morris Carnovsky, Jeff Corey, Howard da Silva, Will Geer, Marsha Hunt, Kim Hunter, Sam Jaffe, Burgess Meredith, Zero Mostel, Jean Muir, John Randolph, Edward G. Robinson and Lionel Stander as well as Paul Robeson. The singers Pete Seeger and Josh White, tap dancer Paul Draper and radio personality John Henry Faulk were also blacklisted. Harmonica player Larry Adler refused to appear and moved to England. Phil Brown and Sam Wanamaker, along with other actors in addition to Charlie Chaplin, were forced into exile. The activities of HUAC are also said to have hastened the death of several actors, including J. Edward Bromberg, Mady Christians, John Garfield, Canada Lee and Philip Loeb.

As well as Larry Parks, among the actors who informed were Lloyd Bridges, Abe Burrows, Lee J. Cobb and Sterling Hayden. Singer Burl Ives and bandleader Artie Shaw joined them.

Hollywood performers, like the profession and to some extent the wider society, were polarised as the blacklist mushroomed along with the number who 'named names'. As in a civil war, families were rent apart in what became a tribal battle involving deeply personal struggles with individual moral conscience. Actors' Equity was opposed to blacklisting but did nothing to protect its members whom it considered had endangered their own careers. The Screen Actors' Guild passed an anti-blacklist resolution, while at the same time barring from membership Communists and 'unfriendly' witnesses. To vote the 'wrong' way in the union could cost employment.

The era spawned many groups allied to one side or the other, though the anti-red camp was more numerous, attracting those who could make a buck out of blacklisting alongside those who joined the fray for ideological reasons. Such was the Motion Picture Alliance for the Preservation of American Ideals, which gave John Wayne an off-screen platform for his machismo persona. In the other camp, following the Hollywood Ten citation, a group of leading actors like Humphrey Bogart and Lauren Bacall supported the ad hoc Committee for the First Amendment. It disintegrated after the 'unfriendly' witnesses attacked HUAC and the press smeared the First Amendment committee as pro-Communist. The studios weighed in and told the stars their public stand was incompatible with continued employment. The cogs of the cultural production system – the agents, managers, producers, PR and marketing people – all played their part in the hegemony of oppression.

The aim of HUAC and its satellite supporters was to exert control over the dominant mass medium of cinema, which was the central production unit of celebrity and American identity. HUAC earned populist appeal in demonstrating that it was more powerful than film stars, whom it could subjugate and if need be destroy. It derived potency from its rituals, from the publicity it generated (often by the very stars it wished to humiliate) and, in contrast to the public aspect of its deliberations, from the secretive and undefined nature of the blacklist itself. It tapped into and fed racist currents, both anti-black and anti-Semitic. It undermined feelings of trust and toleration and closed down space for debate both in private and in public.

The end of the blacklist was signalled in 1960 by the writing credit on *Spartacus* for Dalton Trumbo, one of the Hollywood Ten. Later, the blacklist itself was treated on screen – in a documentary, *Point of Order* (1964), and feature films such as *The Way We Were* (1973), *The Front* (1976), written, directed, produced and featuring blacklistees, *Guilty by Suspicion* (1991) and *The Majestic* (2001).[8]

Attacks on liberal actors did not cease, however: Robert Redford, Jack Lemmon and Gregory Peck were criticised for participation in film festivals held in Cuba. Ed Asner, president of the Screen Actors' Guild and a supporter of medical aid to left-wing rebels in El Salvador, had his *Lou Grant* television show cancelled after an active protest campaign by right-wing groups. State harassment of screen performers had not been completely eradicated, either. Jean Seberg, who played Joan in Otto Preminger's *Saint Joan* (1957) and came to international prominence in Jean-Luc Godard's *À bout de souffle* (1960), supported the Black Panthers, a group targeted by the FBI at the time as the greatest internal threat to the US. In 1970 when she became pregnant, the FBI used a gossip columnist to spread the story that the father was a Panther, Ray Hewitt, and not her husband, the French writer and diplomat Romain Gary. She took an overdose but survived; the baby was born prematurely and died two days later. At the funeral, she opened the coffin to prove that the baby was white. Several suicide attempts later, she eventually succeeded in 1979.

Across the cultural field in the 1960s, however, there was a gradual recovery from McCarthyism, as politics were revivified and theatricalised, particularly during the Vietnam War with the activism of students, the women's movement and black liberation. State surveillance agencies still saw Communists at every turn and harassed solo performers like satirists Lenny Bruce and Dick Gregory as well as groups like the communal Living Theatre, which was closed down in 1963 for tax infringements and went into exile abroad before eventually returning in 1984.

Protest singers were a particular target. The FBI and other arms of the intelligence community kept records on many of them. Joan Baez had to sue the National Security Agency for access to her file. Phil Ochs was harassed even when he had become deeply sceptical of the prospects for any meaningful political change; he committed suicide in 1976.

The major celebrity of this period to be the subject of a surveillance and wiretapping campaign was John Lennon. The trigger was President Nixon's fear of the effect Lennon might have on his re-election in 1972. Lennon was planning a national anti-Nixon tour, culminating in a massive protest concert to coincide with Nixon's reaffirmation at the Republican convention. Nixon wanted him deported; Lennon's visa was withdrawn and, although he won an exhausting three-year legal battle, the deportation dispute had the desired effect of neutralising him politically.

With the demise of the Soviet Union, the internal threat to America was reappraised, and, following the bombing of the Twin Towers in 2001, the 'reds' ceased to be a major threat.

RACISM

If 'reds' had represented a threat linked to the 'other' without, 'blacks' represented a threat linked to the 'other' within. Both were perceived to subvert the American way of life – Communists because of their ungodly beliefs and economic system, and, at an atavistic level, African Americans, because, although they often conformed in every other way to the demands of the myth, they were not white and, therefore, were deemed inferior. While the categorisation of both was presented as self-evident, the instability that lay behind the definitions was constantly revealed in the struggles against them.

As is the case in white European history, racism is endemic to white American history. From Columbus through the settlers and on, its volatility is fuelled by the fact that the whites were emigrants themselves. Myths that embody the American identity are built on this racism; black, after all, is the colour of Christian sin. It is not just black people who are affected; they, however, crystallise the anxiety of the dominant white group by being both the most obvious personification of the 'other' and the greatest potential disruption of that notion.

The attacks on Paul Robeson, who was both 'red' and 'black', were nothing new or exceptional, save in scope and intensity. All African American performers suffered discrimination, and wealth or fame made no difference, apart from partially mitigating the effects. Survival was paramount but resistance was profuse. Defiance did not automatically radicalise, but the effects of achievement, an important index in the aspiration of any marginal group, carried meanings not always easily susceptible to conventional political analysis. Art, or any self-expression, by such a group is in one way or another a statement about its condition, however circumscribed by the economic and ideological grip of those in power. It can, therefore, always be interpreted politically. For African Americans, aspiration through self-expression was especially associated with performance, most notably in sport and entertainment.

In the entertainment world, the few employment opportunities that were available channelled non-white performers into stereotypical roles. In 1910 comedian Bert Williams became the first black performer to appear – against much protest and threats of violence – in Florenz Ziegfeld's popular revue *The Follies*. Yet he was the highest paid entertainer of his day. Being light-skinned, he 'blacked up' so that he could play the Jim Crow 'coon' – possibly a pre-Brechtian example of the 'alienation' effect, which allowed Williams to comment on the very stereotype he was obliged to enact. The pioneering African American educator Booker T. Washington said Williams had achieved more for his race than he had, a judgement about the balance between co-option, resistance and rebellion that all performers from outside the governing group have had – and continue – to face.

It was applied to Robeson and others during the attempts of the Harlem Renaissance in the 1920s to assert an independent African American image within a white-dominated culture. The Harlem Renaissance, also sometimes known as the New Negro Movement, aroused interest in black musicals and supported a number of theatre groups that performed plays by black writers, including an all-black ensemble, the Lafayette Players, from which, among others, the black actor Charles Gilpin emerged. In the 1930s, the Federal Theatre Project dealt with issues relevant to black people and employed black performers in Negro Theatre units across the country. Its Chicago dance unit was for a time led by the pioneering dancer and choreographer Katherine Dunham, who introduced a distinctive vocabulary of African American and African Caribbean movement into contemporary dance. An active campaigner against segregation and for civil rights, in 1951 she premiered *Southland*, a ballet depicting the lynching of a black man falsely accused of raping a white woman. After the première in Santiago, Chile there were no reviews because the performance had offended the US embassy, and Dunham was forced to drop the ballet from her programme. It had one more revival, in Paris in 1953, against official US wishes. She found her subsequent appeals for state support were not heeded, and some commentators have traced the eventual disbandment of her company in 1960 to her stand over *Southland*.

Prejudice was as clearly rife across the 'high' arts as in commercial entertainment. Black soprano Dorothy Maynor was denied access to the main US opera theatres and was forced to limit her career to concerts and recordings. Before becoming a well-known blues singer, Odetta had to give up an opera career because of racism. It was not until 1951 that Janet Collins, who had danced with Dunham's troupe, became the first black performer allowed on to the stage of the New York Metropolitan Opera House. It took four more years before a black singer, Marian Anderson, appeared.

Anderson, who had tried to enrol in a small Philadelphia music school but had been denied entry because of her skin colour, had established her career in Europe before she achieved success in the US. In 1939 she became, involuntarily, a prominent emblem of the reality of racism in the US. Anderson had to change venues for an Easter concert in Washington DC, but the Daughters of the Revolution (DoR), who owned the new venue, the best in the city, vetoed her. Eleanor Roosevelt, who was married to the President, resigned from the DoR and obtained a permit for Anderson to sing at the Lincoln Memorial. The audience for the open-air concert numbered around 75,000, both black and white, and it was broadcast across America. Although a reluctant heroine, Anderson emphasised the importance of performance, of the contact between performer and audience, in the resistance of her people.

The situation was particularly hard for female performers. In addition to the sexism they faced from men of whatever colour, their potential transgressions of both race and gender unnerved those who controlled American culture and the promotion of the American myths.

Dancer Josephine Baker, one of the first international black female celebrities, found refuge in Europe like many black artists when she left the US in 1925 to join *La Revue Nègre* in Paris. There she became – and remained – 'whitecast' as a highly sexualised, exotic fantasy, although in her own life she broke free from this image when she chose to. Baker was not generally accepted in the US, either on her return in the mid-1930s to star in *The Ziegfeld Follies* or after the war when she used her fame to affirm civil rights. During the war she worked for the French Resistance, and she continued to be an activist, participating in the huge 'freedom' march in 1963 – the 100th anniversary of the Emancipation Proclamation that abolished slavery in the US – when Martin Luther King Jr delivered his 'I Have a Dream' speech.

Also on that march was Lena Horne, who became politicised by the racism she encountered in the 1930s when she began a career first as a dancer then a singer and actress. She renewed her acquaintance with Paul Robeson, whom she had known as a child, and became committed to civil rights and anti-racist activity. By the mid-1940s she was one of – if not *the* – highest paid black entertainer in the US yet, despite a seven-year deal with MGM, unprecedented for a black actress, the studio did not offer her suitable roles. Her light skin confused and exposed the superficiality of colour prejudice; she was deemed too light to appear with black male stars and too dark to appear with white ones. For her part, in seeking to avoid the traps that many black performers, including Robeson, had fallen into, she turned down roles that degraded her as a black woman. In the early 1950s she was refused employment because of her political activism.

Dorothy Dandridge challenged the racism of the entertainment industry to become only the second black performer to be nominated for an Oscar (in the Best Actress category, for her role in *Carmen Jones* – she lost to Grace Kelly). Despite her achievements, the Hollywood system – as with Lena

Horne, and before her, Ethel Waters – did not know how to use her talents, and with her fame came increasing isolation from her own community. She died in 1965 of an overdose of anti-depressants. The first Oscar nomination of an African-American performer had been even more controversial; it went to Hattie McDaniel in 1939 for Best Supporting Actress in her role as Mammy in *Gone With the Wind*, a film whose première in Atlanta she and the other black actors in the film were not allowed to attend. The film was unpopular among many in the black community because of its inherent racism, made worse by the fact that McDaniel went on to win the Oscar.

Where success has come, some performers, like Ossie Davis, Ruby Dee, Danny Glover or Harry Belafonte, for instance, have used and risked that success to campaign for a better and just world. But, as happened to Robeson, success in the entertainment world has also brought problems as well as praise for black performers. Sidney Poitier, the first African American actor to win an Oscar for Best Actor (in 1963 for *Lilies of the Field*), was celebrated by some black figures for portraying sympathetic characters but attacked by others for portraying middle-class Uncle Toms. Poitier replied that he was the only black actor who worked with any degree of regularity. When there were more, he said, 'then one of us can play villains all the time.'[9] It took a few decades before this situation of choice for black actors arrived in film.

MUSIC

African American performers have been present in larger numbers in the music industry and for longer, but the exploitation has been even more widespread. Black music, referred to as 'race' music before the 1950s, confirmed the fears of whites and offended their sense of sexual and moral propriety. Live performance was segregated, and black performers were denied both opportunity and their due rewards, usually through surrender or theft of copyright. In the 1950s, when white music was revolutionised by rock 'n' roll derived from black rhythm 'n' blues, black performers were still being barred from recording studios and the most remunerative work. The situation changed in the subsequent years with the extraordinary growth in the commercial success of black music and the expansion of black ownership and power within the industry.

In spite of racism, black musicians found ways of fighting back, as Robeson had tried to do. Before World War II, overt politics was the exception, even in the folk repertoire of Leadbelly, who was 'discovered' in prison by folklorist John Lomax in the early 1930s. Like the blues music of Gertrude 'Ma' Rainey and Bessie Smith, politics, however, infuses the songs because they reflect the lives of black working-class communities and deal with the everyday issues confronting them. Rainey and Smith were strong, independent women who expressed defiance in their performances, itself a political act.

Billie Holiday also sang her politics in her performances. Mostly her repertoire dealt with the theme of love but in 1939 she sang the anti-lynching song 'Strange Fruit' at the Café Society in New York's Greenwich Village, which, possibly uniquely in the US at the time, was an integrated nightclub. For the song, special performance conditions were introduced: all activity by waiters and cashiers was stopped, the lights were turned low and a spot picked her out. Columbia, Holiday's record company, refused to release the song and instead she went to an independent label, Commodore. Written by a white Communist high school teacher, Abel Meeropol, under the name Lewis Allen, the song thereafter became associated with Holiday and her haunting tone. She believed it brought her the later harassment she suffered from the authorities when her rampant drug consumption offered them a different line of attack.

Black music, which took a new turn in the 1940s and broke from the entertainment industry with the creation of bebop, became the musical backdrop to the post-war anti-racist and civil rights struggles. 'Now's the Time' (1945) by pioneering saxophonist Charlie Parker was a call for change, and in 1952 he gave what later was dubbed a legendary concert at Rockland Palace ballroom as a benefit for jailed Harlem councillor Ben Davis Jr, reportedly the last Communist Party member to be elected to office in the US. Bass player and composer Charles Mingus, who in 1950 was dropped from a trio as its only black member to ensure the group appeared on TV, two years later recorded the fiercely intense 'Haitian Fight Song', the performing of which, he said, was inspired by the injustice of racism. In 1959 he recorded his 'Fables of Faubus' – Orval Faubus being the Arkansas governor who used the National Guard at Little Rock Central High School in 1957 to resist federal moves to desegregate.

Many jazz performers, including Miles Davis, John Coltrane and Archie Shepp, openly expressed political views and actively opposed racism. Some also marked the anti-colonial struggle, honouring their African roots and linking the domestic struggle with the liberation struggles abroad. One of the earliest examples was Sonny Rollins' 'Airegin' (Nigeria backwards), a 1954 tribute to the newly autonomous federation, followed by Coltrane's 'Dakar' (1957), 'Black Pearl' (1958), 'Dahomey Dance' and 'Africa' (1961), and Max Roach's 'All Africa' and 'Tears for Johannesburg' (1960).

There was an expectation among activists that celebrity black performers would lend their support to civil rights campaigns. Louis Armstrong, who had made famous the 1929 song '(What did I do to be so) Black and Blue' featuring the refrain 'My only sin . . . is in my skin', refused the many appeals made to him but, in 1957, he was so incensed by the state-initiated violence at Little Rock that he publicly condemned it and attacked the government. By way of protest, he cancelled a State Department-sponsored tour of the Soviet Union. Black jazz musicians like Armstrong and Dizzie Gillespie were sponsored abroad as the epitome of individual freedom in America, while the Soviet Union welcomed such tours because it believed the US was vulnerable on racism at home.

Music was central to the civil rights movement, as it gained fresh momentum in the post-McCarthyite era under the leadership of Martin Luther King Jr, himself an accomplished performer as a preacher influenced by the rhythms of black music. Alongside new songs, songs were adapted from spirituals, gospel, rhythm 'n' blues and other forms to suit the needs of the movement, which ran its own choirs and song groups and published books of protest songs in the same way that the Communist movement had done in the 1930s. At the iconic 'freedom' march on Washington in 1963, Odetta, Marian Anderson and Mahalia Jackson performed along with Joan Baez and Bob Dylan in a 'rainbow coalition' of protest.

Duke Ellington, who openly identified with the US establishment, refused to join the march, but he did financially support the civil rights movement. Ellington was used to fighting segregation his own way; when on tour he hired his own train with dining and sleeping cars, thus sidestepping likely refusal at a hotel or restaurant. He expressed his politics and pride through his music, but he did perform at several Communist Party events in the 1930s and '40s and played for causes such as the defence of the Scottsboro Boys (eight young black men falsely convicted of raping a white woman and sentenced to death). The year of the Washington march Ellington composed the oratorio *My People*, which builds on and incorporates part of his 1943 composition, *Black, Brown and Beige*. He added two new pieces, 'What Colour is Virtue?' and 'King Fit the Battle of Alabam', commemorating a civil rights protest in Birmingham, Alabama, led by Dr King, who was arrested along with two other reverends.

In September 1963, white vigilantes planted dynamite in a Baptist church in Birmingham attended by black worshippers and killed four girls. The perpetrators were protected by local police. This outrage became the subject of Coltrane's song 'Alabama' and, along with the murder earlier that year of civil rights worker Medgar Evers, stimulated Nina Simone to write 'Mississippi Goddam'. A South Carolina radio station destroyed the promotional copy of Simone's record and, when it was released, returned the whole batch with each record snapped in two. Simone, who went on to perform such political songs as 'Four Women' (1966) and 'To Be Young, Gifted and Black' (1970), was strongly associated with the civil rights movement and, echoing Robeson, said: 'I stopped singing love songs and started singing protest songs because protest songs were needed. You can be a complete politician through music.'[10]

A new stage of the civil rights movement arrived in the mid-1960s with the passing of legislation, such as the Civil Rights Act (1964) and the Voting Rights Act (1965), and the growing political purchase of Malcolm X and radical black consciousness in reaction to lack of change at the level of people's lives. Many performers, like Sam Cooke and Curtis Mayfield, recorded songs that reflected the new mood of self-assertion.

This mood was intensified by the assassinations of Malcolm X in 1965 and in 1968 of Dr King and Robert Kennedy, a civil rights supporter and Democratic Presidential candidate. That year saw more rioting across urban America. A month after King's murder, Aretha Franklin released 'Think' with its insistent call for freedom, and three months later James Brown recorded 'Say It Loud, I'm Black and I'm Proud'. In Britain, Diana Ross and the Supremes, who, it was reported, required considerable persuasion to appear at the 1968 Royal Command Performance because it included a black and white minstrel show, interrupted the final song, 'Somewhere (There's a Place for Us)', to appeal for racial harmony and claim a place for 'us'. Jimi Hendrix at the 1969 Woodstock festival played his coruscating version of 'The Star-Spangled Banner', a visceral performance that was regarded as both a protest at the Vietnam War and an endorsement of black power. Hendrix, however, refused to confirm what his intention had been.

Outside America, black American music became symbolic of resistance to oppression. The peace movement in the west adopted civil rights songs, as did the nationalist cause in Northern Ireland. Popular music, rooted in black experience and transformed by white musicians, expressed counter-cultural aspirations on a scale that theatre and dance could not. It helped western youth learn to feel, and this fuelled the social changes precipitated by the political and cultural challenges of the 1960s.

But the entertainment industry had also adopted black protest music as a saleable commodity and turned even aggressive protest rap into a lucrative global business. By this time, black music did not have to accommodate its white audiences; it had become the dominant force. The resisters had to find new ways of being effective.

NEW CONTEXT

Post 9/11, the context altered dramatically. Security agencies took a renewed interest in 'gangsta' rap and hip-hop singers, performers like The Dixie Chicks, who criticised President Bush for the 2003 invasion of Iraq, were boycotted in the US and saw their CDs destroyed, and, in the new climate of suspicion, greater restrictions were placed on performers visiting America from abroad. Performers from the Middle East faced increased difficulties in gaining visas, and tours by Beijing Opera, South African anti-apartheid singer Vusi Mahlasela and Spanish guitarist Paco de Lucia were interrupted or stopped. The seventy-six-year old Cuban singer Ibrahim Ferrer was not allowed into the US in 2004 to receive a Grammy award because he was deemed a security risk. Concurrently, self-censorship became more apparent; plans by a New York theatre to stage a British play, *My Name Is Rachel Corrie*, which tells the story of an American activist killed by an Israeli bulldozer in Gaza, were postponed in 2006 because the theatre did not want to be seen to take a stand in a political conflict.[11] In Britain, at the same time, four actors who played al-Qaida suspects in the film *The Road to Guantánamo* were questioned by police under fresh anti-terrorism laws when they returned from the Berlin Film Festival where the film had won a major prize.

The 'war on terror', like all major wars, changed a way of life and posed serious threats to established rights, such as academic independence and freedom of expression, but unlike other recent wars it held little hope or prospect of an expected resolution. It shows that prohibition comes in many different guises and underlines the need for constant vigilance. Contexts and systems of rule will change, and societies will continue to debate the balance of rights and responsibilities, weighing majority against minority opinion and deciding when censorship is a legitimate form of protection and when an abuse. In that process, rebel performers will continue to feature prominently, giving voice to curiosity, conscience and, where necessary, provocation and dissent.

NOTES

1. From 'Open your window' ('Abre tu ventana'), a song by Victor Jara quoted in Joan Jara, *Victor: An Unfinished Song*, London, Jonathan Cape, 1983, p. 158.

2. Orwell quoted in the *Guardian*, 21 June 2003. A broadly based campaign forced the government to intervene over the People's Convention ban, which was lifted when Churchill was persuaded it would damage the BBC's standing. This brief ban may have cost Redgrave little in terms of lost employment but, according to his son Corin, 'damage of a subtle kind was done , and was far harder to undo' (*Michael Redgrave, My Father*, London, Fourth Estate, 1996, p. 73) and it cast a shadow over his life (*Guardian*, 28 June 2003).

3. Quoted by Agence France-Presse, 8 July 2004, from Elisabeth Schwarzkopf with André Tubeuf, *Les Autres Soirs* ('The Other Nights'), Paris, Éditions Tallandier, 2004.

4. The term Kristallnacht has passed into general usage, although it is a Nazi label that masks the scope, brutality and intensity of this unique pogrom.

5. Mendel Kohansky, in *The Disreputable Profession: The Actor in Society*, Westport, Connecticut and London, Greenwood Press, 1984, p. 9, quotes French sociologist of theatre Jean Duvignaud as saying religions based on transcendence, like Islam, Catholicism, Protestantism and Jansenism, are particularly hostile to performance because they see it as competition.

6. Quoted by Peter Keepnews in 'There Was Thought in His Rage', *New York Times*, 8 August 1999.

7. Wailers lead guitarist Al Anderson dissents from the general view and does not believe the attack was politically motivated, according to an interview on www.bobmarley.com.

8. *The Front* was written by the blacklisted Walter Bernstein, produced and directed by the blacklisted Martin Ritt, and featured the blacklisted actors Herschel Bernardi, Lloyd Gough, Zero Mostel, John Randolph and Joshua Shelley.

9. Quoted by Philip French in the *Observer*, 8 October 2000. In his memoir, *The Measure of a Man*, Poitier deals with attacks on him by black commentators and defends his appearance in criticised films such as *The Defiant Ones* (pp. 103–5).

10. Quoted in the *Sunday Herald*, 27 April 2003. In her autobiography, *I Put a Spell on You*, London, Penguin, 1992, Simone writes about the importance to her of the civil rights movement and how her music is 'dedicated to the fight for freedom and the historic destiny of my people' (p. 91).

11. *My Name Is Rachel Corrie* is edited by Alan Rickman and Katherine Viner from Rachel Corrie's writings, published by Nick Hern Books, 2005.

WHAT IT IS TO BE HUMAN:
ART, POLITICS AND PERFORMANCE

*'There's a contradiction between being involved
in a movement for social change and also being a
movie actress in Hollywood. I am trying to reduce
that contradiction as much as possible'*
Jane Fonda [1]

THE AESTHETIC VERSUS THE POLITICAL

Art and politics have different primary functions; indeed, art
is frequently promoted as the antidote to politics. Furthermore, there is generally a tension between individual artistic
vision, which often involves exploration, questioning and un-
certainty, and programmatic politics, which mostly involves
the opposite.

Nevertheless, they overlap and interact. Despite periodic
attempts to separate the one from the other, their symbiotic
relationship remains robustly insistent and present. History
itself may appear to be absent from certain works of art, and
even from certain periods of art, but sooner or later it comes
knocking, whether as expected guest or uninvited visitor.

During the time of Duncan, Robeson and Chaplin, the relationship between art and politics became a defining preoccu-
pation that supplanted earlier aesthetic obsessions such as the
nature and status of beauty. For much of this period, the art-
politics debate was polarised into 'art for art's sake' versus 'art
as a weapon', a tussle that climaxed in the years between the
world wars when the passionate engagement of the left was
counter-posed to the impersonal detachment of the purport-
edly apolitical aesthetes.

The contest between the aesthetic and the political was the
old argument of form versus content in another guise and
found echoes in other contemporary disputes, such as realism

versus modernism. In one corner, the aesthetic is completely autonomous: there is no subject matter separate from the form, and the medium is the message. In the other corner is found the instrumental view, that content determines everything. On the one hand, art's prime virtue is its ability to transport us out of the 'real' world while on the other its greatest asset is the ability to take us deeper in.

For some, art by definition must exclude politics; otherwise, it is damned as polemic or propaganda (a view frequently promoted by critics who dislike the perceived politics of the art concerned). Such an approach implies a sliding scale: the less the politics, the better the art – despite the fact that apparent neutrality can itself lay art open to the greatest of political manipulation. Yet the vitality of much art is undeniably linked to social compassion or a desire for social change, and often there is a coherent philosophy of the world lying behind it. To condemn and discard all art that imparts a message would be to abandon what has been regarded as art throughout history. A contrary view, as authoritarian and exclusive, judges art against its conformity to and promotion of a particular ideology, and insists art derives its validation directly from society or the 'real' world.

Much of this debate was based on narrow and restrictive notions of art, politics and ideology, which gradually opened up as each became seen as an active process rather than a fixed product. For art, this meant it was no longer merely an object of study separate from the 'real' world. Art *was* the 'real' world – curiously, an echo (in a new context) of a so-called primitive age in which we assume that art, such as 'prehistoric' cave paintings, had not yet become disconnected or privileged. This integrating perspective was reinforced by the revolution in the definition of art symbolised by Marcel Duchamp. He announced at the beginning of the twentieth century that it was the artist who makes art: even a urinal can be art if the artist makes it so. This was both an elitist and simultaneously a profoundly democratic idea because the necessary complement to the artist was the spectator or witness, who was also allowed to decide her or his own interpretation of what was being presented; art became anything that anyone (artist or not) said was art.

Following on from this conclusion was another radical proposition: that those who make art and its meanings – the artists and the audiences – as well as the places in which this occurs are all located in a social structure, and every social structure is an expression, however remote or tenuous, of a place in the hierarchy of power. Art, therefore, is in some way or to some degree inescapably political. If art is politics and art is society, it does not require validation from either, but, equally, it cannot be entirely neutral.

Philosophically, we may decide the artefact is neutral and does not carry inherent value, but the artefact is only contemplated in a social interaction – the very process that defines something as art – and in this interaction it acquires value. What that value is may be hard to discern outside subjective experience because of the variability of individual response, but that does not mean there is no value or that we cannot make useful, albeit provisional, judgements about it. If, however, there is sufficient commonality of response, then perhaps one can argue against the neutrality of the artefact and for the view that the artefact contains the rough equivalent of an artistic genetic code. Whichever way we look at the question, the act of defining something as art carries a social implication, however slight, and that means the act may also be transformed into a political effect, however difficult to identify.

The traditional model for political art in the twentieth century – a model which demanded overt ideological complicity – was an extension of the Enlightenment idea that art *did* have an inherent value. It was predicated on the belief that art was intrinsically civilising and 'good for you', a belief that was shattered by the Nazis. This idea of art saw an obvious connection between intention and effect. Commonly associated with the left, it presupposed an alternative domain, from which political art operated and to which it returned, that lay outside and free from the dominant, oppressive domain. The alternative domain was the embodiment of the relevant political ideology, a utopia of admirable and assured values that could be reached by sticking to the chosen path. When the ideology that supported the alternative domain collapsed, so too did the notion of political art that had arisen from and reinforced it.

POLITICAL REBIRTH

In this context, Bob Dylan becomes iconic. In the early 1960s, he revitalised political song at a critical moment in America, by now the major nation in the West. The Soviet experiment had clearly failed and a post-McCarthy thaw saw the rebirth of mass radical politics but in a new vein. Conventional oppositional activity (marching against nuclear weapons, for instance, or for civil rights) was joined and sometimes replaced by a new militancy (feminist campaigning, occupations supporting the Vietnamese liberation front, community programmes avowing black power). The Duchamp revolution in art had been taken further, in jazz, in happenings, in action painting, in beat poetry, in composition based on chance. All involved forms of performance, and, in their improvisation and fecund creativity, they brought together the influence of two supposedly inferior groups, the 'other' as represented by African Americans and by philosophy from the 'East'. The 'East', for long romanticised as exotic, was the location of the first key post-war defeat of the US, and cultural innovations contributed importantly to that defeat in Vietnam; they were reconfiguring ideas of politics as well as of art.

Dylan was not a political activist but he had a distinct political voice. He sang at rallies and marches and supported campaigns, both locally (voter registration) and on the grand scale (for peace). In terms of albums, his output of what were regarded as protest songs is represented on *The Freewheelin' Bob Dylan* (1963) and *The Times They Are A-Changin'* (1964). Here he draws on blues, folk song and ballad, and is clearly influenced by the likes of Leadbelly, Woody Guthrie and Pete Seeger.

Dylan's identification with the folk protest movement gave him a popular platform but also restricted him. In 1964, he released *Another Side of Bob Dylan*, which, as the title suggests, took him down an altered path. He was reprimanded for becoming inward instead of outward looking, and, despite his denying this shift was a negation of his past, the fact that he was making it just as he was achieving fame as a political singer convinced his critics he was selling out. The counterculture was becoming commercially viable, therefore more potent (because it was reaching a bigger audience) and yet possibly more compromised. Dylan was booed at the Newport Folk Festival for abandoning acoustic guitar and playing rock 'n' roll. Protests dogged his tour around the US and into Britain, where the folk scene, dominated by the Communist Party as a redoubt against the depredations of international capitalism, ensured a hostile reception, including the much-quoted accusation shouted at him from the floor of being 'Judas'.

In his performances and interviews, Dylan made clear he had no desire to act as a spokesman and declared he was not part of any movement. Yet he answered one disgruntled heckler with the reply, 'Oh come on, these are all protest songs.'[2] Indeed, his work retained its political acuity but from a different perspective, removed from politics as a discrete area of activity separate from his songs, to which they referred and from which they derived their potency. The political was to be found within the songs as well as in how he sang them and his choice of instrument. Dylan had moved on from the notions of protest as an expression of ideological purity and of political art delivering *'the'* truth. That route, he believed, led to a dead end both politically and artistically. He also now had claimed the freedom to escape from his fans' and the media's expectations. While some of his later songs do handle conventional political subjects, such as 'Julius and Ethel', a 1983 song about the Rosenbergs, who were executed for spying, most do not but should not be judged as non-political because of that.

Nevertheless, his detachment from a movement and absorption into the music industry circuit opened up questions of the extent to which he was still achieving a political effect, and if this did not matter or could not be assessed, to what extent did this undermine Dylan's new notion of the political? Although his 'protest' output covers only a brief period in an extensive and diverse career, his change of direction in 1964 – or apostasy, to some – still dominates debate about Dylan, who remains decades later, despite the alleged betrayal, the most celebrated of protest singers.

Was Dylan simply challenging the old art-politics relationship, or was he also questioning the associated view of art as beneficial? If art did not of necessity make us better – and, correspondingly, did not harm us – what did it do, and how? What did this mean for its political effect? Art may have made political impact but have had no obvious politics, or it may have appeared to be political because of its subject matter but not carry much political meaning; a play about a political topic like a strike, for example, is not necessarily a political play. Interest moved from political art to the politics of art, and from analysis of content to assessment of the ideological implications of the process and apparatus of production and presentation.[3]

Many artists like Dylan were allusive and elusive, refusing to be tied down as to meaning, as if to do so would result in an unacceptable reduction of their art. Given that forms of McCarthyism had appeared throughout the western democracies, this might have been understandable caution, or it might also have been signalling the shortcomings of the Communist project that had dominated notions of political art for so long.

The interconnected process of the redefinition of art and politics, which Dylan encapsulated, accelerated swiftly in the latter decades of the twentieth century, when the importance of ideas and culture gained new prominence with the rise in material comfort in the West. This was part of the wider process of expanding commodification and globalisation, which involved an increasing emphasis on subjectivity, as modernism gave way to post-modernism and 'high' art notions gave way under political pressure and technological innovations to a more egalitarian view of culture.

IDENTITY

Central to this shift was the changing status of identity, underpinned by major developments in the understanding of what constituted its main determinants, such as class, gender, sexuality and ethnicity, and the roles they play in making us who we become (itself a constant and unfinished process). How we live out 'who we are' was no longer seen as being shaped by a set of fixed givens but by what we do, our quotidian interactions, and in this process the importance was recognised of the relationship between the subjective 'I' and group solidarity or consciousness.

In terms of an activist idea of art and politics as opposed to the passive elitism of 'high' art ideas, such self-awareness places agency at the core. Agency challenges the assumptions of 'high' art, which exclude those 'not in the know' and treat them as the objects, not the subjects, of history. Agency allows marginalised groups (however loose or provisional their boundaries), which define themselves in opposition to an oppressor, competitor or outsider, to generate their own histories and find self-recognition and self-affirmation in art, for example gay drag culture or political murals in Belfast. Such self-assertion goes beyond opposition to the mainstream towards the creation of an autonomous cultural identity.

The old idea of politics as a battle of rival armies, of revolutionary change as a moment of glorious insurrection, was increasingly challenged by alternative ideas of hegemony, of the role of the personal in the political, and of politics as a broader concept of process than previously allowed for. The political vocabulary of left, right, progressive and radical was questioned, as were the apparent verities of political discourse, just as post-modernity challenged conventional notions of art and culture.

The post-modern, nevertheless, retained the aesthetic at its heart. The aesthetic, however, does not exist in a vacuum and it cannot be 'innocent'. It carries multiple and complex encodings, both pre- and post-expressive, drawn from social discourse as well as from artistic practice itself. We may try to experience art on its own terms, but those terms cannot be wholly divorced from the world in which they were created and in which we experience them. The relationship of the process of cultural production to a wider set of social and political activities becomes critical in attempting to analyse the political effects of art or whether it is possible to be politically effective through art at all.

For those who acknowledge a political effect, art can be complicit as well as defiant – or both at the same time. Whilst political art has usually meant 'of the left' or 'progressive', it can, therefore, be 'of the right', too. Art can function within an open or a closed ideological arena, as the examples of Leni Riefenstahl filming for the Nazis or D.W. Griffith's cinematic portrayal of the Ku Klux Klan show.[4] The imagination can produce what we deem to be good as well as evil. Art – even the same art – can play its part in oppression as much as in liberation, and liberators can censor and suppress art as much as oppressors.

Unless we define art very narrowly, its function overwhelmingly is to confirm the values of the dominant culture (and in doing this it may be classified as a form of propaganda or it may be intentionally propagandistic, which is a distinct aim, and just one of the many ways that ideology is expressed). It is exceptional art that is committed and radical, that challenges, transgresses or transforms. Whether or not it is better art is a different question.

If all art is politically implicated, not only does the issue arise of how to distinguish politically between different art but also of how those artists who express a political commitment avoid incorporation and achieve effectiveness. Commerce has been adept at exploiting the possibilities opened up by rebellion. After famously co-opting the image of Che Guevara, business has developed a broad swathe of cause-related marketing, ranging from Fair Trade and economic empowerment of black people to promoting anti-war campaigns. The most lucrative area has been performance-related, in the sales of rebellious music, which, since the counter-cultural days of the Vietnam War, has proved highly profitable.

Has rebellion become a commodity with a market value like everything else, and, far from challenging the system it opposes, is required by that system to fuel its cycle of development? If that were the complete picture, then human agency and a belief in the possibility of change would have been eliminated, unless change is seen as associated with the development of the system instead of being its antithesis. Accommodation may be a part but not necessarily the whole of the process; art may still retain its ability to challenge and defy even if it is also simultaneously reproducing or reinforcing dominant values.

In trying to elaborate a theory that would explain art's subversive quality, the problem of differentiation and incorporation has led to the use of the adjective 'radical' in place of 'political' and an emphasis on exploring the entire apparatus of a particular cultural practice and its place in a broader ideological set-up. Radical, however, is not seen as necessarily being transformative or transgressive, and, therefore, analysis of possible political effect has been further refined to focus on the audience and, as far as performance is concerned, on the transformative potential of the transaction that takes place between performer and spectator. Resistant art in the post-modern sense is seen actively to encourage the audience to author meanings in that transaction but without intending the audience to revert to making simple interpretations associated with the old notion of political art. The focus has become the making and disputation of meaning rather than the meaning itself. The denial of coherence in such art means that control over effect has been loosened and the gap between intention and effect inevitably widened. In such a scenario, it can become very difficult to define what is political.

Within this new emphasis, art becomes a site of many struggles involving all the elements of the process, internal and external to the art, touching on ownership, authorship, distribution and reception. The relative influence of each element and its importance to political intention becomes vital in examining how – and why – certain art at certain times and places is seen not only to reconsider but also to recon-figure the world.

INTENTION

Intention is hugely problematic, however. Like other artists, those who have radical or political aims will have many intentions – to entertain, to educate, to gladden, to sadden, to reflect, to question, to provoke, to oppose. How the political dimension is expressed may not be clear, and even if it is, who is to judge what connections the audience has made? Even if intention can be inscribed in the aesthetic, there is no control over either audiences' interpretations or subsequent reinter-pretations by different artists, both of which are affected by time, place and individual circumstance.

The fact that art can transcend its own ideology – for example, Renaissance art detached from its religious inspir-ation, the music of Wagner no longer bearing his ideological views or the multifarious manifestos applied to Shakespearean production – throws into doubt any concept of an immanent

intention, message or meaning (unless very loosely interpreted). The question of where responsibility might lie in
relation to the original and whether there are any limits to
freedom of interpretation is a different matter altogether.

There are no theories yet that adequately explain how art
works in any, let alone different contexts, particularly in
different eras – why certain plays, for example, fall out of
vogue for decades and even centuries and then become fashionable again. Recourse to the 'universal' as an explanation is
inadequate, as many works that can be said to treat 'universal'
themes clearly lack any purchase in the present day. Ironically,
the materialist's counter view – a direct challenge to the
Enlightenment notion of longevity as a benchmark for artistic
merit – finds common cause between political art that celebrates the moment, for instance an agitprop play, and post-
modernism's embrace of the disposable to undermine art's
supposed victory over mortality. For performance pieces that
are not intended to be repeated beyond their original life, any
political intention or effect resides in the immediate experiences of the piece and in the subsequent memories, debates
and comments that ensue. Posterity is not the arbiter.

As far as reception is concerned (whether by a reader, a
listener, a viewer or a spectator), each one of us reacts differently, and our own reactions can alter to the same piece,
depending on the situation. Paul Robeson's African American
audiences may have reacted differently to the white audiences
yet neither audience was monolithic; they could not be
correlated in any simple way to the perceived views of the
category to which they belonged. Both black and white
responses were differentiated and changed as Robeson's performing career and political circumstances changed. Whilst,
therefore, there is no uniformity, there is evidence of sufficient
similarities in response not only to suggest that art does have
a discernible political effect but also to begin to investigate it.

To explore the issue of reception fully would require an
advanced theory of the individual and the nature of ideas and
the imagination, and of how they relate to collective behaviour. Developments in biology, psychiatry and neuroscience
underscore the materiality of ideas and the complexity of
individual responses as well as their common physiological

roots. Individual reactions may be subjective but that does not invalidate them nor remove the basis for objective assessment; it merely undermines the notion of the absolute in aesthetics.

While no theory will fully uncover how each individual receives and interprets a work of art, that does not mean art has no effect or that it defies description and analysis. In searching for a political effect, the context of the reception or transaction may offer the best clues, along with examination of the art itself. An example might be a documentary drama created in support of a local campaign, with local people involved, performed to them and their community as part of that campaign in a space they consider part of their world. Such a production might justifiably lay claim to the description 'political' in a way that a banal West End performance of an avowedly political play by Bernard Shaw might not. Another instance might be the role of Shakespearean production in providing a focus for criticism of the Communist regimes in post-war Eastern Europe, or the rock music of the 'West' that was banned in the Soviet bloc and acquired there as a consequence a more political and subversive tone; when western powers bombed Serbia in 1999, however, such music was denounced as 'NATO rock'.

PERFORMANCE

In terms of performance, the art-politics debate has been heavily influenced by a significant social shift: performance, a notion associated with the aesthetic sphere, has become widely used in other contexts as both a descriptor of and a conceptual framework for analysing not only associated realms of human activity (e.g. literature and language) but also broader social activities (e.g. role play in therapy and management skills). Performance has become a metaphor for society and life itself.

While this convergence has not erased the distinction between the performance we undertake in the various roles we play in everyday life and performance undertaken as a specialist professional activity, the two have come closer together in certain theatre practices, such as theatre anthropology. This has been the result of a more general and sustained challenge to prevailing naturalism, which has had consequences for political analysis. The dominant analogical and mimetic model of performance, in which the audience is led to unwrap a referential meaning latent within the illusion, has been supplanted in political performance by dialectical forms (in the theatre, most notably by Brecht and subsequently by post-modern practitioners like the Wooster Group, and in film, for example, by Sergei Eisenstein or Jean-Luc Godard). In this process, the nature of performance itself has been questioned.

Ranging across theories of spectatorship and expression, a great deal of the discussion on the nature and politics of performance has revolved around the performers' interaction with the audience (a term that has been seen as problematic and in certain contexts has been replaced by 'spectator' or 'spect-actor' and other neologisms). This interaction is different in different types of performance, but involves an active and structured conversation in which the performers propose and the spectators/audience suppose. What performers and audience/spectators both bring to this conversation is themselves: their own histories and individual experiences, their own personalities and temperaments, and their own preoccupations and political views as well as their own understanding of performance.

Live performance is potentially a more open conversation than that enjoyed in recorded performance, and it is differently focused because the audience can interact with the performers. There are also differences within live performance, between, for example, a play, a ballet, a musical and a rock concert, but they all share this element of live interaction. The key to understanding this interaction, its distinctive and defining quality, has been an exploration of what 'liveness' means and how this relates to notions of the performer's 'presence', issues of representation and authenticity, and the ephemeral nature of the experience of live performance.

Live performance can open up its own special possibilities for change because it is social and connecting in a way that reading a novel, looking at a painting, watching television or even going to the cinema is not. These possibilities are not inherently superior to those afforded by other art forms, merely different.

The peculiar intimacy of live performance, of human beings having this sensory conversation in the same space, allows questions to be put in a unique way, and, because of the social nature of the experience, this can relate to political effect. It could be argued, however, that this intimacy is in fact complicity and that live performance, therefore, is more likely to contain and accommodate any critique than, for example, the distance or separation involved in viewing a film.

To test this contention would require analysis of the totality of procedures that constitute the experience of performance. This totality ranges from the position performance occupies in the wider cultural landscape – theatre in 1960s Britain, for example, held a prominent place in national debate – through the nature of the performance itself to the apparatus that supports performance (such as marketing, the 'front of house' experience or even transport accessibility).

In a conventional theatre experience, the supporting apparatus may not carry much apparent weight, yet disrupting any aspect might be making a statement (for example, when cast and director greet the audience as they enter the auditorium). For performance in a 'non-theatre' environment, its appropriation and use may carry significant weight on its own; street theatre, for instance, might exploit the symbolism of a 'non-conventional' location, like a particular local or historical association in a town square or similar gathering place. In these situations, the connection might be direct – such as a performance in support of, and being itself a part of, a demonstration – or it might be more oblique, using the anonymity of the setting (perhaps a hotel lobby or a carriage on the underground network) to reflect on contemporary alienation.

The supporting apparatus of a performance affects what might be called the aesthetic signature of the conversation between performers and audience. The aesthetic signature, which will probably carry the maximum weight in the conversation, comprises all the images that are created, whether presented traditionally, with, for example, the word at the apex of the hierarchy, or more fluidly, within a greater plurality and equality of significances. Sound, movement, speech and use of language as well as setting, costumes, objects and how they and the performers are lit – even the framing signals within which the performance can be said to take place (e.g. a curtain being raised and lowered) – will contribute. Above all, the aesthetic signature will include the physicality of the performance, its sensual pleasure and allure.

The process of choosing, editing and presenting transforms everything in the performance into an imaginative reality, as the performance negotiates between the world of the audience and the representation of that world being put before them. Representation, which may be rooted in or combine any number of aesthetic styles, from verisimilitude to fantasy, has thrown up many political and ethical issues, from whether or not a white actor should play Othello to how a western actor could 'act' a poor Vietnamese peasant or an emaciated concentration camp prisoner. Indeed, there are some who have argued that the magnitude of certain horrors of human experience, such as those of the Nazi genocide, has placed them beyond any attempt at representation.

The aesthetic signature of performance will also determine to what extent the conversation with the audience is open or closed. The signature, for example, may mask aspects of ideology inherent in the performance, such as the sexism or racism embedded in daily experience, or it may invite the audience to reflect on and challenge them. Similarly, the signature might transform the potential bestowed by the intimacy of live performance into either disinterest or engagement. It might appeal to a collective rather than an individual ethos; it might confirm the status quo or suggest the possibility of different ways of seeing, and might even challenge its own limitations. In terms of seeking a desired political effect, the signature and its context might need to reach beyond a multiplicity of elements and offer synthesis or coherence.

Performance that calls attention to the political processes by which a desired change might be brought about is likely to be seen as more politically driven than performance that does not. It is more likely to be dismissed by its critics as propaganda and excluded from the cannon of art. Yet in these cases – perhaps a guerrilla theatre performance or some other interventionist event of applied theatre – the implied notion of art being invoked ('good' art in the Enlightenment tradition) is frequently irrelevant.

The interventionist strand, which often involves exchange between performers and political activists, has become the standard-bearer for a committed, overtly political practice, albeit marginalised by conventional commentary and historiography. This theatre for social change has become associated with post-colonial 'theatre for development' and the work of Augusto Boal (himself the victim of torture and imprisonment). His systems of participatory techniques, from the 'theatre of the oppressed' to 'legislative theatre', have been used in a variety of situations, among, for example, prisoners, the homeless, the unemployed, asylum seekers and casualties of war. Related to this strand of work is the 'third theatre' movement inaugurated by director Eugenio Barba in the 1970s as an alternative to both mainstream and avant-garde theatre, in which theatre has journeyed beyond being a tool in the process of change to being a way of life and, therefore, embodying change itself.

In such contexts, it may be easier to assess the collective response of the audience and its subsequent relationship to relevant external processes. But, while it is possible to estimate the effect of performance as a whole, it is clearly impossible to evaluate let alone quantify the necessarily untraceable and incalculable effects of performance at the individual level, except (and then still only partially) where individuals choose to record them in reviews or other commentaries. For political performance, this returns us to the totality of procedures as the site of debate, with the aesthetic signature at its centre.

THE PERFORMER

For the audience, performers lie at the core of the conversation. Sometimes, an audience may be asked to engage with the performers in an overtly physical sense (for example, in promenade), but mainly the interaction comes through the exercise of the audience's imagination and a learned vocabulary of responses, like silence, laughter, clapping. For the performers, their contribution in most cases will be circumscribed by many factors, over which they will have little control. This raises important issues for all performers, but in particular for those who are politically conscious.

Many performers are politically active, either away from work or, more rarely, at work (perhaps as a member of a cast, company or band performing a benefit for a campaign, or maybe even striking for improvement in conditions or to further a cause). In terms of the work itself, performers, especially those who do not originate their material, have a different relationship to the art-politics debate to that of others on the production side, such as directors or choreographers. The relationship has become more complex as collaborative creation has increased. How does a performer, who is not the conceiver of the role or material s/he is presenting, understand and express its political importance, and how does that relate to personal political views, especially when performing an unsympathetic role or a role at odds with one's own personal views? Is the performer's aim to impart a truth or to help produce knowledge? In other words, what is the moral responsibility of the performer?

For a performer, there is no direct or necessary relationship between personal opinion and artistic expression, although the former will have a bearing on the latter through the critical intelligence a performer applies while preparing for performance and in the performance itself. In many instances, such as in interventionist performance, proximity between viewpoint, intention and expression would clearly be advantageous, if not essential.

How performers 'come across' is informed by the different and powerful drives that compel them to perform, as well as by the ways in which they have prepared for and met the intellectual and physical demands of their particular role. How performers look, sound and move carries meaning, even if different members of the audience interpret this and its components differently. In openly political work, the performers are often performing as much for themselves as for the audience, with whom they may believe they share an affinity. In less overt work, performers may believe they are performing for the work itself, for the art, and in that distinction might lie another redefinition of how the political is embedded within a cultural practice.

In the activist theatre and dance of the 1960s and '70s, for example, whether under the banner of progressing a Socialist, feminist, 'ethnic' or gay/lesbian cause, the performer was clearly being liberated as much as the audience, but it was assumed to be a joint venture. Performance was redefined by those groups and their target audiences in relation to, and as an assertion of, their own identity. Performance allowed both to share in a public affirmation at a time when it was important to make such a declaration. However, such declarations could also be accompanied by an exclusive and even authoritarian use of presence (related to the totalitarian aspect of utopia). The symbolically named Living Theatre, for instance, demanded personal liberation through performance; in several shows, the audience was forced either to be 'with them' or 'against them', and the company offered no space outside this choice. Such an approach may not have reduced the group's political impact but it may have narrowed its scope.

As far as expressing commitment in one's work is concerned, being part of an ensemble with a distinct political or cultural identity is one avenue, but one that is difficult to find or to sustain. Applied or interventionist theatre in its various forms may offer such opportunities, as the activist theatre and dance of the 1960s and '70s attempted. Some rejected the dominant practice of building-based theatre companies and the hierarchies of authority associated with them; collective creation replaced authorial creation and in certain cases performers tried to replace the traditional power relationship of performance ('we speak, you listen') with an inclusive aesthetic. A few performers went further and resisted the commodification of their art by turning to their own bodies as the site of the art itself.

Mostly, however, performers do not work in such contexts and have to accept whatever work is offered. Few who are progressive can sustain a career without many compromises, as it is rare to find work that regularly expresses a similar world outlook to one's own. Even when performers are able to choose sympathetic material, and possibly be involved at the outset in its creation, there is no guarantee that the effect will be as desired. Any number of things can intervene, from the activities of the collaborators to media and audience reception. The performer, nevertheless, would have exercised an active, ideological choice, but individual decisions by performers mostly pass unnoticed unless the person is famous.

While not always able to choose the material, performers do control the deployment of their selves in the performance and embodiment of that material. They may not control all the elements and, hence, the overall ideological expression of the performance, but that expression is differentiated and they can often control their own contribution to it. They can control their gesture, tone of voice, and posture and their relationships to the other performers, even though these are negotiated with a director or choreographer and may not always represent a choice with which the performer is completely satisfied. In front of a live audience, however, the performer takes charge; in cinema, how performance is lit and shot becomes critical and then editing intervenes, and few performers have control over that.

Similarly, few performers have any control over the means by which the ephemeral in their careers becomes set in history through the recording and reporting of performance, whether that resides in associated artefacts (CDs, videos, photographs, programmes), reflections of collaborators (diaries, sketchbooks) or in material produced by critics and academics (reviews, articles, monographs).[5] The archive is partial and, in that sense, political, too.

CELEBRITY

The individual performer who does appear to exercise control over many aspects of her or his work is the celebrity, and for this reason the first part of this book concentrated on the lives of three stars.

Celebrity represents the apogee of the autonomous individual, broadly speaking a product of the era of bourgeois culture that has its roots in the Renaissance. While, therefore, by no means a modern phenomenon, celebrity has come to occupy a special place in contemporary culture, abetted by and indivisible from the development of technology. Mass communication meant fame could spread immediately not just beyond one village or town to the next but from one country or culture to another. It was a performer, Charlie Chaplin, who could justifiably claim to have been the first global celebrity, and performers remain the most popular of stars.

The use of the word 'star' to describe an exceptional person can be traced back to the late eighteenth century theatre in England. By the early nineteenth century its use had become well established as a promotional tool. Star turns and star billing could be found later that century in the music hall, and in the 1920s Hollywood studios gave the word its contemporary gloss through promotion of the star system. 'Star' quality is a matter of negotiation between the entertainment and public relations industries, the media, the star in question and the final arbiter, public opinion. Stardom has even been divided into leagues, the 'A' list as opposed to a 'B', 'C' or even 'Z' list, and there is a huge difference between being a celebrity in one field, the theatre, for example, and being a star who is recognised as such in wider popular culture.

Stars play a major role in the way we see ourselves and lead our lives by helping determine our sense of who we are, our nationality, ethnicity, sexuality and class (and this is true of Socialist as well as capitalist systems). Celebrities are not created in a void but serve to reinforce a particular set of ideologies, through the lives the media and publicity apparatus select for us to see and though the art in which the stars' celebrity is made and remade. The complex matrix of interactions between celebrity and role and between star and audience usually carries its ideological effects by excluding or hiding alternative viewpoints. Difficult notions are made simple. Aspirations are realised. The assumptions of the system are validated. As each individual juggles her or his jumble of identities, both imposed and desired, celebrities can appear in sharp relief, realistically or not, to present a model or guide, either through positive identification or its converse, what not to do or think.

Just as the distinctive quality of performers is described in terms of presence, the essential quality of a celebrity is described in terms of charisma. This intensification of presence has a dual function. It separates the celebrity from an already separate caste as extra-special (and therefore to be taken note of) while at the same time removing through apparent familiarity the threat of that necessary remoteness (hence the increase in images of stars undertaking 'ordinary' activities, like shopping or jogging). In this way the extraordinary is reflected back to the ordinary in what one author calls the notion of the 'intimate stranger', which allows a star to be both symbolic *and* highly individualised.[6] To become extraordinary requires loss of the ordinary, and represents a gamble as well as a surrender in return for the advantages of stardom.

Stardom is not constant, however, and has to be sustained through the apparatus that creates as well as destroys it. It is in the nature of the process that stars can and do wane, to be replaced by the next 'supernova'. The growth of celebrity-based magazines, which has raised the pursuit of stars to a lucrative global sport, shows that turning fame into notoriety and wrecking a reputation is just as popular and imperative as manufacturing a new one: stars are powerful but their power is limited and provisional.

Identity lies at the root of attempts to control or influence the trajectory of stardom. To begin with, performers often have to abandon their own names, occasionally to avoid duplication but more commonly to acquire what might be considered a more attractive or apposite name. The choice already locates a new identity. In Diaghilev's time, the association had to be worthy of the exotic Ballets Russes: Lilian Marks became Alicia Markova, Edris Stannus became Ninette de Valois and Patrick Healey-Kay became Anton Dolin. Decades later, in hip hop, the choices were theatricalised and self-consciously invented yet had clear metaphorical power: Dr Dre (Andre Young), Ice Cube (O'Shea Jackson), Puff Daddy (Sean Combs). Performers like Bob Dylan (Robert Zimmerman) and David Bowie (David Jones) used multiple identities to remain creative and escape the stereotyping of their identity, which happens to all stars at the moment they achieve their fame. Their identity increasingly becomes assessed in terms of conformity to or divergence from the typecast (including that of the rebel), and, in the process, the space for renewal and development becomes increasingly diminished.

Celebrity identity is a tangled totality that is always changing. It changes in relation to several factors: the star's own persona and its different dynamics, both socially and in the work, depending on time, place and audience; the star's own industry and the other stars of that industry as well as its non-star contributors; and the stars of other industries, and the place each occupies in social and cultural life. History plays another part, too; stars can be interpreted differently at different times, both within their own life and after their death. Within this totality, the particular mix of social and cultural power (the star in society) and the values of representation (the star in art) lies beyond the control of both the star and the audiences, although both can influence, dispute and challenge. How and to what extent they do this can constitute a cultural political effect.

Stars develop an identity most obviously as a public face but also as a mask behind which they attempt to protect the private self, often the source of their creativity. It becomes difficult for celebrity performers to maintain a rooted sense of themselves, especially as the gap between the public persona and private person is open to manipulation by both the entertainment industries and the media. Any celebrity wishing to challenge the star apparatus has to negotiate this gap between the private and the public.

Unlike 'ordinary' performers, who, from the point of view of the audience, have no 'off-stage' or 'off-screen' persona and, therefore, can become completely the role they are performing, stars bring with them a defined persona. The audience sees both the celebrity and the role s/he is performing, though they most likely have paid their money to see the celebrity. Depending on the material and how the celebrity handles this duality, the star can offer complex readings between the extremes of identification either with the content (being the vehicle of the 'message') or with the persona (being seen as the star regardless of content). With politically committed stars, whatever their politics, the tension between the two, or the reinforcement of one by the other, contributes significantly to the overall effect, and when the link between the person, the persona and the performance is unambiguous, the effect is strongest. This is best achieved when the performer can exercise a significant degree of control over material and its distribution and reception. Celebrity is seen to provide the leverage that allows this, although the power is frequently revealed as temporary, if not illusory.

Should a celebrity wish to challenge dominant forms and content of representation through the material s/he has chosen, the relationship with the audience remains critical. Such a relationship is at its most direct in amateur performance, which allows for uncomplicated political statement beyond the demands of presentational technique in a social transaction free of the mediation of commerce. It is not clear when dealing with a star, however, whether the ability to represent authentically either a celebratory or an adversarial politics is enhanced by the appeal and focus of fame or limited by its otherness, distance and the mediations that celebrity brings with it. For a star, the relationship to an audience afforded by identification with a political movement can bring respect, self-respect and purpose, but it can also be restricting artistically and, therefore, counterproductive. Striking a balance can be difficult.

While the politically active star may reinforce the notion of individual heroism, being a star reinstates the notion of the artist as special, as elevated above the common herd. This characteristic is at odds with mass activism and the self-liberating democratic impulse, hence the attempts of politically conscious stars to seem ordinary and to belong. Without some distinction, a performer cannot offer an imagined other way of seeing or being. As 'intimate stranger', the star can gain attention for a cause, intensify identification with it and its values, and make them seem 'natural', both as an outsider (offering the objectivity of one 'who is not us') and as an insider (one 'who is us and understands us'). On the other hand, the star might simply attract more attention to her or his own celebrity, and the cause becomes a servant to fame not the other way round. The star may parachute in and out of a campaign and act independently without regard to an agreed strategy, while, from the celebrity's point of view, he or she may be trying to avoid becoming the property of the cause. Given the sectarianism and coterie aspect of much political activity, this can be a tricky problem for a star and, if not handled carefully, deleterious to the very quality that makes the star politically valuable.

If a star does achieve positive effects for a campaign, it may be difficult to assess whether this has affected only audiences already associated with the cause rather than those yet to be won to its side. The public's suspicion of those who protest from safety and advantage might counter the fame effect and snap the tension between their regard for, even delight in, a celebrity taking a political stand and their disregard for and distrust of the material comfort that allows it. The star may have to make a judgement as to which audience s/he wishes to address, or to which to give more attention. Sometimes audiences can be addressed differentially, with different messages being offered to different audiences at the same time, just as artists like Paul Robeson or Ray Charles appealed differently to black and white audiences yet successfully to both. In this way, a star might be able to satisfy the commercial need, which supports the material trappings of celebrity, as well as the political or ideological need, which supports the personal motivation. Again, this is not often possible, or not for long.

To what extent does being a celebrity, which presupposes incorporation and commodification, allow or inhibit a challenge to the very system of incorporation and commodification that has promoted the particular individual into stardom in the first place? The tools available to stars to exploit their advantage are the same tools they used to become a celebrity. What a celebrity does is always described in terms of their celebrity, and in that process the politics may be submerged, if not lost. Unless a radical soloist is not to be a contradiction in terms, does the way a politically committed star relates to her or his audiences – and this may involve a relationship to political movements – have to endanger the very status that has provided their leverage? Does a rebel celebrity have to live the image by renouncing wealth and privilege, or even embracing 'failure' in relation to the mainstream (and, thereby, endangering celebrity status) in order to avoid accusations of 'selling out'? And does the fact that political movements turn such distancing into its own kind of celebrity carry its own dangers?

LINK TO POLITICS

The role of the famous individual, which involves different dynamics to those of a collective, is often dismissed, as was the case with critics of white-supported black stars in the Harlem Renaissance. Yet celebrity can link people to politics through performance and can have significance to beleaguered groups, without being a substitute for political activity, which is required for change. Sometimes context is sufficient; the young violinist Yehudi Menuhin performing during the years of Nazi and fascist oppression brought hope to many fellow Jews and inspired the Allied troops in more than five hundred concerts he played for them. He also played for prisoners recently liberated from the concentration camps where music had been savagely debased, and, as part of his desire to honour what he saw as the best in German culture, he helped the rehabilitation of Wilhelm Furtwängler, the conductor condemned for alleged pro-Nazi sympathy. Acts of solidarity, such as the writer Susan Sontag directing *Waiting for Godot* during the siege of Sarajevo in 1993, had an immediate as well as a long lasting resonance. In the case of musician Daniel Barenboim and cultural scholar Edward Said, who together founded the West-East Divan Orchestra in 1999 and set up a Palestinian music kindergarten, important practical effects accompanied the powerful symbolism of uniting musicians from Arab countries and Israel.

Celebrities can intervene politically in a number of ways outside their work. They can join demonstrations, lend their name to campaigns or use prize-giving ceremonies as platforms (it is a time when performers are sometimes but not always able to speak with their own voice).[7] Several performers across the political spectrum, such as Harry Belafonte, Ewan McGregor, Roger Moore and Bono, have represented the UN and its agencies while others, like Melina Mercouri in Greece, Ion Caramitru in Romania or Glenda Jackson in Britain, have entered conventional politics. In the US, Ronald Reagan became US President, and bigger film stars, like Clint Eastwood and Arnold Schwarzenegger, have won elected positions. Ignacy Jan Paderewski, the internationally acclaimed virtuoso pianist and signatory to the Peace Treaty at the end of World War I, was Poland's Prime Minister and its first delegate to the League of Nations, where he demonstrated oratorical skills almost the equal of his musical ones. He was also noted as a humanitarian, contributing to causes and establishing funds that helped composers, writers, war victims and the unemployed.

Many stars, however, operate outside the established political structures, as exemplified by two iconic contemporaries,

Jane Fonda and Vanessa Redgrave. Both come from acting dynasties and inherited famous names, both became stars in their own right through their work and through their activism, and both suffered professionally for the risks they took, as if it were especially astonishing and unacceptable that actresses should engage in politics.

Redgrave, who first became politically active in the anti-nuclear movement of the late 1950s/early 1960s, became notorious in the media as a member of the Trotskyist group, the Workers' Revolutionary Party. Her support for Palestine liberation was seen in a 1977 documentary, *The Palestinians*, which she produced and narrated. This stance led to strong criticism when she was cast as Fania Fenelon, a Jewish musician who survives Auschwitz, in the TV film scripted by Arthur Miller from Fenelon's book of the same name, *Playing for Time* (1980), for which Redgrave won an Emmy award. In 1984 she sued the Boston Symphony Orchestra for cancelling her contract to narrate Stravinsky's *Oedipus Rex*. She was awarded damages for breach of contract but the jury dismissed her charge that the breach derived from political motives. Her political activities, which have continued throughout her adult life, have affected though not blighted what is nevertheless a distinguished career.

In 1977, Redgrave and Fonda appeared together in the film *Julia*; Redgrave plays the anti-fascist eponymous heroine while Fonda plays the liberal left author Lillian Hellman. It was a film in keeping with Fonda's political commitment yet also a departure for her, in that it placed women and the friendship between them at its centre. For much of her time, Fonda had been defined in relation to men, not only because of her famous father Henry but also because the media had projected her early on as a 'sex kitten'. Some of the vitriol aimed at her subsequently was a consequence of her publicly abandoning that role in the name of politics.

Her particular misdemeanour was to campaign over Vietnam against the US military, a central strand of American national identity. This connection has overshadowed her support for other causes, such as black self-determination and equal rights for women, but that is not surprising because, as is the case with Robeson, Duncan and Chaplin, Fonda's image is constructed and contested from different points of view (a process to which she has actively contributed). She toured a political vaudeville *FTA* (*Free the Army*, which became known as *Fuck the Army*) to venues near army and naval bases in association with the anti-war GI movement, and, in a much-publicised and criticised visit to North Vietnam in 1972 (to document US attacks on the crucial dyke system the Americans denied had taken place), she made anti-war broadcasts and was photographed beside a North Vietnamese anti-aircraft gun.

In her autobiography, she says she agreed to the visit in order to use her celebrity 'to get people's attention'.[8] Unfortunately, the image of her by the gun was interpreted in the US as her shooting at American planes, and earned her the pejorative nickname 'Hanoi Jane', which has stuck. As well as suffering virulent condemnation for what was seen as treachery at a time of war and being forced from film locations by angry Vietnam veterans, she was also smeared with false stories, such as betraying American prisoners of war to their captors. The security agencies kept her under surveillance, and there were attempts to blacklist her as well as calls for her to be tried for treason. She kept making films and the storm around her abated, as attitudes to the war changed and America became consumed by the Watergate scandal.

Fonda was acutely aware of the committed celebrity dilemma, and set up her own film production company to explore how to make politically effective films. It began with the Vietnam documentary, *Introduction to the Enemy*, in 1974. Then she changed tack and decided not to desert Hollywood but to work within the system. The result was films such as *Coming Home* (1978), in which she plays the wife of a Vietnam veteran who helps the war wounded; *The China Syndrome* (1979), in which she plays a reporter who witnesses an accident at a nuclear power plant; *Nine to Five* (1980), a comedy of female empowerment at work; and *On Golden Pond* (1981), a family drama that had parallels with her own daughter-father relationship. The political journey is clear.

In spite of her subsequent description of the Vietnamese gun episode as an unintended lapse, her stand on the war survives her remaking of herself as the leader of an aerobic trend and latterly a Christian. Such is the potency of her activist image that during the 2004 Bush–Kerry presidential election campaign, a falsified photograph of her and Kerry apparently sharing a platform at an anti-war rally in the early 1970s was circulated in order to damage him.

Like Duncan, Fonda has been criticised for her sexuality. Like Duncan, she has also been criticised by the left as a 'cause junkie' and for symbolising white, middle-class radicalism as well as for her changes of view and the accompanying changes of image. Yet she has remained politically involved, and, as she notes in her book, the bombing of the dykes stopped a month after she returned from her Vietnam visit.

CELEBRITY ACTIVISM

Since the days of Duncan, Chaplin and Robeson the number of performers associated with political issues has grown enormously. The range of issues with which they are associated has likewise mushroomed, from union rights, nuclear disarmament, abolition of the death penalty, gun control (for and against) and saving the environment to AIDS, autism, breast cancer, rape, gay marriage, poverty and the liberation of Tibet. In addition, following the example of left-wing cultural events and campaigns, there have been massive pop music campaigns run by celebrities, such as the 1971 Concert for Bangladesh, the Band Aid and Live Aid projects of the 1980s and the more politically directed versions, such as Amnesty International's 'Human Rights Now!' world tour of 1988.

The day of the celebrity activist has arrived, and that in some ways has made it harder for the long-term committed to be effective, especially when journalists report that to be associated with an issue is indispensable for stars, who hire PR consultants to get the right fit; some people's despair is evidently more fashionable than others.

Political awareness has become, instead, a duty for the famous (known sometimes in the profession as 'giving something back'), a duty that if fulfilled in public can form an important part of fame creation. Much of this commitment is not political but charitable, and follows in the long history of the rich who give in order to assuage guilt at their privileged situation. Others with a determined commitment do seek to reach beyond charity. The fact that the border between charity and politics is crowded with celebrities reflects poorly on the lack of achievement by politicians, who resent the stars for apparently winning public favour in this arena without having to put in the unsung hours of hard but often dull work.

The very apathy politicians complain about is the inevitable consequence of the political system they promote, and it is into this vacuum that celebrity performers such as Bob Geldof have inserted projects like Band Aid, Live Aid and Live 8 to raise mass consciousness and funds.

Celebrity musicians, not celebrity actors, have taken the lead in trying to mobilise audiences. Music remains globally the main cultural voice of protest, from Christy Moore in Ireland to Djordje Balasevic in Serbia, censored and exiled by the Slobodan Milosevic government but whose songs were central to toppling that regime. Thanks to globalisation such rebel music from across continents has found lucrative sales outlets in a similarly wide range of countries, marketed under the label World Music. Its spread is impressive, as a random selection shows: Colombian singer Shakira, Iraqi singer Kazem al-Sahir, Cameroonian saxophonist Manu Dibango, Zimbabwean singer Thomas Mapfumo, the nomadic Tuareg band Tinari-wen, who were persecuted in Mali and trained as guerrillas in Libya, and the Mauritanian singer Malouma Mint Maideh, silenced because of erotic songs. It is important that such voices are heard, yet international exposure has caused many of those labelled in this genre great difficulty in sustaining their commitment, sense of meaningful representation and connection with their roots.

In a politicised but commercial environment, Live 8 in 2005 encapsulates the dilemma. Comprising ten concerts in nine countries, it played to an unquantifiable audience of billions via television to coincide with a meeting of the industrial world's select leaders, and linked performers with mass activism in order to put pressure on politicians to end poverty in Africa. Very little of the music played was political – political information came in traditional dissemination of humanitarian facts and images – and the potential for building on the consciousness raising through connections to political movements and sustained activity was compromised by mixed messages. The line-up, chosen by volume of sales and celebrity rating, resulted in a white bias, and the response of the organisers to the politicians' weak declaration on Africa was overly praising and reflective of mainstream political diplomacy, as if the organisers were scared of harnessing the mass power into which they had tapped.

To what extent the self-proclaimed purpose of moving beyond charity to justice is achieved will depend on the extent to which the political pressure is maintained, and that is likely to have an artistic as well as a political dimension. Celebrities can and will play their part, but the movements and institutions that will deliver will draw their strength from a much wider base, as Robeson recognised. The role celebrities will have played in politicising that wider base will be hard to determine, which is not to deny its significance. Stars are not measured against the same benchmarks as those in politics, but the choice facing celebrities is no longer whether to use their fame, but how. People, after all, will go on fighting for a better life, with or without the famous.

IN PRAISE OF PERFORMANCE

Art will also play its part in that fight, whether or not its contribution can be determined with any precision or confidence. In the epoch of globalisation, the enormous power to accommodate political challenge demonstrated by the systems of the highly industrialised countries has cast further serious doubt on whether art can or does have any political effect. If, as has been proposed, tragedy is no longer possible in the modern age, perhaps political art is no longer possible either. Maybe it is a delusion that sustains art, without which its primary purpose would be revealed as commerce.

The continued desire of authority to control art suggests, however, it can and does have a political effect: the issue is 'what effect?' And how can that effect be judged as political?

Within the interplay of commitment, intention and outcome, performers and the other artists with whom they necessarily collaborate are still grappling, and will continue to grapple, with these and other questions. Is resistance sufficient? Is transgression possible? How can images move people beyond affirmation or provocation into a realm of action and, if need be, adversarial engagement? Are the answers to be found in aesthetics or in politics, or in both? Does it matter if the answers cannot be found?

If context – a relationship to a wider movement or set of movements – is crucial, the problems remain as to how art connects, especially when the art forms are marginal pursuits, and what happens when the movements to which art wishes to connect are minimal or weak. A movement requires more than common cause in order to become the dynamo of collective action, which is what makes the individual most politically effective. Yet the very element that defines and forges a movement – its ideology – became suspect after the Cold War, resulting, paradoxically, in the recrudescence of religious and political fundamentalism in the twenty-first century.

Against the new totalitarianism, a new politics is being developed that goes beyond the models of the Cold War promoted by both 'left' an 'right'. It resists the imperial imposition of 'free' market solutions and offers alternative forms of globalisation from below, defying the idea that globalisation and post-modernism are forces of nature rather than sites of major struggle. With a greater emphasis in the new politics on moral questioning and debating rather than asserting the truth, perhaps connections are less obvious and more tentative, if no less important. The more we know, the more we know we do not know.

This suggests a more variegated notion of political performance than before, one that can chronicle and celebrate struggle, but one that can also offer a potent critique as well as a rallying cry. Performance can provide both and much else across the spectrum from the oblique and circuitous to the direct and immediate, from education to entertainment.

Performance is affected by fashion; just as activism in art was modish once, indifference replaced it as a prominent aesthetic signature. An apparent embrace of nihilism or neutrality, however, may be a defence of private space and a rejection of traditional public politics rather than a lack of concern for public or political issues. Such a defence may be a crucial public issue itself in a contemporary society of massive alienation when culture has become integral to supporting the status quo, and the commitment associated with conventional political activity is relentless, frequently humdrum and often socially debilitating.

Performance can challenge the absolute and authenticate the increasingly disjointed and isolated experiences of individuals forced to retreat into a less public and more private relationship to the world. This intensifying subjectivity has its corollary in the importance attached to authentication of the 'actual'. It is expressed in the rise of hugely stage-managed 'confessional' and 'reality' television and in the emphasis on 'liveness testing' in the growing world of security, where individuals have to convince a computer they are who they claim to be by means of a variety of biological checks.

Indeed, the authenticity of the actual is in crisis because of the increasing prominence of the virtual. Immediacy of communications, which allows armchair viewers to see on their television screens the bombing of a foreign country as it happens, can at the same time distance us, just as the avalanche of accessible information symbolised by the internet can also hide understanding.

Performance has the ability to affirm a different kind of authenticity, to counter atomisation and reassert a collective or interrelated and public view of life. It can bridge the gap between political and artistic truth. It can offer a social experience that can have an effect beyond the aesthetic, re-imagining notions of shared community, based on active and independent citizenship, and on pluralism that does not deny ethical values or drown in relativism.

To some – individually or collectively – forgetting or ignoring may seem necessary in order to endure in the modern world, and performance can play its part in that, too. In fact, most institutionalised performance, whether mainstream or alternative, can and does help sustain the established system. But performance can also help us remember and question. With its own rules and time frames, performance can help us recall things we prefer to forget or cannot recollect or articulate. It can call collective as well as individual memory to account. It can help us look at the world anew. It may even go beyond describing a world in flux to embodying and enacting change itself.

Performance can challenge the role of culture in keeping certain groups, both marginalised minorities and ignored majorities, in secondary and often silent roles. It can also move beyond the separateness of identity politics, which may set tribe or clan against society and be as authoritarian as the grand old ideological narratives it has sought to replace. It can connect the realities of lived experience among different groups and individuals, and contrast those realities with the images of that experience promoted by the powerful. It can empower audiences through validation of self and the meanings we make of our lives. In so doing, it can also offer more than meaning. It can offer an emotionally charged elucidation and complex consideration, not in order to explain away but in order to confront the world we live in, whether through irony or indignation, anger or amusement.

Performance can do all these things because it is a flexible form of cultural and human knowledge that reaches beyond simple cause and effect. It has proved to be an indispensable activity for allowing humans to reflect upon their humanness, to test or show the possibilities of what it is to be a human – to be human – not in the compartmentalised structures beloved of ideological systems but in all its messiness, intricacy and unpredictability, using doubt, perplexity and enigma as much as if not more than the certainties of life.

This role is all the more important in our technological era, an era that has been able to map the brain but not the mind and in which the subjective 'I', through which we make sense of the world and our place in it, may well turn out to be an illusion, albeit one that we humans need in order to survive.

Like ideology, the illusion that is performance can inspire the noblest of human impulses as well as strip people of their humanity, which is why, to borrow a 1930s metaphor that seems to have become appropriate once again, the war of ideas is as important as the war of physical power. The use of the metaphor should not imply, however, that victory is possible. The struggle is continuous and complicated, and, in that struggle, the effect of art will always be hard to assess. For art, the judgements will never be the same as for politics. Art may not be able to 'change the world' but it can play an essential role in doing so; liberation begins in the imagination, and the prerequisite for changing the world is changing the way we see the world.

The title of this book refers to one battlefront in that permanent war of ideas, a battlefront occupied by the prime intermediaries of performance, the performers. The title is a description of appearing before an audience as well as a declaration of defiance. Those performers, whether celebrities or not, who proclaim 'Here We Stand' are refusing their consent and saying to their audiences, 'Together we are going to remake the world in a different image.' It is a declaration heard through the ages and across the continents. Its reverberations have echoed from the past into the present and will surely continue to resound far into the future.

NOTES

1. Quoted in Christopher Andersen, *Citizen Jane: the Turbulent Life of Jane Fonda*, London, Virgin Books, 1990, p. 199.

2. Quoted in Mike Marqusee, *Wicked Messenger*, New York, Seven Stories Press, 2005, p. 212.

3. For those on the left, this process was associated with the broader challenge to the mechanical interpretation of Marx's views on the relationship between 'base' and 'superstructure'.

4. The years after Griffith released *The Birth of a Nation* in 1915 saw massive race riots throughout the country, peaking in the North in 1919 in what became known as the 'red summer' because of the blood spilt (see 'Charlie Chaplin: Citizen of the World', p. 106). Many historians lay the blame for this racial conflict on *The Birth of a Nation*.

5. In addition to the personal bias that underlines the selectivity of archives, there is the often unacknowledged reality of absence and loss from the record of history; for example, when talking about early cinema, it is worth remembering it is estimated that 80 per cent of silent films has been lost.

6. Richard Schickel in *Intimate Strangers: The Culture of Celebrity*, New York, Doubleday, 1985.

7. For instance, the organisers of the 2004 Academy Awards ceremony banned any mention of the invasion of Iraq.

8. Jane Fonda, *My Life So Far*, London, Ebury Press, 2005, p. 290.

BIBLIOGRAPHY AND REFERENCES

Alexander, Karen, 'Fatal Beauties: Black Women in Hollywood' in Christine Gledhill (ed.), *Stardom: Industry of Desire*, London, Routledge, 1991

Alexander, William, *Film on the Left: American Documentary Film from 1931–1942*, Princeton, New Jersey, Princeton University Press, 1981

Andersen, Christopher, *Citizen Jane: the Turbulent Life of Jane Fonda*, London, Virgin Books, 1990

Archer-Straw, Petrine, *Negrophilia*, London, Thames & Hudson, 2000

Arden, John, *To Present the Pretence: Essays on the Theatre and its Public*, London, Eyre Methuen, 1977

Auslander, Philip, *From Acting to Performance: Essays in modernism and postmodernism*, London, Routledge 1997

———— , *Liveness: Performance in a Mediatized Culture*, London, Routledge, 1999

Baldwin, James, *The Devil Finds Work*, London, Corgi, 1978

Bharucha, Rustom, *Theatre and the World: performance and the politics of culture*, London, Routledge, 1993

Baxandall, Lee (ed.), *Radical Perspectives in the Arts*, Harmondsworth, Penguin, 1972

Bentley, Eric, *Are You Now or Have You Ever Been? And Other Plays*, New York, Grove Press, 1981

———— (ed.), *Thirty Years of Treason: Extracts from hearings before the House Committee on Un-American Activities, 1938–1968*, London, Thames & Hudson, 1972

Betz, Albrecht (trans. Bill Hopkins), *Hanns Eisler, Political Musician*, Cambridge, Cambridge University Press, 1982

Blair, Frederika, *Isadora: Portrait of the Artist as a Woman*, Wellingborough, Northants, Equation, 1987

Blau, Herbert, *To All Appearances: Ideology and Performance*, New York and London, Routledge, 1992

Bloch, Ernest, *et al.*, *Aesthetics and Politics*, London, New Left Books, 1977

Boal, Augusto (trans. Charles A. and Maria Odila Leal McBride), *Theatre of the Oppressed*, London, Pluto Press, 1979

———— (trans. Adrian Jackson), *The Rainbow of Desire: the Boal Method of Theatre and Therapy*, London, Routledge, 1995

Bogle, Donald, *Dorothy Dandridge: A Biography*, New York, Amistad Press, 1997

———— , *Toms, Coons, Mulattoes, Mammies and Bucks: An Interpretive History of Blacks in American Films*, New York, Continuum, 1989

Bourne, Stephen, *Black in the British Frame: The Black Experience in British Film and Television*, London, Continuum, 2001

Brown, Jared, *Zero Mostel, A Biography*, New York, Atheneum, 1989

Bruce, Lenny, *How to Talk Dirty and Influence People*, New York, Simon and Schuster, 1992

Brustein, Robert, *Who Needs Theatre: Dramatic Opinions*, London, Faber and Faber, 1989

Buckle, Richard, *Nijinsky*, London, Penguin, 1975

Buhle, Paul, and Wagner, David, *Radical Hollywood; the untold story behind America's favourite movies*, New York, the New Press, 2003

Buñuel, Luis (trans. Abigail Israel), *My Last Breath*, London, Jonathan Cape, 1984

Burke, Thomas, *City of Encounters: A London Divertissement*, London, Constable & Co, 1932

Campbell, Russell, *Cinema Strikes Back: Radial Filmmaking in the United States 1930–1942*, Ann Arbor, Michigan, UMI Research Press, 1982

Carey, John, *What Good are the Arts?*, London, Faber and Faber, 2005

Case, Sue-Ellen, and Reinelt, Janelle (eds.), *The Performance of Power: Theatrical Discourse and Politics*, Iowa City, University of Iowa Press, 1991

Chambers, Colin, 'Socialist Theatre and the Ghetto Mentality', *Marxism Today*, August 1978

———— , *The Story of Unity Theatre*, London, Lawrence and Wishart, 1989

———— , *Inside the Royal Shakespeare Company: Creativity and the Institution*, London, Routledge, 2002

———— , and Prior, Mike, *Playwrights' Progress: Patterns of Postwar British Drama*, Oxford, Amber Lane Press, 1987

———— , and Steed, Maggie, 'Playing on the Front Foot: Actors and Audience in British Popular Theatre, 1970–1990' in Jane Milling and Martin Banham (eds.), *Extraordinary Actors: Studies in Honour of Peter Thomson*, Exeter, University of Exeter Press, 2004

Chaplin, Charles, *My Autobiography*, London, Bodley Head, 1964

———— , *My Life in Pictures*, London, Bodley Head, 1974

Chaplin Jr, Charles, *My Father, Charlie Chaplin*, London, Longmans, 1960

Clark, Vèvè A., and Johnson, Sara E. (eds.), *Kaiso! Writings by and about Katherine Dunham*, Wisconsin, University of Wisconsin Press, 2005

Cohen, Rachel, *A Chance Meeting*, London, Jonathan Cape, 2004

Coleman, Wanda (ed.), *High Performance*, special issue on Los Angeles riots, September 1992, Los Angeles, CA, Astro Artz

Conner, Lynn, 'What the Modern Dance Should be: Socialist Agendas in the Modern Dance, 1930–34' in Janelle Reinelt (ed.), *Crucibles of Crisis: Performing Social Change*, Ann Arbor, University of Michigan Press, 1996

Cripps, Thomas, *Slow Fade to Black – The Negro in American Film 1900–1942*, New York, Oxford University Press, 1977
———— , *Black Film as Genre*, Bloomington and London, Indiana University Press, 1978
———— , *Making Movies Black: the Hollywood Message Movie from World War II to the Civil Rights Era*, New York and Oxford, Oxford University Press, 1993
Croft, Andy (ed.), *A Weapon in the Struggle: The Cultural History of the Communist Party in Britain*, London, Pluto Press, 1998
Cruse, Harold, *The Crisis of the Negro Intellectual*, London, W.H. Allen, 1969
———— , 'The Creative and Performing Arts and the Struggle for Identity and Credibility' in Harry A. Johnson (ed.), *Negotiating the Mainstream*, Chicago, American Library Association, 1978
Daly, Ann, 'The Continuing Beauty of the Curve: Isadora Duncan and Her Last Compositions', *Ballet International*, vol. 13, no. 8, August 1990, Köln, Verlag
———— , *Done Into Dance: Isadora in America*, Bloomington and Indianapolis, Indiana University Press, 1995
Dandridge, Dorothy, and Conrad, Earl, *Everything and Nothing: The Dorothy Dandridge Tragedy*, New York, Abelard and Schuman, 1970
Davies Andrew, *Other Theatres: the Development of Alternative and Experimental Theatre in Britain*, Basingstoke, Macmillan, 1987
Davis, Ossie, and Dee, Ruby, *With Ossie and Ruby: In This Life Together*, New York, William Morrow, 1998
Diamond, Elin (ed.), *Performance and Cultural Politics*, London, Routledge 1996
Dickinson, Margaret, *Rogue Reels: Oppositional Film in Britain, 1945–90*, London, British Film Institute, 1999
Dorinson, Joseph, and Pencak, William (eds.), *Paul Robeson: Essays on His Life and Legacy*, North Carolina, Jefferson and London, McFarland, 2002
Duberman, Martin Bauml, *Paul Robeson*, New York, Ballantine Books, 1990
Duncan, Irma, and Macdougall, Allan Ross, *Isadora Duncan's Russian Days and Her Last Years in France*, New York, Covici-Friede, 1929
Duncan, Isadora, *My Life*, New York, Award Books, 1966
———— , *The Art of Dance*, New York, Theatre Art Books, 1969
Dyer, Richard, *Stars*, London, BFI Publishing, 1998
———— , *Heavenly Bodies: Film Stars and Society*, Basingstoke, Macmillan, 1986
Fonda, Jane, *My Life So Far*, London, Ebury Press, 2005
Foner, Philip S. (ed.), *Paul Robeson Speaks: Writings, Speeches, Interviews 1918–74*, London, Quartet Books, 1978
Fortier, Marc, *Theory/Theatre: An Introduction*, London, Routledge, 1997

Foster, Hal (ed.), *The Anti-Aesthetic: Essays on Postmodern Culture*, Port Townsend, WA, Bay Press, 1983

Franko, Marc, *Dancing Modernism/ Performing Politics*, Bloomington and Indianapolis, Indiana University Press, 1995

——— , *The Work of Dance: Labor, Movement, Identity in the 1930s*, Middletown, Ct, Wesleyan University Press, 2002

Franko, Mark, and Richards, Annette (eds.), *Acting on the Past: historical performance across the disciplines*, Hanover and London, Wesleyan University Press, 2000

Fusco, Coco (ed.), *Corpus Delecti: Performance Art of the Americas*, London, Routledge, 2000

Gledhill, Christine (ed.), *Stardom: Industry of Desire*, London, Routledge, 1991

Goldstein, Malcolm, *The Political Stage: Amateur Drama and Theater of the Great Depression*, New York, Oxford University Press, 1974

Golub, Spencer, 'Charlie Chaplin, Soviet Icon' in Sue-Ellen Case and Janelle Reinelt (eds.), *The Performance of Power: Theatrical Discourse and Politics*, Iowa City, University of Iowa Press, 1991

Goodman, Lizbeth, and de Gay, Jane (eds.), *The Routledge Reader in Politics and Performance*, London and New York, Routledge, 2000

Gottlieb, Vera, and Chambers, Colin (eds.), *Theatre in a Cold Climate*, Oxford, Amber Lane Press, 1999

Grabs, Manfred (ed., trans. Marjorie Meyer), *Hanns Eisler: A Rebel in Music – Selected Writings*, Berlin, Seven Seas Books, 1978

Grimshaw, Anna (ed.), *C.L.R. James Reader*, Oxford, Blackwell, 1992

Guiles, Fred Lawrence, *Jane Fonda: The Actress in Her Time*, London, Michael Joseph, 1981

Haskins, James, with Benson, Kathleen, *Lena – A Personal and Professional Biography of Lena Horne*, New York, Stein and Day, 1984

Henze, Hans Werner (trans. Peter Labanyi), *Music and Politics: Collected Writings 1953–1981*, Faber and Faber, 1982

Herman, Gary, and Downing, David, *Jane Fonda – All American Anti-Heroine*, London, Omnibus, 1980

Himelstein, Morgan Y., *Drama Was a Weapon: The Left-Wing Theatre in New York 1929–1941*, New Brunswick, New Jersey, Rutgers University Press, 1963

Hogenkamp, Bert, *Deadly Parallels: Film and the Left in Britain, 1929–1939*, London, Lawrence and Wishart, 1986

——— , *Film, Television and the Left, 1950–1970*, London, Lawrence and Wishart, 2000

Horne, Gerald, *Class Struggle in Hollywood 1930–1950: Moguls, Mobsters, Stars, Reds and Trade Unionists*, Austin, Texas, University of Texas Press, 2001

Horne, Lena, and Schickel, Richard, *Lena*, London, Andre Deutsch, 1966

Huggins, Nathan, *Harlem Renaissance*, New York, Oxford University Press, 1971

Index on Censorship, London, Writers and Scholars International Ltd., monthly magazine first published May 1972

Itzin, Catherine, *Stages in the Revolution: Political Theatre in Britain since 1968*, London, Eyre Methuen, 1980

James, C.L.R., *Modern Politics*, Detroit, Bewick, 1973

————, *The Struggle for Happiness and American Civilization*, Oxford, Blackwell, 1993

Jara, Joan, *Victor – An Unfinished Song*, London, Jonathan Cape, 1983

Johnson, Harry A. (ed.), *Negotiating the Mainstream*, Chicago, American Library Association, 1978

Jones, LeRoi, *Blues People: The Negro Experience in White America and the Music that Developed from it*, Edinburgh, Payback Press, 1963

Kamin, Dan, 'Teaching Charlie Chaplin to Walk' in Nicole Potter (ed.), *Movement for Actors*, New York, Allworth Press, 2002

Kater, Michael H., *The Twisted Muse: Musicians and Their Music in the Third Reich*, New York and Oxford, Oxford University Press, 1997

Kaye, Nick, *Postmodernism and Performance*, Basingstoke, Macmillan, 1994

Kermode, Frank, *Epiphanies and Puzzles: essays and reviews 1958–61*, London, Routledge and Kegan Paul, 1962

Kershaw, Baz, *The Politics of Performance: Radical Theatre as Cultural Intervention*, London, Routledge, 1992

————, *The Radical in Performance: Between Brecht and Baudrillard*, London, Routledge, 1999

Kiernan, Thomas, *Jane Fonda*, London, Talmy Foundation, 1973

Kohansky, Mendel, *The Disreputable Profession: The Actor in Society*, Westport, Connecticut, and London, Greenwood Press, 1984

Kosky, Frank, *Black Nationalism and the Revolution in Music*, New York, Pathfinder, 1970

Kurth, Peter, *Isadora: A Sensational Life*, London, Abacus, 2003

Kuziakina, Natalia (trans. Boris M. Meerovich), *Theatre in the Solovki Prison Camp*, London, Routledge 1996

Leab, Daniel J., *From Sambo to Superspade: The Black Experience in Motion Pictures*, London, Secker and Warburg, 1975

Let Paul Robeson Sing!, a celebration of the life of Paul Robeson, a Paul Robeson Cymru Committee/Bevan Foundation/Theatre Museum publication, 2001

Let Paul Robeson Sing!, education and resource pack, Theatre Museum, London, 2001

Lynn, Kenneth S., *Charlie Chaplin and His Times*, London, Aurum Press, 1998

Margolick, David, *Strange Fruit: Billie Holiday, Cafe Society and an Early Cry for Civil Rights*, Philadelphia, PA, Running Press, 2000

Marland Charles J. (ed. and intro.), ' "Are You Now, Or Have You Ever Been . . . ?": The INS Interview with Charles Chaplin', *Cineaste*, vol. xiv, no 4, 1986, New York
———— , *Chaplin and American Culture: the Evolution of a Star Image*, New Jersey, Princeton University Press, 1989
Marqusee, Mike, *Wicked Messenger*, New York, Seven Stories Press, 2005
McCabe, John, *Charlie Chaplin*, London, Robson, 1978
McCann, David, *The Hanns Eisler Hearings – Hollywood, Washington and Beyond*, Workshop, University of California at Los Angeles, 1971
McConachie, Bruce, and Friedman, Daniel (eds.), *Theatre for Working-Class Audiences in the United States, 1830–1980*, Westport, Ct, Greenwood, 1985
McGilligan, Patrick, and Buhle, Paul, *Tender Comrades: A Backhistory of the Hollywood Blacklist*, New York, St. Martin's Press, 1997
McRae, Donald, *In Black and White: The Untold Story of Joe Louis and Jessie Owens*, London, Scribner, 2002
McVay, Gordon, *Isadora and Esenin*, Ann Arbor, Michigan, Ardis Publications, 1980
Milling, Jane, and Banham, Martin (eds.), *Extraordinary Actors: Studies in Honour of Peter Thomson*, Exeter, University of Exeter Press, 2004
Milton, Joyce, *Tramp: The Life of Charlie Chaplin*, New York, Da Capo Press, 1998
Mitchell, Tony, *Dario Fo: People's Court Jester*, London, Methuen, 1984
Mostel, Kate, Gilford, Madeline, Gilford, Jack, and Mostel, Zero, *170 Years of Show Business*, New York, Random House, 1978
Navasky, Victor S., *Naming Names*, New York, Viking Press, 1980
Perkins, Tessa, 'The Politics of "Jane Fonda" ', in Christine Gledhill (ed.), *Stardom: Industry of Desire*, London, Routledge, 1991
Phelan, Peggy, *Unmarked: the Politics of Performance*, London, Routledge, 1992
Phillips, Caryl, *Dancing in the Dark*, New York, Alfred A. Knopf, 2005
Pines, Jim, *Blacks in Films: A survey of racial themes and images in the American film*, London, Studio Vista, 1975
Poitier, Sidney, *The Measure of a Man: a Memoir*, London, Pocket, 2001
Porter, Eric, *What Is This Thing Called Jazz?: African American Musicians as Artists, Critics and Activists*, Berkeley, CA, University of California Press, 2002
Potter, Nicole (ed.), *Movement for Actors*, New York, Allworth Press, 2002
O'Connor, John, and Brown, Lorraine (eds.), *The Federal Theatre Project: 'Free, Adult, Uncensored'*, Eyre Methuen, London, 1980
Radford, Robert, *Art for a Purpose: The Artists' International Association, 1933–1953*, Winchester, Hampshire, Winchester School of Art Press, 1987
Ramdin, Ron, *Paul Robeson: The Man and his Mission*, London, Peter Owen, 1987

Redgrave, Corin, *Michael Redgrave, My Father*, London, Fourth Estate, 1996

Redgrave, Vanessa, *An Autobiography*, London, Hutchinson, 1991

Reinelt, Janelle (ed.), *Crucibles of Crisis: Performing Social Change*, Ann Arbor, University of Michigan Press, 1996

Reynolds, Simon, *Rip It Up and Start Again: Postpunk 1978–1984*, London, Faber and Faber, 2005

Robeson, Eslanda Goode, *Paul Robeson, Negro*, New York, Harpers & Brothers, 1930

Robeson, Paul, *Here I Stand*, Boston, Beacon Press, 1988

Robeson Jr, Paul, *The Undiscovered Paul Robeson: An Artist's Journey 1898–1939*, New York, John Wiley and Sons Inc, 2001

Robinson, David, *Chaplin, His Life and Art*, London, Penguin, 2001

Samuel, Ralph, *et al.*, *Theatres of the Left 1880–1935: Workers' Theatre Movements in Britain and America*, London, Routledge and Kegan Paul, 1985

Saunders, Francis Stonor, *Who Paid the Piper? The CIA and the Cultural Cold War*, London, Granta Books, 1999

Schechner, Richard, *Performance Theory*, London, Routledge, 1988

Schickel, Richard, *Intimate Strangers: The Culture of Celebrity*, New York, Doubleday, 1985

Schlossman, David A., *Actors and Activists: Politics, Performance, and Exchange Among Social Worlds*, New York and London, Routledge, 2002

Schneider, Ilya Ilyich, *Isadora Duncan: The Russian Years*, New York, Da Capo Press, 1968

Seroff, Victor, *The Real Isadora*, London, Hutchinson, 1972

Seton, Marie, *Paul Robeson*, London, Dennis Dobson, 1958

Simone, Nina, with Cleary, Stephen, *I Put a Spell on You: the Autobiography*, London, Penguin, 1992

Smith, Eric Ledell, *Bert Williams: A Biography of the Pioneer Black Comedian*, Jefferson, NC, 1992

Smith, Julian, *Chaplin*, London, Columbus, 1986

Sobel, Raoul, and Francis, David, *Chaplin, Genesis of a Clown*, London, Quartet, 1977

Steegmuller, Francis (ed.), *Your Isadora: The Love Story of Isadora Duncan and Gordon Craig*, Basingstoke, Macmillan, 1974

Stewart, Jeffrey C. (ed.), *Paul Robeson: Artist and Citizen*, New Brunswick, New Jersey and London, Rutgers University Press, 1998

Stourac, Richard, and McCreery, Kathleen, *Theatre as a Weapon: Workers' Theatre in the Soviet Union, Germany and Britain, 1917–1934*, London, Routledge and Kegan Paul, 1986

Szanto, George, *Theatre and Propaganda*, Austin and London, University of Texas Press, 1978

Taylor, John Russell, *Strangers in Paradise: the Hollywood émigrés, 1933–1950*, London, Faber and Faber, 1993

Taylor, Karen Malpede, *People's Theatre in America*, New York, Drama Book Specialists, 1972

Terry, Walter, *Isadora Duncan: Her Life, Her Art, Her Legacy*, New York, Dodd, Mead & Co., 1963

Werner, Craig, *A Change Is Gonna Come*, New York, Plume, 1998

White, Timothy, *Catch a Fire: the Life of Bob Marley*, London, Omnibus Press, 2000

Wiener, Jon, *Come Together: John Lennon in His Time*, London, Faber and Faber, 1985

Witham, Barry B., 'The Playhouse and the Committee', in Sue-Ellen Case and Janelle Reinelt (eds.), *The Performance of Power: Theatrical Discourse and Politics*, Iowa City, University of Iowa Press, 1991

Zarrilli, Phillip B. (ed.), *Acting (Re)Considered*, London, Routledge, 1995

Daniel, Curt, *Theatre in German Concentration Camps* in *Theatre Arts*, November 1941, New York, Theatre Arts, Inc, reproduced at http://www.theatrehistory.com

Dickinson, Margaret, 'Film and Politics', http://www.screenonline.co.uk

http://www.bbc.co.uk/music/classicaltv/holocaust/holocaustmusic.shtml

http://www.bobmarley.com

http://www.fadetoblack.com/foi/charliechaplin

http://foia.fbi.gov/foiaindex/robeson.htm

http://www.inplaceofwar.net

http://memory.loc.gov/ammem/fedtp/ftwpa.html

http://www.peace-not-war.org/Jukebox

Paul Robeson in Live Performance, CBS 61247

Peace Arch Concerts, Folk Era FE 1442

Soul Music, BBC Radio 4, 14 March 2006

A Woman of Paris, DVD, Warner Brothers, Z1 37976, 2003

INDEX